E. Neumann '41

DATE DUE

CANADA

THE FOUNDATIONS
OF ITS FUTURE

CANADA

THE FOUNDATIONS
OF ITS FUTURE

by STEPHEN LEACOCK

Illustrated by Canadian Artists

PRIVATELY PRINTED IN MONTREAL, CANADA
MCMXLI

OF ALL

THE NATURAL RESOURCES OF CANADA

THE GREATEST IS ITS PEOPLE

TO WHOM THIS VOLUME

IS RESPECTFULLY DEDICATED

BY

THE HOUSE OF SEAGRAM

THE HISTORY OF CANADA is the sum total of the biographies of all its citizens. In its unfolding, all have a share; from its narrative, all derive that pride which comes of participation. Written in national terms, it is yet, in so far as every Canadian is concerned, a deeply personal record; for here, fashioned into a composite picture are the activities, in peace and war, of industry and commerce, of labour and capital, of the great and the humble. Other departments of letters may perhaps have a special appeal; history belongs to all. ❡ The House of Seagram, it is true, is not a publishing house. That under its imprimatur is issued Professor Leacock's inspiring history of our country is the result, both of an appreciation of the extreme timeliness of the subject, and of a consciousness of the wider civic interests of industry. For Canadian business, it seems to us, is not merely availing itself of a privilege, but is also fulfilling a duty, when it lifts its eyes from the narrow confines of its 'powers' as described in its charters, to regard the wider panorama of that country to the history of which it contributes its record of achievement. The horizon of industry, surely, does not terminate at the boundary-line of its plants; it has a broader horizon, a farther view, and that view embraces the entire Dominion. ❡ There is no doubt but that the most important document among the records of any commercial enterprise is its balance-sheet. That document, of course, owes its importance not to the facts and figures it contains, but to the people, the human effort and striving, represented by its mathematical symbols. For a business is constituted, to paraphrase a well-known dictum, 'of people, for people, and by people'. We feel that Appendix A to each and every business balance-sheet, an appendix unwritten yet undeniably there, is the general history of the Dominion, itself a projection in deeds of the personality of all its citizens. That, in fact, is the larger balance-sheet, without which all others are meaningless, purposeless, motion without progress! ❡ It was with this motivation, that, as our country stood engaged in battle for the defence of its most precious ideals, this volume was conceived, planned and prepared. We felt that it ought to be done, and done now; and that no one could do it better than Professor Leacock. ❡ Certainly it is meet and fitting at this time of struggle, as with might and main we strive to preserve our Canadian way of life against the onslaught of a ruthless foe, that we cast a backward glance upon our history to find those ideals and aspirations which made that way of life, and to realize anew the solid and enduring principles for which we have taken up arms. Certainly it is well, as we measure our resources in man-power and in armament, that we take into account the true strength of our national character, which achieved so much in the past and which to-day is the mightiest weapon in our arsenal. Such a survey, surely, would intensify our sense of privilege in our Canadian citizenship, and hearten us in all the changing circumstances of war. For the inspiration of the men and women of the past who with valour, faith and self-denial brought our Dominion thus far in its journey, is, in itself, in the hour of destiny, an army with banners. Let the chronicles be taken down again, therefore, and the tale be re-told, from its early beginning until this very day, and let not the occasion when yesterday we defeated the same foe who now shows his fangs again, be forgotten.

❡ It is an heroic saga, this of our Dominion, told in Professor Leacock's brilliant and inimitable style, and it is a story full of the profoundest moral implications. Here, for centuries, lay the vast expanse of Canada, stretching, in the words of the Psalmist and of our national motto, *from sea unto sea*, rich in natural resources, enjoying a climate which was vigour calling unto vigour and waiting for man, bearing in his hand the conjuror's rod of civilization to turn that untouched domain of yesterday into the flourishing Dominion of to-day. Here, indeed, was God-given bounty, but none to benefit therefrom.

❡ But not forever. From the British Isles and from Old France they came, followed later by many of the peoples of Europe — men of Norway, Denmark, Holland, Poland, Czechoslovakia, Russia, Greece—Canadian kin of our present allies—and other ethnic groups too, who crossed the sea to build a new life in a free Canada—many peoples, from near and from far, each of a different historic past, all of a single

Canadian future. The perils of the sea are braved; a path is blazed through the wilderness; a way is blasted through the mountains. Land is about to become a country! The makers of Canada are upon the scene! Adopting criteria which were in themselves to be a triple standard in the land, they follow the lofty traditions of their origin, they apply the genius of their craftsmanship, with integrity of purpose they strive ever onward, and they build—Canada. ❦ Labour and capital make their respective contributions to the common weal, and statesmanship conceives confederation, and gives birth to national unity. Our railway-builders view the trackless wilderness, and endow the vast land with a vertebral column of steel. Banking, industry and commerce begin to flourish. The prairie is made to give forth the gold of its wheat; and men descend into the bowels of the earth to wrest from their hiding-place the treasures, sealed so long. Cities arise, with their towering structures, and harbours are builded whence men may go down to the sea in ships. The forests are felled; the mills are in motion, supplying their products to a free and untrammelled press. Places of worship, and places of learning dot the land. Where yesterday there was only the forest primeval and the whispering pine and the hemlock, there is to-day the multifarious activity of a great country. ❦ It is no magic fiat which achieves this: it is the people of Canada who have made and are making Canada. The coureur de bois; the merchant-adventurer; the explorer; the colonist; the homesteader; all who came early, wrestled with Nature, and won —these are the precursors who made our country. Without them, Canada would be still a beautiful but uninhabited Xanadu, "of caverns measureless to man." The splendid history which Professor Leacock has written is a just tribute to those intrepid and inspired pioneers. ⁌ But while we pay tribute to the forerunners of Canadian history—the pioneers who left their heritage to this generation — we cannot but realize that this generation itself is chosen by opportunity, and bound by duty, to constitute the pioneers for the generations yet to come. For pioneering is not a static thing, done and accomplished. To us, too, is given the occasion so to fashion, and build, and defend our way of life, that our children and our children's children may look back upon the men of this age as the pioneers of the twentieth century. ⁌ The opportunities which lie open to Canadians inflame the imagination. Certainly the future decades of this century, which in the words of the late Sir Wilfrid Laurier "belong to Canada," will see Canadians zealously dedicating themselves to the further development of the boundless resources of our country, and will see, too, those resources flowing to the farthest corners of the world—a Canadian contribution to the welfare of humanity. At this moment Canada is already playing its high role. The position which our Dominion occupies within the Empire—a position, born of our common loyalty to the Crown, and now emphasized by our comradeship in arms—places our country proudly among those which are to-day the bulwark of world civilization. ⁋ Nor can we leave unmentioned the part which Canada is playing and will continue to play as intermediary between the two greatest forces for good that exist in the world to-day. Because of our geographic location upon this continent, and our spiritual location within the Empire, we are destined — as we, indeed, have already seized that destiny—to bring closer together the best of the Old World and the New. Nature itself seems to have intended us as the intellectual corridor between England and the United States, already bound one to the other by common ideals, a common culture, and a common peril. In the hand-clasp which to-day symbolizes British-American relations, the respective forearms may well extend over an ocean and a continent, but it is through Canada that the firm grip of friendship meets. ⁋ They are high objectives which the future holds for Canada. To encompass them the vision of the early pioneers must be with us still, for where there is no vision, the people perish. It is the vision of a free Canada, a united Canada, a mighty Dominion. To-day as we come to grips with the barbarian foe, not only of the Empire, but of all mankind, we shall find in these the pages of our history the signposts which shall serve us, not only during the struggle, but also after the inevitable victory. Here are enshrined the ideals of liberty and democracy upon which our way of life is based, and here in the activity of our people, are manifested the various groups of different origins and separate creeds, working together in harmonious unison, each making its own contribution to the completed achievement which is the Canadian mosaic. Here, too, the firm resolve of all to follow the one increasing purpose of progress, and to develop still further the untold possibilities of our country, a blessing to ourselves and a boon to all mankind; and here above all, glowing upon every page, is courage, courage to defend our rich heritage, and maintain what is dearest of all, our freedom and our principles. These, indeed, are "the foundations of our future"!

Samuel Bronfman

THE HOUSE OF SEAGRAM
MONTREAL, P.Q.
OCTOBER, 1941.

TABLE OF CONTENTS

LIST OF ILLUSTRATIONS

✐   ✐   ✐

TITLE PAGE DECORATION AND COVER DESIGNED BY . . . . . H. R. PERRIGARD, A.R.C.A.

END LEAVES: NATURAL RESOURCES OF CANADA, BY . . . . ERNST NEUMANN

CHAPTER DECORATIONS BY . . . . A. SHERRIFF SCOTT, A.R.C.A.

LAYOUT AND TYPOGRAPHY BY . . . . JOHN W. MORRELL

LIST OF MAPS

The maps in the present volume are intended only as sketch-maps to elucidate the reading of the text. Names not relevant are omitted.

AUTHOR'S FOREWORD

I AM very glad to have my name associated with the preparation of this volume. While it is being written and prepared, our country and our Empire are passing through the shadow and storm of war. But this dark hour is illuminated by the white light of human courage; the bitterness of this suffering is alleviated by the inspiration of patriotism; and this dark cloud carries a silver lining that foretells the coming dawn.

It is at the present hour that a book such as this is meant to be may well come forth. The strength and unity of our Empire, which is proving its salvation in our present crisis, rests upon its past. We have built on this bedrock of human freedom. This structure still shall last when those erected on the dead sands of despotism shall be washed away by the rising tide.

We can best learn to value this heritage of freedom by reflecting on its history. We can best appreciate the present in the light of the past, and in the same light we can realize the measure of our duty and obligation towards the future.

Here then is the story of the making of Canada. The aim of the narrative is to show the foundations of our present national life. The large canvas of our Canadian history carries a wonderful wealth of light and colour, in the romance of exploration and adventure. In its foreground are the waving banners that mark the alternating fortunes of war. But set within all this is the real picture, the deeper colours and the quiet shades that reflect the life of a people, the silent growth of a nation.

Our country carries upon its surface the traces of over three hundred years of settlement. It has already its antiquities, its mouldering stones, its sites and shrines, its venerable buildings falling to decay. It has already in places its "long, long ago." With this are the annals of three centuries of history unrivalled in its varied and picturesque interest. But we realize on reflection that the vastly greater part of our country, as regards civilized settlement and occupation, is a thing of yesterday. Here are great cities that within living memory were solitary prairie, crowded harbours where but half a century ago the sea rolled in unheard, unheeded.

This very novelty is an inspiration. This very lack of history is the foundation of history itself. We can begin at the beginning. We can mark the site of the earliest cabin, the grave of the first settler. Those short and simple annals of the lowly, too humble for narration in our older world, overlooked in the majesty of royal records and titled genealogies, can be the basis of our Canadian story.

It is in this light, this fading light if you will, that those of us now grown old view our Canadian history. For much of English-Canada our own memories and our own recollection of those before us carry it all. While we have time we should set it down so that for those who come after the record shall endure with its proper surrounding and setting.

If it may be said with becoming modesty, I myself can claim a certain qualification as such a witness. I was a child of six when my father came, sixty-five years ago, to settle in the Lake Simcoe district, thirty miles from the nearest railway. We lived in an isolation not known to-day even in the Arctic. The nearest village was four miles away, over rough roads and through cedar swamps. Newspapers we never saw. No one came and went. There was nowhere to come and go. And the stillness of the winter nights was as silent as eternity. So I am qualified to speak of settlement.

This part of Canada was never settled till the new migration from the old country, after the great war with France, supplemented the earlier opening of Upper Canada by the American Loyalists. Till after 1815 it was one vast stretch of unbroken forest, dense cedar and close-packed tamarack and the tall hemlocks and pines that overtopped it. The earliest grants of land were to retired officers and men, mustered out after the war. I can myself remember some of these oldest settlers who had first come to settle in the woods around the Lake, and, among them, old men who had been rebel and loyalist in the rebellion of 1837 and carried still something of its angers, fading out with age.

I speak of such recollections not in a personal way but as a heritage common to so many of us in Canada. Carry them back through a generation or two of memory and hearsay, and you can reach to the days of the American Revolution and the founding of the Maritime Provinces. With our French-Canadian fellows such memories and recollections carry back even further, till they are lost in the golden mist of the royal history of France. In our Western Canada the annals of settlement are still for the most part those of a single life, and memory and history are one. It is to this softened light of a history that blends so largely with living memory that this narrative looks for its colouring.

But this relative shortness of the past serves to lengthen and enlarge our future. Canadians instinctively think more of what is still to come in their country than of what has happened in the past. People of older lands typically and commonly look back. They think of their thousands of years of history, they see all about them the monuments and the majesty of the past. The face of the earth beneath their feet has been changed and refashioned at the hands of man. Of nature as it was there is but the unchanging sea and the sky, fickle with the changes of the hours but in centuries the same. Thus people in England or Scotland turn their aspirations towards living up to their past, keeping their country as great as it has been. "There'll always be an England" sings the Englishman, and the Scot doesn't even have to sing. But Canadians would never sing that there will always be a Canada—like this one. This is just a beginning. We have hardly started. Wait a hundred years and see.

Hence any proper story of Canada, even in narrating the past, must open the windows of every outlook to the sunshine of the future.

I would like to add one further word. It may well be that in the writing of this book the execution has fallen short of the aim. But there is no doubt of the value to our country of such a record of the history and the life of its people as this book was designed to be by those who collaborated in planning it. Canada has always been fortunate in the generous help given in the past to education, art and science by those eminent in commercial life. The House of Seagram in their public-spirited design in the production of this volume, worthily take their place in this honoured company.

Stephen Leacock

"... *the oldest country in the world*" — PAGE 3

ORIGINAL PAINTING BY ADAM SHERRIFF SCOTT, A.R.C.A., MONTREAL, P.Q., 1941

Adam Sherriff Scott

CHAPTER I

THE EMPTY CONTINENT

The New Discovery of America—Formation of the Continent—Man's Transit to America —The Norsemen in America—The Aborigines and the Empty Continent—European Expansion and the New World—The Search for the East—Voyages and Explorations of the Fifteen Hundreds—Misdirection of Effort—The Empty Continent still waits.

THE poet Jemmy Thomson, in writing *Rule Britannia* in 1740, tells us that Britain originally "arose from out the azure main." This is exactly what it did, except that the main was not azure. It rose, very properly accompanied by the rest of the British Empire and in fact preceded by Canada. The "main" was not azure because there was no sunlight to make it so. Around our unformed globe was still wrapped the dense volume of steamy cloud that shrouded it in the half-darkness that still holds the planet Venus. Under this moved and stirred the heaving and silent water later to be the windswept, sunlit ocean. Within the first crust that thus emerged and remained above the water, was the rim of desolate rock that surrounds the Hudson Bay, the central ring of inner Canada. This is perhaps the oldest country in the world. Till yesterday it seemed destined to eternal solitude. The discovery of America has begun again. Much of it, and especially of Canada, such as the El Dorado in the northern wilderness or the Aladdin's cave of radium beside the Great Bear Lake, moves from useless desolation to the foreground of human interest. In the world's production of wealth and search for welfare the emphasis of human effort has shifted from tropic plants to northern minerals, from the jungle to the rock, from the forced labour of the Egyptian slave to the leaping power of the northern waterfall. This alters entirely the outlook of the world towards Canada. Less than a century ago the famous British historian, Sir Archibald Alison, could state that "probably seven-eighths of this immense surface, British North America, are doomed to eternal sterility from the excessive severity of the climate, which yields only a scanty herbage to the reindeer, the elk and the musk-ox." But it is now as if the globe had shifted on its axis and tilted Canada towards the sun. Thus does history reveal that continued migration of civilization so finely called the "northward course of empire." The palaces of Nineveh are buried under the Mesopotamian sand, and the Assyrian, who once came down like a wolf on the fold and whose banners were gleaming in purple and gold, now sells rugs in a palatial hotel in what was once the "desert of the Saskatchewan." This sense of the illimitable resource of our future—not boastful but earnest—should be the inspiring idea of a proper study of Canada.

"History of Europe," Chap. 76.

"Northward Course of Empire," V. Stefansson, 1922

These great changes have had much to do with the change and development of our globe itself. Where nature built and fashioned broadcast, man has groped and burrowed. Every last thing was thrown down lavishly for us millions of years ago. Only knowledge lingered. So we can perhaps best understand the structure and resources of our country or our continent by turning back to the earliest hour of earth's time and seeing it in its formation. Our globe, once a ball of fire torn from the sun, cooled, shrank and solidified. As it cooled, so the geologists tell us, it underwent the same pressure of stress and strain as attend the collapse of a balloon losing gas, or a football losing air. Like these it tried to draw itself into a solid figure of four sides, each side a triangle, like the little four-sided glass pyramids seen as table ornaments. Its own rotary motion counteracted this, trying to re-make it to a smaller sphere. But the enlightened eye can still see in the structure of our continents and oceans, the huge outline of these four triangular faces, washed by the

J. W. Gregory, "The Making of the Earth," 1912

seven seas. One great triangle outline, the easiest to detect, is that of America—all America with the Atlantic—from its wide base along the arctic rim to its "toe" in the antarctic. The great gash where the Gulf of Mexico is torn out of the continental outline is said by scientists to mark the place where it was detached in its formation from the side of Africa that once joined it. Slide our American continent east again along its parallels and it would refit with Africa. But as a matter of fact—of science—it is still slowly sliding the other way, west. Canada is estimated to be moving away from Europe at the rate of a few yards a year. This is excellent, except that it brings us nearer Japan. But this picture at least emphasizes, if only as in a parable, the unity of all America.

Per contra, what we call the Old World, Asia with its appended Europe, along with Africa and the Indian Ocean tapering south, forms another face. The Pacific Ocean gives the natural and simple outline of another triangle, sunk beneath the sea. The broad cap of the arctic regions, unfamiliar as a unit in our maps, marks the fourth face—the top, or lid, as it were, as we generally picture the upright globe. As the outline formed, as the ridges rose and the seas retreated, there may well have been alternate rises and falls, lost land, land bridges and bygone islands, such as human fancy, ever since Plato, has loved to restore. All this for the most part long before man; but not of necessity before emerging life.

The globe cooled; the clouds lifted; the sun came; the waters sparkled and there was life. How it came in we do not know. What it is, we cannot tell. We mark its self-adapting change, its will to be. Its mystery we cannot read. Even before the sunlight, great plants, giant ferns, rose in the half-darkness to sink and submerge as future coal fields. Animate life no doubt appeared under the water and then crawled hideous to the land. It grew in size before it grew in adaptability. Huge animals dragged their flabby length, pulpy, non-resistant and premature. But nature always toned the process to strength, endurance and beauty. There came a time when the prairie blossomed with flowers and the birds sang in the woods, and the earth waited for man; waited and waited for such uncounted thousands of years that science cannot count them now. Indeed our scientists seem to lengthen their conjectures with every passing decade.

Sir Arthur Keith, "The Antiquity of Man," 1925

Lord Kelvin estimated the age of the earth at 100,000,000 years. Our later knowledge of radio-active elemental change alters the estimate to perhaps 4,000,000,000 years. Life may have existed hundreds of millions of years ago. But the space between the first appearance of life, and the first appearance of man, perhaps 500,000 years ago, seems inconceivably vast.

But at last man came. He was by descent a sort of super-baboon, or a first-cousin ape. The scientific name is an "aberrant primate." Like most of us he cannot trace his direct family—just his "people" at large. Such as they were, he parted company with them. Man came down from the trees, stopped climbing, stood to attention and began using his hands. His particular trick was that of "opposing" his thumb to his fingers. They say that that *made* him.

At any rate man set to work to make something of himself, and presently succeeded, and there he was! Body and mind, man beat his cousin apes on every lap; turned growls and chuckles into speech; made sticks into tools; and so parted company with all the rest of the world.

This was in Asia. Man undoubtedly was evolved in one area and from it spread out over the globe. But our New World of America knew nothing of man for a long time. We have never found, as in Europe and Asia, those ancient skulls buried deep under rocks that prove their age by the calendar of geology. Here is the famous "Piltdown" skull of some man who once lived in Sussex; the Pithecanthropus of Java; or the recently found Mongolian man, the last addition to the "old gang." Now and then a false alarm, as started by the Los Angeles find of 1924, awakens vain hopes of ancestry. But so far all our discoveries of skulls in rock betray a later burial, and not the solemn, primeval rest of the Sussex man.

Man, then, came to America from the Old World. There was no difficulty about it, as we see it in the light of modern knowledge. Indeed there were so many ways of coming, and man probably came by so many different ways, that the only surprising thing is that there was no regular coming and going to the mainland of America till the time of Christopher Columbus. That was the trouble—the coming and going. Primitive people might come, and did come, but they couldn't go back; or they came by so slow a journey, spread over generations, that they forgot where they came from and presently thought they came from the sky.

Here are some of the ways in which mankind came to America. A glance at the globe shows that Asia and America are almost connected territory. We seldom realize that the long peninsula of Alaska, which is part of the United States, reaches out so far west that the most westerly of the Aleutian Islands, which form its continuation, are due north of New Zealand. In other words this long peninsula and its island stepping-stones reach to within 200 miles of the Peninsula of Kamchatka, in Siberia. Early men, even with only primitive means of water transport, could have drifted or been blown across this gap. It could never have been in prehistoric times a known and travelled passage. It was at best a disappearance into the black night of the ocean, like the passage beyond Gibraltar to the early Mediterranean people. But the Bering Strait itself, though about 800 miles farther north, is only fifty-six miles wide, with two small islands that reduce its longest water gap to thirty-five miles. In some winters the whole strait freezes to a solid stretch of ice. Nothing but the climate of this desolate Asiatic region prevented mankind from moving eastward out of Asia as easily as westward into Mediterranean Europe. But between the truly habitable parts of Eastern Asia—as the valley of the Amoor River—and the Bering Strait, there lies a stretch of two to three thousand miles of the coldest and most forbidding territory on the globe. Life shudders in the cold, its flame almost extinct. The winter temperature at Verkhoyansk, the "cold pole" of north-east Siberia, shows a January average of 59 degrees below zero, while the minimum recorded (so far) is 94 below. In such a region the means of life are scant and precarious, the winter an unending darkness, the summer a glare of meaningless sunshine. Scholars do not doubt that prehistoric man crossed this territory, but never as a single and remembered transit. It was a slow migration, generation after generation long, farther and farther

Ellsworth Huntington, "The Red Man's Continent"

Ellsworth Huntington, "The Red Man's Continent"

into the mist and cold, till it filtered down the Alaskan coast of
America into the sunshine—its origins forgotten. But where
man's memory fails, the stamp that nature sets on him persists.
Our Eskimos of Canada and our Indians reproduce beyond all
doubt the Mongolian type of man. The native custom and mode
of life of our Pacific Indians, as first discovered, still connects
with Asiatic culture.

It is true, the bridge of language between Asia and America
is broken beyond recall, the connection, if any, a mere matter
of guess-work. Language in America is multiplied and divided
even more than in the Old World. It is estimated that there
are at least 1,000 original distinct languages on the American
continent, that is to say, languages, mutually unintelligible and
not, as dialects, mutually comprehensible. These all interconnect
from the Eskimos to the Patagonians. But nowhere do they connect with the speech of other continents. This is the more striking
since elsewhere surviving similarities of language stretch over a
connection of thousands of miles of distance and forgotten centuries of history. You may trace the Uro-Altaic family of languages, from Finland and Turkey across the whole stretch of Asia.
The numerals from one to ten, as existing in Turkish, are virtually the same as those used at Yakutsk. This marks the track
of the great Asiatic migration westward and north-eastward
from its first starting point. Similarities of language, as said, run
through and across all America. But as from continent to continent there is no bridge. Yet this only bespeaks the vast
antiquity of the migration and its slow transit.

H. de Windt,
"Paris to New
York by Land,"
1903

But this undoubted movement of man into America was no
doubt supplemented in some small degree with arrivals by other
routes. We need consider but little the possibility of land bridges
joining America to the Old World. Such there undoubtedly were.
The American continent, as has been said, may once have
adhered to Europe and to Africa, from which we may imagine
it, as in the fancy of love songs, reluctantly drifting apart. But
few scientists would allow us to imagine man as part of its
reluctant flight. His time was yet to come. Similarly the North
Atlantic may have had its Atlantis, now sunk beneath the
waves, and the "banks" of Newfoundland, the "continental shelf"

of Greenland, may once have joined to Iceland and the British Isles. But there is a lack of any evidence that this was in man's brief yesterday.

But in one direction from America there is such evidence. The Polynesian Islands of the Pacific which are the still projecting heights of the earth-face that collapsed, reach all the way from the Australian waters to where they end at a distance of some 2,000 miles from South America. Across the whole island world of the Pacific, there is, and always has been, transit and intercourse reflected in the bond of language and culture. The phrase "the cannibal isles," once covered them all. Now Easter Island, the farthest outpost towards South America, is distant from it 2,000 miles. To the nearest inhabited island on the west, Pitcairn, the distance is 1,100 miles. But on Easter Island are huge stone monuments, fashioned, beyond all doubt, by man and not by nature. Some of them represent human figures, as high as 37 feet and 50 tons in weight, evidently cut from the still traceable quarries in the island lava. Who put them there? Not the puny population of an island of 55 square miles. It was, at first discovery (1722), estimated at perhaps 2,000; never more; at present 250. This original population knew nothing of either stone work or mechanics. The monuments were certainly not transported from Asia or America. The only conclusion is that Easter Island was once part of a much bigger place with a great population and with arts unknown now, and that most of it subsided under the ocean. The tidal wave of its subsidence may well have washed its people away, or perhaps they left in terror. New-comers, thousands of years later perhaps, took the island and the stones as they found them. If this were true, a lot of queer resemblances between South America and Polynesian culture would find an easy explanation. Constructive imagination, once started, could make the mystery of Easter Island rival the life of William Shakespeare.

On the other side of America is another "dead certainty" of primitive migration. There is no doubt that long ago men from the old world made their way—or had their way made for them—to Central America. Physically this is all too easy since the direction of the winds, blowing over temperate seas, makes

G. Routledge, "The Mystery of Easter Island"

such a transit a simple accident of storm and weather. Here
then in Yucatan, and in adjoining regions of Central America,
overgrown in the jungle, lost from memory for centuries, are
the stone walls and sunken corridors that mark what was once
the seat of Mayan civilization. Painstaking scholarship has
deciphered its calendars, its star pictures and its records, only
one degree from alphabet writing. Now primitive people, tending
their flocks, know and watch the night sky—a thing unseen
and forgotten in our cities. They note imaginary resemblances
in a group of stars—highly fanciful mostly—to a dipper or a
wagon or a chair. By these resemblances they name the stars,
by word or picture. And the Mayan symbols for the stars around
the Zodiac—the ram, the bull, the heavenly twins, etc.—are the
same as ours, the ones the Old World made up thousands of
years ago. The likeness between the constellation and the thing
from which it is named could never account for this. There is
too little likeness. Mathematically the chance of twelve "same"
names in a line, beats out infinity. The only conclusion is that
the "Mayans" blew in from "home." Unfortunately that seems
all of it. After the first glow of our comradeship, the realization
that they too are of European descent, there is nothing left.

But of far greater meaning and with a bearing on the future
as well as on the past, is the coming of the Norsemen to America,
five hundred years before Columbus. A thousand years ago the
Norsemen roved the seas of north-west Europe. Their home
was on the coast of Scandinavia and on the narrow seas below,
but their toil was on the sea, and every settlement their harvest.
They were themselves driven forward by the eternal pressure of
Asia upon Europe. They turned from piracy and plunder to
settlement. All the east and south of Britain became theirs in a
slow conquest that in a century and a half pushed back the
Britons to the mountains and to the far west coast and islands.
They settled down, turned Christian, and presently their inland
farms and homesteads heard the village church bells in place of
the sound of the sea—and that was England. The fire of the
maritime spirit died down, to be kindled again five hundred
years later with the winds of American discovery, to blaze in
glory in the beacons of the Armada—as yesterday in the night

*"Narrative and
Critical History
of America,"
8 Vols.
Edited by
Justin Winsor,
Vol. I,
Chapter II*

ADAM SHERRIFF SCOTT, A.R.C.A., MONTREAL, P.Q., 1941

"A thousand years ago, the Norsemen roved the seas . . . ."—PAGE 10

sky above Dunkirk. Thus leads a main thread of our history from the Norsemen till to-day.

But other Norsemen clung to the far north. They passed Great Britain by and settled in Iceland (A.D. 874). They built up a cultured civilization, a community of some 50,000 souls. There in a treeless land of lava, fiord and open grass, adventure could not fall asleep as in the Sussex farmstead. They blew westward on the wings of the wind and established a farther settlement in Greenland. The chance voyage of a boat driven in a storm (Gunnbjörn, about A.D. 900) first revealed this land. Two generations later an outlaw leader, Eric the Red, led his followers to Greenland, (A.D. 980), and a little later a whole company of settlers to this new home. It also was treeless, but that mattered to them less than nothing. There was a bright carpet of summer grass glistening on the hillsides, like Ireland in the rain, and so they called the place Greenland. This Greenland establishment lasted for four hundred years. The settlers raised cattle and sheep, built stone houses and churches and traded back to their homeland, and so to Europe, with cattle hides and seal skins and walrus ivory.

It was inevitable that the Norsemen should blow on from Greenland to America. The transit was nothing to people whose *Fridtjof* great open boats, often over seventy feet long, strong and *Nansen,* buoyant, driven with banks of oars or a huge square sail, could *"In Northern* ride the seven seas. Due west from the Greenland settlement is *Mists,"* the mouth of the Hudson Strait, at a distance of about 600 miles; *1911* south-west about 800 miles is the Strait of Belle Isle, leading to the Gulf of the St. Lawrence and the heart of the continent. There was nothing to stop the Norsemen from "discovering" America. They did. The record of it all is preserved for us in the Sagas of the Norsemen and in a sort of Domesday Book, the *Land-Names-Book*, kept in the Icelandic settlement. Chance led the way. We read how Biarni, son of Heriulf, striking westward from Iceland for Greenland in the year 986, was driven too far, and found a land covered with woods and with low coasts without mountains in sight. So Biarni knew it was not Greenland and steered away. Then came a great wind from the south and blew the ship in four days to Greenland. After Biarni came Leif, the son of the Red Eric who first colonized Greenland itself. Leif bought Biarni's ship, and sailed on set purpose with a crew of thirty-five. This was in the year A.D. 1000. They easily reached land, but this time it was all covered with snow, and on the shore were great slabs of stone and in the background empty and desolate hills. Leif called it Helluland, which sounds in our English like what it was, but he meant the "Land of Stones." There is little doubt that this was Labrador.

Leif and his crew sailed on down the seas—south and east and then south it must have been, but there is no count of days, no landmarks of places. No doubt they caught sight here and there of the coast and stood out to sea and on. They landed

again at a place where they saw broad beaches of white sand. Here there were thick forests all along the shore. So they called it Markland, the country of trees. This could have been Newfoundland, or Cape Breton, or Nova Scotia. There is no way to tell. They sailed again, a north-east wind behind them, and then, in two days, landed again. This time they had reached the place that every schoolboy knows as Vinland. Here were lakes and rivers filled with salmon, and beautiful woods and trees easy to fashion into houses. It was not cold, though the autumn was well on, and the days had not drawn in so short as in Greenland. They found patches of wild grain and one day one of the sailors found bushes with berries on, which he said were the grapes from which wine was made in southern countries. None of the Norsemen had seen such things as vines, but the man who brought the grapes is called by the saga a "Turk," meaning a man from the south, and so they took for granted that he knew. They gathered boatloads of American wild grapes, and presumably made wine and anticipated the horrors of the prohibition era by nine hundred years. Leif called this place Vinland and they stayed all the winter through. When they got back they told all about it and others came in new voyages, Leif's brother Thorvald and different people.

For a few years there were many Vinland voyages. One leader, Thorfinn Karlsefni, tried to make real settlement (A.D. 1007), with a hundred and sixty men in his ships, with many of their wives, and with cattle. They built houses and traded with the savages and were there four years. At least one child was born in America, and christened Snorri, the first hundred-per-cent white American. Then came hardship and quarrels with the savages and the settlers learned for the first time the lurking danger of savage ambush in the woods, that darkens the annals of America. Karlsefni saw his people killed by savages who did not fight like men. Presently so many settlers were killed that the terror of it drove the rest away—back to God's country, all bright ice and snow, and with no trees to shelter savages.

So that, except for the mention in the saga of odd journeys to the Labrador coast and to the mainland elsewhere for timber, was the end of Vinland. And presently the night fell on the

Greenland settlement itself. We do not know how and why it
ended. Transit and communication with Iceland seem to have
grown less. After the year 1410 the record ends. The last known
voyage from Greenland to Norway is dated in that year. When
John Davis, the Elizabethan navigator, saw the coast in 1585,
there was no sign of any habitation. When settlement was
started again by missionaries in 1721, there was no population

V. Stefansson, found but the native Eskimos. Of the Norsemen's colony there
"Unsolved remained nothing but ruined stone and scattered rubble; no
Mysteries of record; no writing; and over part of it the eternal glacier of
The Arctic" Greenland had made its burial of ice. We do not know how the
settlement met its end. It may have been that the plague of the
Black Death, which passed westward across Europe in that
epoch, laid its hand on the little colony. It may be that food ran
short and the settlers moved westward, to become long afterwards the "blond Eskimos" of Coronation Gulf. Perhaps the
Eskimo fell on the settlement and wiped it out. Readers who
wish to pursue the topic further may find it in the fascinating
pages of Vilhjalmur Stefansson's book, *The Unsolved Mysteries
of the Arctic.*

Meantime, whereabouts was Vinland? The simple truth is
that we don't know. It may have been anywhere down the east
coast of Canada or of the United States. The saga tells us exactly
how long the shortest winter day was. That would locate its
latitude to a nicety; but we no longer understand the method of
time measurement used in the chronicle. Fond fancy traces the
Norsemen over a wide area. There is an old mill assigned to

For illustration them at Newport in Rhode Island. There is the famous Dighton
of the rock, see Rock, with marks like Nordic runes traced on it, lying in the
"Leif Ericson" Taunton River in Massachusetts, and other tokens elsewhere.
But, unfortunately, Nordic runes are extremely hard to distinguish from scratches, and old mills without a miller mean nothing.
The latest speculations and investigations, of lively interest to
us in Canada, are the attempts to prove that the Norsemen went
due west from Greenland into the Hudson Bay and from there
south into the interior. Evidence of this is offered in certain
resemblances of language (a shaky matter to the trained philolo-
gist) and in the avowed discovery of Norse armour, swords, etc.,

all of which is set forth in Mr. James Curran's recent volume, *Vinland the Good*.

In summary, it is perfectly clear from the record that the Norsemen discovered the mainland of America, visited it from Greenland again and again, and once at least attempted a settlement. But the main point of the episode has been, I think, entirely missed. They discovered America and had no particular use for it. To us the words "discovery of America" are so portentous with meaning that we stand aghast at the idea of people finding it and leaving it. We know now that it was really *America!* and behind it were New York and Hollywood and all sorts of things. To the Norsemen it meant nothing—an empty shore of slate, or at best a forest of wood; but with treacherous savages in ambush among the trees—not to be compared with the bright, clear sky of the north, the glittering icebergs all adrip, and the carpet of green grass and flowers, and the long winter sleep, and the goodwill towards man that drinks and sings and fights but knows no treachery. That is how the Norsemen must have viewed America.

But although it remained for centuries a closed chapter, this coming of the Norsemen to Canada is of more than academic or historic interest. It bears directly on our future. We want them back again. Of all the people who have come to settle among us, there are none to whom the Canadian climate and environment is as congenial as to the Scandinavian races. They are, in a sense, more Canadian than ourselves. I have heard it argued by one of the most illustrious scientists of McGill that the peculiar tone and rigour of our climate, or of most of it, will turn us all into Scandinavians before it has done with us. The Nova Scotian and such may well remain damp enough to be a Scotchman, but the rest of us, especially in the North-West, will "go Norwegian." This may be a far cry, but even a far cry may have a nearer echo.

And the nearer echo is this. Immigration from the Scandinavian countries should be a major feature of our Canadian policy when at last British victory imposes peace on Europe. Such a peace will undoubtedly bring us a new migration from our home-lands such as never was seen before. But we can no longer dream of the open door of migration thrown wide to all nations. The British Empire can restore and impose peace and humanity and fair play, but it cannot create in the poisoned organism of continental Europe the trust and honour and mutual reliance now lost for generations in race hatred and in the creed of brute force. The hope of world peace, resting on power—for it can rest on nothing else, and on the humane use of it, or else it rots away—this hope lies only in our Empire and in America. The British Isles will be our European bulwark, buttressed with the adherence of nations kindred in race and ideals. In such companionship alone we can place our full faith.

One other bearing on our present world has this bygone chapter of our annals. It throws into a strong light the anomalous position occupied by the territory of Greenland. An accident of history, broken from all meaning, connects it with European sovereignty. Till yesterday this fact was of no consequence. This vast region, one-fifth the size of the United States, is nothing more than a huge bed of ice such as once buried all Canada. Alaska, at first sight its western counterpart, was derisively called, when Secretary Seward bought it in 1867, "Seward's ice box." Yet when the box was opened the Alaskan birds began to sing. But Greenland is, and remains, a chunk of ice. Of its area of 730,000 square miles, all but 30,000 is buried under ice. The "green" of Greenland is too small to matter. The fact is that Greenland is suited only for the Devil's work of air bases and hidden stations of attack from which to threaten the real continent. Even such mineral deposit as its cryolite, known since 1784 and found on the Arksut Fiord, in the ice-free corner of Greenland, is contributory rather to the uses of war than to those of peace. No one can think that the inhabitants of Greenland wish their territory to be a continuing menace to the peace of the world and of themselves. Their parent country, in chains or out, can never guarantee its own security, let alone that of a territory of 730,000 square miles, three thousand miles away. These Danes can play an important role in the world's future and one that will not be inconsistent with an accepted change in the international status of Greenland after the war.

With the close of the Norse voyages all definite connection between the mainland of North America and Europe came to an end. The continent remained, as it had been for uncounted centuries, empty. We think of prehistoric North America as inhabited by the Indians, and have based on this a sort of recognition of ownership on their part. But this attitude is hardly warranted. The Indians were too few to count. Their use of the resources of the continent was scarcely more than that by crows and wolves, their development of it nothing. Estimates of their numbers varied. But a recent scientific survey gives the figure of 1,100,000 to cover all the Indians in what is now the United States and Canada. This estimate, according to other authorities, is, if anything, an overstatement. But even at that, it only means one Indian to every seven square miles. But that again gives a false impression. The great bulk of the continent was far emptier than that. Such Indians as existed were in many places grouped together in considerable bodies; such as the 17,000 Iroquois between the Mohawk River and the Great Lakes, or still more, the coast Indians of British Columbia.

Mooney, Smithsonian Institute Papers, 1928

This meant that enormous stretches of territory such as those around the Great Lakes and on the Atlantic seaboard, were made up of unbroken forests, impassable except by lake and stream, where the voyager might wander for days without meeting, or expecting to meet, the face or trace of other human beings. The fiction of Fenimore Cooper and the history of Francis Parkman have preserved for us the aspect of what it once was. "Seen from above," says Parkman, in speaking of this primeval forest, "the mingled tops of the trees spread in a sea of verdure basking in light; seen from below, all is shadow, through which spots of timid sunshine steal down among legions of lank, mossy trunks, toad-stools and rank ferns, protruding roots, matted bushes and rotting carcasses of fallen trees." Even more lonely, but with the strange attraction of its very loneliness of grass and flowers, were the wide savannahs, the open prairies that stretched "in airy undulation" from where William Cullen Bryant saw them in the Ohio territory till they reached the sunset of the far Canadian West below the Rockies. As late as at the first establishment of Manitoba (1870) Captain Butler

Francis Parkman, "Half Century of Conflict," Vol. I, Chap III

"The Prairies," 1842

Captain (later General Sir William) Butler, "The Great Lone Land"

could write of our North-West, "there is no other portion of the globe, in which travel is possible, where loneliness can be said to dwell so thoroughly. One may wander five hundred miles in a straight line without seeing a human being." Such, and no more, is the meaning and extent of the Indian ownership of North America.

From this long sleep the continent was awakened by the tumult of the age of discovery that brought the voyage of Christopher Columbus in 1492. His discovery came, like everything else, because it had to. It was a part of the new awakening of Europe when the night of the Middle Ages gave way to the dawn of the modern world. Many causes contributed. The invention of gunpowder ruined feudalism. There are in warfare two permanent enemies, the attack and the defence. First one and then the other is uppermost. In the Middle Ages defence had utterly beaten attack. Huge stone castles on hillsides and escarpments, with well-water and ample provisions, could resist indefinitely. Then came the train of artillery and the castles fell. The attack prevailed and stayed uppermost for centuries, till the Boer war of 1899 first showed trench warfare, that was to mean the deadlock of triumphant defence in the Great War. Now has come the new chapter of aerial bombardment; attack leads as never before.

De Revolutionibus Orbium Celestium, 1543

A.D. 1610

Thus the close of the Middle Ages saw feudalism give way to great national states with trains of artillery and the cannon of ships of war. That meant a new political order. With it came the awakening mind; the art of printing; the rediscovery of Greek learning; the new mathematics and astronomy, Copernicus and Galileo's telescope. The old heaven and earth literally passed away.

Justin Winsor, "Narrative and Critical History of America," Vol. I

Not one but many scientists and navigators revived the Greek theory that the earth was a sphere. Sail west long enough and you would get east. Several model "globes," like that of Martin Behaim, had been made before Columbus sailed. Hence came new power and confidence in navigation and transport—the compass and the quadrant, and the art of sailing against the wind. Galley oars were packed away for ever in the new triumph of sail. Longer voyages were possible with new opportunities for

STANLEY ROYLE, R.B.A., R.C.A., SACKVILLE, N.B., 1941

*"From this long sleep the continent was awakened . . . by the voyage
of Christopher Columbus . . ."*— PAGE 20

commerce. The Portuguese ships reached farther and farther down Africa.

Then came the precipitating cause that set all others into operation. The invading Turks overran Eastern Europe, took Constantinople (1453) and blocked the trade route to the East. From time immemorial trade had passed from Asia to Europe by overland caravans and by the Red Sea. The route was so long and varied that the Asiatic end was lost in the mist. When Marco Polo told Europe about it, they classed him with Herodotus and other such liars. Thus the East remained a place of myth and fable and magic attraction, containing somewhere Arabia Felix, and Prester John, and the Great Khan of Tartary, the Empire of Cathay and the Islands of Zipangu. These were the names that later lured Europe to discover empty America, where Cathay turned into New York, and Arabia Felix was Manitoba.

A.D. 1298

Such is the background of the voyage of Christopher Columbus. Let it be noted how filled with paradox are the annals of the discovery of America. It was accidentally found in their path by men who were certain it was not there. As Goldwin Smith has said of Columbus, "the new continent was discovered by the man who had staked most on the belief that no such continent existed." Columbus died still thinking America part of the East Indies. Even when it had to be admitted that the continent was there, its "discoverers" still hoped to find a way round it or through it. They found it hard to believe that the globe is divided, as it is, by one huge mountain barrier reaching virtually from pole to pole. Cabot and, after him, the Elizabethans and Henry Hudson were trying to get round the top of the continent. This was the famous "North-West Passage" to Asia, the arctic mirage that ended only when Roald Amundsen's voyage in the *Gjöa* in 1903 proved it feasible and worthless. Others tried to get through by going up the St. Lawrence. The name "Lachine," even if given in irony, chronicles this waning belief in a passage to China. As late as 1634 Champlain sent Nicolet up the lakes to Wisconsin, which he thought was part of Asia. For it was hoped that the rivers of the interior might somehow lead to a portage "over the top," as indeed they do in Central America. John Smith, in going up the Chickahominy in Virginia, carried

"The United States," 1893

R. G. Thwaites, "The Colonies," 1901

letters to the Grand Khan. These eager hopes passed by as of no account the dense forests, the broad savannahs, and the silent waters of an empty continent—its real wealth. This frenzied expectation of palaces, of stores of gold and silk and precious stones, misdirected and distorted all the discovery of America. When the expectation turned to reality in the treasures of the Aztecs and the Incas, the wrong turn became the main highway. Thus the real America, our northern continent, had to wait for a hundred years. We have but to recall the calendar and course of discovery in the sixteenth century, to realize that this was not yet settlement, but search. Columbus landed on Watkin's Island in 1492. John Cabot sailed the coast of Newfoundland in 1497. It was in the year following that Vasco da Gama successfully carried the Portuguese trade-route around the Cape of Good Hope to India. This eastern reality strengthened western effort. In 1501 Corte-Real, another Portuguese, explored the North American coast south of the St. Lawrence. In 1513 Nuñez Balboa made his way through the jungles of the Isthmus of Panama and looked out on the illimitable Pacific, "silent upon a peak in Darien." In the same year the ageing Ponce de Leon searched the "land of flowers" (Florida) looking for the Fountain of Youth, which was not there. Old men still seek it there in vain. Hernando Cortez (1519-20) first achieved reality in his seizure of Mexico and its treasure of precious metals. Velasquez landed in "Chicora," now South Carolina, in 1625 to catch slaves, but found instead Indian savages. Narvaez tried again for Florida in 1528, landed at Pensacola, was lured inland by the savages and perished in the swamps with all of his three hundred followers except four. These men, eight years later, reached the California coast and were saved by Spaniards from Mexico. Coronado (1540) and other Spaniards explored the Rio Grande and spent three years on the south-western plains, looking for the fabulous "Seven Cities of Cibola." These things are not part of the history of Canada except that they show the reason why there was no history of Canada. The search went on. The brothers Pizarro (1532) achieved an even greater result than Cortez in their discovery and conquest of Peru. Fernando de Soto went overland through the swamps and reached the Mississippi, where

Keats
of Cortez,
in error

he died of swamp fever. Where the lure of gold failed, the sign of the Cross held firm. After the adventurers came the missions from Santa Fé in 1598 till the end of the chain in San Francisco (1776).

With this Spanish adventure went that of France. It was conspicuous in the voyages of Jacques Cartier (1534-41), as discussed later. But it failed signally in attempted establishments in Florida and Carolina (1562-64) and on Sable Island, off our Nova Scotia (1568). The British calendar of exploration in North America showed a long gap after the Cabot voyages. Attention had turned elsewhere, to the Russian seas and to the Levant. Hakluyt chronicles a voyage to Newfoundland made by a leader called Hore, ending in misery and cannibalism, a poor "ad" for this country, as we should say. Then no one came till Martin Frobisher (1576), who sailed into our arctic seas, "for the search of the strait or passage to China." He brought home what seemed gold ore, came again and fetched back quite a cargo of "fool's gold" (iron pyrites). Then came, just at the end of the chapter and of the century, when exploration was to be exchanged for settlement, Sir Humphrey Gilbert's glorious but futile voyage and first attempt at English colonization.

A.D. 1536

C. P. Lucas, "History of Canada," 1891

Thus practically all this early enterprise in the New World was vitiated by its inferior purpose. It was based on the search for treasure, domination and the rapid fortune of conquest. It did not carry with it the fundamental justification of settlement and of a new home beyond the sea.

But even apart from this misdirection of enterprise towards gold and treasure, there were other reasons why much of the best part of the continent slept, and sleeps, so long; why the worst was taken and the best left. These reasons lay in the peculiar geography of access from Europe to the North American continent. One can hardly deny that the western, the Pacific, coast, offers the more attractive area of settlement. To realize this, one has only to think of the sunshine of California, the island paradise of Vancouver and the adjacent shores, and the soft climates and the warm currents that wrap these latitudes.

But there was no way to reach this western side of the

A.D. *1519*
A.D. *1577-80*

continent. The voyages of Magellan through the straits named after him, and those of Drake and others round the Horn, proved that the Pacific could be reached by a sea voyage. But the route could not serve for commerce and migration till later centuries brought better means of transport and better control of scurvy. Balboa's discovery made it possible to reach the farther ocean through the jungles and fever of Panama and to build ships on the Pacific coast. This served for Peruvian adventure and for the establishment of the Pacific missions but it also was out of

J. M. *Gibbon,*
"Steel of
Empire,"
1935,
Chap. IV

the question, for centuries, as a broad path of migration. The Pacific indeed could be reached by an overland journey, as it presently was by Alexander Mackenzie in 1793. But this journey through a savage country of prairie, desert and mountain ranges could only become feasible long after Atlantic settlement had opened the way. Hence the far west stayed empty and unknown, and most of all the part of it that now is Canada. The penetration of North America on the east is facilitated by a coast line easy of access, with innumerable harbours. But the coast once occupied, access to the interior is impeded by the ranges of the Alleghanies. Hence the coast was first settled while the region of the Great Lakes and the Ohio territory remained empty. Access was found through the break offered by the Hudson River and the Mohawk Valley, and by the gap of the Potomac. On the south the tortuous channels of the Mississippi in a land of back-waters and bayous, waited long for commercial use. On the north-east, however, the St. Lawrence offers with the Great Lakes the widest fairway into the very heart of North America, a route still fully to come into its own. But it is ice-blocked in the winter, and in the early days of settlement the hostile tribes of the Five Nations lay across the path. North of the continent is the wide entrance of the Hudson Strait and Hudson Bay and James Bay and the tributary rivers that offer access to the western plains. But here the desolation of the ice-bound sea echoes to the desolation of the barren land. It is not without meaning that the names Hudson Bay and York Factory and Albany River, reproduce, as the counterpart of their christening, New York and Albany and the Hudson River. But the ports of this northern region, when occupied by the Hudson's Bay Company, remained, as it were, island outposts in the frozen seas with no access to the main settlements in America. At as late a date *A.D. 1811* as Lord Selkirk's Red River Settlement, this isolation still prevailed.

Reflecting on these facts of geography and history, we can realize why the earlier settlement of North America left much of the best of it still untouched. The Western Peninsula of Upper Canada lay empty and untenanted. The fertile valleys of British Columbia and its fortunate islands called in vain. The North-West prairies blossomed and withered with each forgotten season while the moving sails, the waving banners and the marching feet of three hundred years of history passed them by.

Our country waited. Its mighty rivers moved, silent and mysterious, from the heart of an unknown continent. The waves thundered on the rugged coast where it fronted the Atlantic Ocean. For the passing ships that explored its shores all was silence and mystery. Beyond it was the unknown East and from it breathed, as the sun set behind its forests, a sense of history still to come, the murmur of many voices caught as the undertone of its rustling woods. Our country waited—whereby in the fullness of time it might play the larger part.

MEMORABLE DATES

1535
Jacques Cartier discovers the St. Lawrence

1605
Founding of Port Royal

1608
Champlain founds Quebec

1610
Hudson discovers Hudson Bay

1642
Maisonneuve founds Montreal

1670
Charter of the Hudson's Bay Company

1672
Count Frontenac comes to New France

1682
LaSalle descends the Mississippi to the Sea

1689
Massacre of Lachine

1713
Treaty of Utrecht

" . . . the Indians led Cartier . . . . to the top of the nearby mountain"
—PAGE 41

CHAPTER II

THE COLONIAL ERA
1534-1713

The Voyages of Jacques Cartier—Hochelaga and Stadacona —The Fisheries of the Gulf and the Banks—Sir Humphrey Gilbert—Champlain and New France—Port Royal and Quebec—Maisonneuve and Montreal—Penetration of the Interior—Hurons and Iroquois—Missions, Massacre and Indian War—Life and Growth of New France —The Seigniorial System and the Fur Trade —Pathfinders of the Mississippi —Frontenac and the Indian and English Wars —Treaty of Utrecht.

THE settlement of New France, like that of New England, does not begin until the seventeenth century, which brought actual and permanent colonization by Champlain, by the Puritans and by the Virginia Company. But a prelude to this settlement is found in the preceding voyages of Jacques Cartier, in the opening by both French and English of the Newfoundland fisheries, and in the unsuccessful attempts at colonization made by Sir Humphrey Gilbert and Sir Walter Raleigh.

The voyages of Jacques Cartier came as an interlude in the unending wars of Europe, preceded by the wars in which France and Spain struggled for the conquest of Italy, and followed by the long series of wars called with unconscious irony the 'wars of religion.' In this pause the restless and energetic Francis I of France, the king who has left to the world after his defeat at Pavia the immortal phrase, "All is lost but honour," found a new field for honour to occupy. He turned his eager ambition

J. Winsor— "The Narrative and Critical History of America," Vol. IV.

towards overseas empire and the western route to Asia. This last was, so to speak, the 'grand prize' that such a sovereign as Francis I would naturally covet. The first commission given to Jacques Cartier, a St. Malo pilot recommended to the king by his admiral, has not been preserved. But other documents show that the voyages of Cartier and of Roberval, his later associate and superior, aimed at the expected opening up of Asia by way of the Western Sea. The discovery of the St. Lawrence and of Hochelaga only strengthened this belief, or at least led the pilots to make capital of it. The new commission to Cartier after his great discovery, speaks of "Canada and Hochelaga" as "forming one end of Asia in the direction of the west."

But higher purposes and more real ambitions were mingled with this search for imaginary empire. For Cartier himself the conversion of the savages to the Christian faith was throughout a leading motive, as witness his setting up of the great cross at Gaspé. Moreover the prospect of treasure from America itself presently became as bright as the vague vision of Cathay. We are told in the opening of the narrative of Cartier's third voyage (the new voyage after the discovery of Hochelaga), that King Francis enjoined him to "attain to the knowledge of the country of the Saguenay, where there are, as is declared, great riches and very good countries." Such is the background of the famous voyages of Jacques Cartier which remain, in spite of their confused and uncertain terminations, one of the great episodes of world history.

The first voyage (in 1534) was little more than a reconnais-
Cartier's sance. Cartier left St. Malo on April 20, 1534, with two ships,
Narrative in each of about 60 tons, and, in all, a company of 61 men. They
Hakluyt's sailed across to Newfoundland waters in three weeks and passed
Voyages through the Strait of Belle Isle and into the Gulf of St. Lawrence. There was nothing unusual or novel in this. For a whole generation already the fishermen of four nations had flocked to these grounds. Cartier himself, after he passed the strait, met "a large ship from Rochelle," looking for anchorage. But his design was to continue westward, beyond the familiar coastal fishing ground, and to find the passage to Asia.

Cartier followed the north shore of the Gulf a little way

westward from the strait. He found it empty and desolate. "I believe," he wrote in his narrative, "that this was the land that God allotted to Cain." This sounds like a jest, the first, the original of the jokes on Canada. But it is not. After the pious fashion of the age, Cartier meant what he said; he had found where Cain went to, and he quite understood it. He left this shore in disgust, turned south along Newfoundland, then struck out westward across the Gulf past the Magdalens and along the west end of Prince Edward Island. Here was a different country indeed, a land of delight. "It is the fairest land," he said, "that could possibly be seen, full of goodly meadows and trees." He skirted the New Brunswick coast and beyond it, on the Gaspé Peninsula, set up a tall wooden cross, thirty feet high, carrying a shield and three fleurs-de-lis, and at the top the legend *VIVE LE ROI DE FRANCE*. The scene remains in our history, a picture that never fades.

Here and there the explorers saw Indians, especially on the warm waters that Cartier called the Baie des Chaleurs and on Gaspé. They were friendly, frightened people, half naked and so destitute that Cartier thought they must be the poorest in the world. He noted that they had their heads shaved "except for a tuft on the top of the crown, as long as a horse's tail." The ominous meaning of this 'scalp-lock' was as yet fortunately hidden from the Frenchmen.

Cartier crossed to Anticosti, rounded the east end of the island and made his way westward along the north shore. Where the island ends, rough winds and adverse currents blocked his advance. But in turning back he at least felt sure that he had found a westward passage. His homeward voyage was through the Strait of Belle Isle for as yet he knew no other way out of the Gulf. In spite of terrific storms from the east that delayed him in mid-ocean he reached St. Malo (September 15) one month after sailing from the 'north shore.'

There followed next year the famous voyage that disclosed Hochelaga and the water gateway to the continent. Cartier himself wrote a narrative report of his first voyage in a manuscript now lost. It was not printed during Cartier's lifetime, though printing was in its first flower, but the report gained for Cartier ample royal support for a new voyage. The king gave him three good ships, the *Grande Ermine* (120 tons), the *Petite Ermine* (60 tons) and the *Emérillon*, otherwise the *Merlin* or *Sparrow Hawk*. To this was added supplies for eighteen months, so that the expedition might winter overseas—all very different from the treatment accorded by the stingy Henry VII of England to John Cabot, who was sent out to make discoveries, like the later despatch of Mr. Pickwick by the Pickwick Club, at his own charges. The ships' companies numbered in all 110 souls, mostly sailors of St. Malo, together with a few 'gentlemen adventurers,' those 'younger sons' who figure so largely in the making of Canada. But whoever they were, Cartier's men played a brave part in adversity. Included in the crew were two Indians who had been taken on board the year before at Gaspé and invited, without option, to spend the winter in France.

The ships left St. Malo on May 19, 1535. A tempestuous voyage parted them in mid-ocean but they came together at their rendezvous off the White Sands, inside the Strait of Belle Isle (July 26). The great Gulf was now familiar ground. This time Cartier was able to pass Anticosti on its north side and then cross to the Gaspé side of the St. Lawrence. Time was wasted in a fruitless detour back to the north side of the river in the vain hope of a passage-way, from which they turned again west, heading up the St. Lawrence.

S. E. Dawson,
"The Saint
Lawrence"
On the first of September the ships reached the mouth of a great river, which fell into the St. Lawrence from the north side through a gloomy gorge of rock. Cartier's two savages told him that this was the river that led to the Saguenay country, and so the river was called and is called the Saguenay—to the great confusion of all readers. For it would seem that the fabulous 'Empire of Saguenay' ought to be somewhere north of this river mouth. But when Cartier reached Stadacona, 83 miles on, and Hochelaga another 160 miles west, the Indians still pointed westward and talked of the Saguenay country. The confusion ends for anyone who looks at the map with an enlightened eye. For the Saguenay River comes down from the north-west, in the

first place from the great Lake St. John, which lies west of the city of Quebec (Stadacona) and from this lake begins the ascent of great rivers that lead to the portages of Lake Mistassini, and to the Nottaway River and thus to the Hudson and the James Bays—our new El Dorado of the north. The fabled kingdom of Saguenay passed into the class of the Cities of Cibola and the Land of Prester John, but in reality it was there all the time with treasures of copper and gold and silver, waiting for its discovery three and a half centuries later.

So Cartier passed on from the Saguenay, and as he moved up the St. Lawrence the shores of the great river narrowed in, and the scene about him changed from desolation to a land of enchantment. All about him was the blaze of the autumn woods of Canada, a thing unseen in Europe. The forest was festooned with hanging vines, here were islands where hazel-nuts hung from the trees, and another so heavy with clustered grapes that Cartier called it Bacchus Island. He presently thought better of this and gave the island a more reputable name as the Island of Orleans. But whether of Greek god or French prince, the island still keeps the charm that Cartier found.

Now when Cartier reached this point the Indians told him that here began the land and province (*terre et prouvynce*) of Canada. With that enters into history the perplexing mystery of the name of our country, and with it the lesser perplexities of the territories Saguenay, Canada and Hochelaga.

This first mystery remains unsolved. We still do not know where the word Canada comes from. All are familiar with the fantastic derivation that makes the word mean, 'nothing here.' The idea was that, before Cartier came, some Spaniard or Portuguee, angered at not finding gold, said in disgust, "*Aca nada!*" The polite natives picked up the word and repeated it to Cartier to mean "That's us." Equally silly is the gross slander involved in the derivation from the Sanskrit 'Kanata'—"a small feeder." Put beside this the derivation once current in Puritan New England to the effect that Canada is called after William Kane who went up there in 1621—a patron saint lost to history. Much better is the claim that Canada is an old Portuguese word to mean the 'narrows' or 'the channel,' that is, the route leading on

Winsor,
Vol. IV, p. 67

to the supposed Western Sea. It is true that such foreign words were now and then dropped on to our map without trace of origin; as witness the Spanish 'Orillia' that fell mercifully out of the sky as an improvement over Champlain's 'Cahiagué.' But the simplest derivation and the best is that 'Canada' was not the name of any one place but was the Huron-Iroquois word for the collection of lodges (such as Stadacona, Hochelaga and Onondaga) which the explorers called a town. Indeed the narrative of Cartier's second voyage has at the end of it a vocabulary of the language of the natives which says in exact terms. *"Ils appellent une ville—Canada."* This might seem to settle it. So high an authority as Dr. S. E. Dawson has said that we may save all waste of "learned labour" by "permitting the Huron-Iroquois to know their own language." But unfortunately the narrative itself keeps using the word as the name of the territory, not the town, as when it says, in the text quoted, "Here begins (at eight leagues above Ile aux Coudres) the province and territory of Canada." At this point of the story Cartier had not yet seen the town (Stadacona). Still, we have to remember that the narrative was written later; indeed, as will be seen, the text has certain suspicious peculiarities about it. Perhaps the word was used in a double sense, as 'town' is used to-day. People in England talk of London as 'town' and 'go up to town' from their own town, without getting muddled.

S. E. Dawson, "The Saint Lawrence," 1905

Cartier anchored his ships in the channel between the Island of Orleans and the north shore. The savages, hitherto seen only at intervals, as in canoes that danced in the foam of the Saguenay, or lurking in the woods, now appeared in numbers. Their first fright disappeared in tumultuous welcome when they recognized Cartier's two Gaspé guides as long-lost kinsmen of their own. The good news spread. The day after their arrival the Lord of Canada—'Le seigneur' Donnacona, appeared with twelve canoes and a great company of people. Cartier gave out presents. There were dances and long Indian harangues of welcome, a first experience of what Indian oratory has bequeathed to our continent. Cartier moved his ship up the stream till he saw the panorama of the "very beautiful and pleasant bay," the basin of Quebec.

Text of Narrative, H. P. Biggar, "Voyages of Jacques Cartier," 1924

Cartier decided to make his winter quarters here. He warped his two larger ships up the stream of the little River St. Charles which here falls into the St. Lawrence. The Indians would have had him stay but Cartier was all anxiety to go on while yet the season allowed it. All that he heard of Hochelaga and of Saguenay made him believe that the great Indian kingdoms and the opening to Asia were farther on. The town of 'Stadacona' was just an outpost. Cartier, so far as we know, heard nothing of 'Quebec.' The term begins with Champlain, and is Algonquin. Cartier's Indians, as we recognize from his list of words, were Huron-Iroquois.

Finding persuasion, dances, and even oratory of no avail, the Indians tried to frighten Cartier with dressed-up devils and a spirit message, specially sent by the great god Cudragny of Hochelaga. But in spite of signs of treachery and ill-will, Cartier left for Hochelaga. His main company stayed with the ships. With Cartier went his gentlemen adventurers and fifty seamen. They had with them the *Emérillon* and two boats. Low water made it wise to leave the *Emérillon* (at the upper end of Lake St. Peter) and use only the boats.

This happy ascent of the river, bright with autumn colour, occupied thirteen days. Thus it was that towards the close of day of October 2, 1535, Cartier and his companions halted their boats where an island blocked the river and made a swift rapid. Here at the foot of St. Mary's current they landed and a great concourse of Indians flocked joyously around them. This was Hochelaga. Here are the words of the *Narrative* that depicts one of the most notable scenes in our history:

"And on reaching Hochelaga, there came to meet us more than a thousand persons, both men, women and children, who gave us as good a welcome as ever father gave to his son, making great signs of joy; for the men danced in one ring, the women in another and the children also apart by themselves. After this they brought us quantities of fish, and of their bread which is made of Indian corn, throwing so much of it into our long-boats that it seemed to rain bread. Seeing this the Captain, accompanied by several of his men, went on shore; and no sooner had he landed than they all crowded about him and about the others, giving them a wonderful reception. And the women brought their babies in their arms to have the Captain and his companions touch them, while all held a merry-making which lasted more than half an hour. Seeing their generosity and friendliness, the Captain had the women all sit down in a row and gave them some tin beads and other trifles; and to some of the men he gave knives. Then he returned on board the long-boats to sup and pass the night, throughout which the Indians remained on the bank of the river, as near the long-boats as they could get, keeping many fires burning all night, and dancing and calling out every moment *'aguyase'* which is their term of salutation and joy."

Next morning at the break of day the Indians led Cartier and his men through woods "as beautiful as any forest in France," to see the town of Hochelaga. On the way they had a rest beside a fire—a brisk October morning—and more Indian speech-making which, as the narrative sadly remarks, "is their way of showing joy and friendliness." After their rest, their way led to the famous stockaded 'town' of Hochelaga, where they were received by a tumult of Indian welcome. The appearance of the place is chronicled in the narrative of the voyage.

"The village is circular and is completely enclosed by a wooden palisade in three tiers like a pyramid. The top one is built crosswise, the middle one perpendicular and the lowest one of strips of wood placed lengthwise. The whole is well joined and lashed after their manner, and is some two lances in height. There is only one gate and entrance to this village, and that can be barred up. Over this gate and in many places about the enclosure are species of galleries with ladders for mounting to them, which galleries are provided with rocks and stones for the defence and protection of the place. There are some fifty houses in this village, each about fifty or more paces in length, and twelve or fifteen in width, built completely of wood and covered in and bordered up with large pieces of the bark and rind of trees, as broad as a table, which are well and cunningly lashed after their manner. And inside these houses are many rooms and chambers; and in the middle is a large space without a floor, where they light their fire and live together in common. Afterwards the men retire to the above-mentioned quarters with their wives and children. And furthermore there are lofts in the upper part of their houses, where they store the corn of which they make their bread."

The above description of the palisade of Hochelaga has been a standing puzzle for the ingenuity of interpretation for over three centuries. That it means some kind of tall stockade fence, is clear; but we must remember that it was made by people with no better tools than axes of stone and some few, perhaps, of native copper such as Champlain found later. Whatever the place was really like, we may be certain that it in no way resembled the famous old woodcut often reproduced, a product of artistic imagination—or of despair. But the picture is worth mention for the history that it carries. As has been already said, the narrative of Cartier's first voyage was not printed. Cartier's own *"Relation* script was lost but copies were made and one still survives. It is *Originale"* generally agreed that it was composed by Cartier. The language is Breton French, and the terms are those of the sea, the style the plain narrative of a pilot. There survive also several manuscript narratives of the second voyage of which this Hochelaga description is a part. But authorities agree that this was not composed by Cartier himself. It is prefaced with a florid and fulsome address to the king and with a denunciation of Lutherans, as people to be put to death. It bungles the sea terms. It strongly suggests, in its description of Hochelaga and later in its visions of the Kingdom of Saguenay, that the writer was trying, as advertising men would say, to 'sell' America to King Francis. This narrative of the second voyage was printed in 1545 but only *"Bref Récit"* one copy of the book survives, in the British Museum.

Now all copies of the manuscript narratives of the voyages were lost from sight for centuries. Meantime the story of Cartier was only known by a translation into Italian in the collection of *Navigations and Voyages* printed by Giovanni Battista Ramusio *G. B. Ramusio,* in 1556. One of the surviving copies of this book is in the pos- *"Navigationi* session of McGill University. It contains also an Italian trans- *e Viaggi,"* lation of the *Bref Récit* of 1545, and this was translated back *1556* into French and printed in 1598. Richard Hakluyt, the famous clergyman of Queen Elizabeth's time, who promoted seafaring by gathering *Principal Navigations, Voyages,* etc., had Ramusio's text translated into English and put it into his volume of 1600. These were the narratives of Cartier's voyages as known to the world till the fortunate discovery in Paris (1867) of a copy of the original manuscript of the narrative of the first voyage, and the reprint of surviving manuscripts of the second, gave us back the text. The woodcut of Hochelaga was made for Ramusio's text and copied and recopied ever since—venerable in its ridiculous inaccuracies. It shows carpenters working with sawn lumber; makes Hochelaga so large that it would reach from the mountain to the river, its houses utterly confused in number and shape, and Mount Royal dwarfed into a hillock.

W. D. Lighthall, "The False Hochelaga," Roy. Soc. Canada, 1932

Some years ago (1925) the writer of this book had the honour of unveiling the Hochelaga Stone that stands at the foot of the McGill grounds—unveiling, or dedicating, or whatever is done to a stone. He felt the same perplexity about the location and real size of the place as Ramusio's artist himself. We have to remember that Hochelaga had apparently disappeared when Champlain came in 1603. All that has been found of it are buried remnants of fireplaces, the debris of kitchen middens, arrows and implements, pipes and human skulls. There are none of the half-burned timbers that might mark the site of such a structure. It seems possible that the 'wigwams' and the palisades of Hochelaga were lighter and more completely combustible than the text suggests. Such relics as have been found indicate for Hochelaga a site along the foot of the McGill grounds, extending down to Burnside (once its protecting river) and east and west from Metcalfe to near Victoria. The centre of Hochelaga was therefore (as in a sense it still is) in the lounge room of the present University Club.

The Indians who crowded about the French in the open square of Hochelaga—it was a stone's throw either way—greeted them with every sign of welcome and devotion, as towards superior beings. They laid mats for them to sit on. They brought their sick and infirm to be touched. Cartier read to them aloud from the Gospel of St. John, the Indians lifting rapt eyes to heaven, in pious imitation. After the presentation of beads, hatchets and trinkets, Cartier and his people left the stockade with a grand flourish of trumpets.

From the stockade the Indians led Cartier and his companions, his attendant gentlemen and twenty sailors, to the top of the nearby mountain, which he named Mount Royal. From its points of vantage they could see some parts of the rapids later to be called Lachine, the broad expansion of the river above, the mountain background to the north, the valley where lies the Ottawa, and, far away in the other direction, the downward river, the broad flat forest and the cone-shaped mountains beside the Richelieu—a view in all of thirty leagues, they said.

The Ottawa Valley seized their interest. This must lead to the Kingdom of Saguenay. Their hopes were raised when the Indians, of their own accord, took hold of the silver chain of Cartier's whistle, touched the yellow metal handle of a sailor's dagger— and pointed up the Ottawa. The meaning of this was long obscure to historians. They thought it meant the silver of the river. The discovery of silver in the road-bed of the Temiskaming and Northern Ontario Railway, over two and a half centuries later, makes the Indians' meaning as clear as it seemed to Cartier.

The season was growing late. Cartier and his men left Hochelaga forthwith, regained their boats and the *Emérillon*, descended the river and rejoined their men beside Stadacona. In their absence the men had built a solid fort of log walls around the ships, defended with the ships' cannon. It was to stand them in good stead. But at first the savages were friendly. They took Cartier with his gentlemen and fifty sailors to see their 'town' of Stadacona. This was a group of lodges and storehouses, far less of a place than Hochelaga. But there were the same dances of welcome, the same 'after-dinner' oratory. Here the French first saw tobacco-smoking. Their narrative reports that the Indians "fill their bodies full of smoke till it cometh out of their mouth and nostrils." Here, too, the sight of human scalps drying on frames, revealed to them what the scalp-lock meant.

It was now in the middle of October. The winter set in and there followed at the fort a season of privation, of danger and anxiety, that deepened into horror. The Canadian cold struck with all its rigour. The ships, as early as mid-November, froze at their anchors, in ice that thickened to two fathoms. The demeanour of the savages changed. Cartier learned from secret sources that they intended to overwhelm and destroy the French. The fort was strengthened. Guards were set and trumpets sounded day and night at the change of watches.

Then came the onslaught of a hideous plague. Students of history who have shuddered at the account of the plague at Athens in the great civil war in ancient Greece, may read with interest the grim story of the pestilence of Cartier's winter.

Thucydides, "History of the Peloponnesian War"

"Some lost all their strength," runs the narrative. "Their legs became swollen and inflamed, while the sinews contracted and turned as black as coal. In other cases the legs were found blotched with purple-coloured blood. Then the disease would mount to the hips, thighs, shoulders, arms and neck. And all had their mouths so tainted, that the gums rotted away down to the roots of the teeth, which nearly all fell out."

This was *scurvy*, the dread and horror of all long voyages till modern medicine and hygiene loosened its fatal grasp. Of Cartier's company of 110 by February only ten, himself among them, remained in health; later not more than three. As best they could, they must man the ramparts, keeping the Indians away, misleading them by noise and clatter. Twenty-five died and lay frozen and hidden under snow; the ground, congealed to stone, forbidding burial. Then came a miracle. The Indians, little knowing the truth, were deceived into revealing a remedy. This was a decoction, brewed from some species of Canadian balsam, that worked a cure as sudden as it was complete.

The worst was past. But with the spring the Stadacona lodges began to fill with new and fiercer savages from the north, far different from the gentle people of Hochelaga. There was no doubt now of their purpose. Cartier determined to be gone. With the break-up of the ice, he hastened his preparations. But he believed himself to be in the very gateway of a land of gold and treasure and he determined to bring to King Francis the visible proof of it. The treacherous chief Donnacona, still intermittently friendly, had astonished Cartier with his talk of the Kingdom of Saguenay. He had spoken of "immense quantities of gold, rubies and other things," of men "as white as in France." He threw in, for good measure, tall stories of a race of men with no stomachs, who never ate, of a race with only one leg and

April 15, 1536

"other marvels too long to tell." As Cartier saw it, Donnacona was too good to lose. He must take him along to the king. The unhappy chief fell a victim to his own imagination. When Cartier's ships were ready, he had his men seize Donnacona and four *May 6, 1536* others. There was a rough scene. The chief's Indian braves fled in panic. Donnacona and his fellows were taken on board the ships, round which the Indians howled all night like wolves. The next day, before sailing, Donnacona, appeased and flattered by the promise of the king's favour, appeared on deck to wave good-bye to his tribe. He made, we are told, "several harangues" and sailed away, apparently still talking.

Those who condemn Cartier for kidnapping Donnacona should better understand the spirit of the age. Columbus had sent home in 1495 five shiploads of Indians to be sold as slaves in Seville. *Article "Columbus," Encyc. Brit., 1929* John Hawkins was presently to be knighted by Queen Elizabeth for opening the Guinea trade in kidnapped negroes. We may see in Donnacona and his mates not slaves, but household curiosities, gay with trinkets and vain with self-importance. All of the Indians brought over died in France, except one little girl. But, like Lady Macbeth, they would have died tomorrow. It is unfair to sully a great reputation for an imaginary wrong, or one at least devoid of cruelty.

For Cartier is one of the heroic characters of his age—courageous, patriotic, devout. There was nothing in him of the brutality of the Peruvian conquerors. Wherever he went, the Cross and divine service went with him. To him the savages were God's children. He braved all dangers but made no attempt at conquest in arms. He faced undismayed the onslaught of the pestilence and the treachery of the savages that seemed to preclude all hope of a return to France. His followers appear to have evinced a faith in their leader worthy of his leadership.

Reflecting on Cartier's part in the foundation of our commonwealth, we realize how deeply graven on it is the seal of France; how necessary it is that we should regard this heritage and recognize the permanence of French nationality and language as one of the corner-stones of this our British Dominion.

Cartier sailed from Stadacona on May 6, 1536, and reached the port of St. Malo on July 16, 1536. The king's abounding

favour promised new expeditions. But Cartier's later voyages
and his association with Roberval need not concern us here. The
record is confused. We cannot rightly follow their coming and
going. Nor was anything thereby accomplished for the further
development of colonization.

After Cartier's voyages the 'Canada' that he had disclosed and
named fell back from the foreground of interest. There were still
the fisheries and many individual voyages into coastal waters.
But the energies of the nation were turned elsewhere. Canada
still slept under its forests, while 'religion' thundered its wars
over Europe.

To Newfoundland is commonly conceded the rank of Britain's
oldest colony. Modern research scholars, who can never let a good

thing alone, have lately disputed this title. It is claimed that actual settlement in Bermuda began in 1610, several months before actual settlement in Newfoundland. But this is only the pleasant nonsense of research scholars, unable to understand a plain thing in a plain way. Under Sir Humphrey Gilbert's patent, the sovereignty of Queen Elizabeth was proclaimed over Newfoundland in 1583; and the "New Found Land," to mean the island and the mainland coast adjoining, was familiar to English sailors for nearly a hundred years before Bermuda is known to have been visited by them.

Indeed the occupation of Newfoundland, and with it, of Labrador and the Gulf coast, by English and other fishermen begins with the voyages of John Cabot. Wonderful stories came home with Cabot to England. There has been preserved a contemporary letter from an Italian in London to the Duke of Milan, in which he says that Cabot's sailors "practically all English from Bristol, affirm that the sea is swarming with fish which can be taken not only with a net but in baskets let down with a stone." With this begins the development of the maritime fisheries of the Gulf and the Banks which fill so large a page in Canadian history. Soon after Cabot's second voyage the Atlantic passage was familiar to a whole fleet of fishing boats out of Bristol and the Channel ports of France, from La Rochelle and from Portugal. As early as 1522 the energetic Henry VIII sent a royal ship of war down the Channel to protect the "coming home of the New Found Island's fleet." Apart from seasons of tempest, the voyage was no great matter. The vessels only came and went in the summer season. At its close they drove home with the north-west wind, filled to the hatches, in a voyage often hardly more than a fortnight. They fished at first in the shallows of the Gulf, then out, and farther out, on the Grand "Banks" a hundred miles from land, where the continental shelf of North America falls steeply into the deep sea.

H. A. Innis,
"The Cod
Fisheries,"
1940

It is true that for the first half-century the English boats still kept chiefly to their familiar Iceland fishing grounds, the vessels sailing from the east-coast ports of England and out of London —149 vessels in 1528. But after the middle century the Newfoundland fisheries grew apace and engaged a fleet out of the

English ports which numbered by the reign of James I about 300 vessels.

The fishermen made no lodgement. They landed to dry and salt their fish, to get wood and such supplies as might be. The winter they never saw. They carried with them their wine from Portugal and it was found that by a kindly miracle of the sea the wine improved with the journey. Later—ideas came slowly in those days—they carried wine back and forward on purpose and Newfoundland port added its lesser glory to Newfoundland cod.

Thus went on these nameless voyages through the unwritten annals of nearly a century. But some men in England dreamed of wider enterprises than fishing. Among them was Sir Humphrey Gilbert, half-brother to Walter Raleigh. He had all the force and inspiration of the Elizabethan age; studied charts of the sea, dreamed of empire and wrote a *Discourse of a Discovery of a New Passage to Cathay*. Gilbert it was who made the first attempt at British colonization overseas. Queen Elizabeth gave him a charter (1578) "for the inhabiting and planting our people in America." Under this he made a voyage to the Florida coast

(*Sir*) *C. P. Lucas, 'New France' (Part I of "Canada") 1901*

that came to nothing; then in 1583 he sailed again with five ships and a company of two hundred and sixty men bound for the Newfoundland coast. They were a varied lot, carpenters and artisans to build a settlement, "mineral men and refiners"—in case of gold—and "morris dancers" (meaning Moorish dancers) "for the solace of our people and allurement of the savages." Thus came Vaudeville to America.

It is typical of the times, and illustrates our limited acquaintance with them, that when Gilbert sailed into the harbour of St. John's (August, 1583) there were thirty-six ships lying in port.

F. Parkman, "Pioneers of France," Chap. I

The name (St. John's) was there long since. Like those of many capes and bays in Newfoundland, it seems to date back even before Cartier; as witness similarly our Cape Breton Island. Gilbert took formal possession, no one opposing. But his colony came to a premature end. Gilbert and part of his fleet were lost on the homeward voyage. Such men, if any, as he left behind, were merged among the fishermen. Yet the 'sovereignty' remained, and permanent settlers wintered after 1610. Gilbert's

STANLEY ROYLE, R.B.A., R.C.A., SACKVILLE, N.B., 1941

". . . . *the Newfoundland fisheries grew apace* . . ."—PAGE 45

best legacy to his country was his last known words, called from his doomed ship, "We are as near heaven by sea as by land."

Equally lofty in its motive and equally disastrous in its fate was the attempt of Gilbert's half-brother Raleigh to found a colony to the south. Two vessels sent on a summer voyage of reconnaissance (1584) landed on Roanoke Island, in what is now North Carolina, and brought marvellous accounts of a land of delight. Raleigh was knighted and in 1587, with royal help, sent out seven ships with 108 colonists to colonize this new 'Virginia.' The Roanoke settlement struggled for six years against Indian treachery and the inexperience and false hopes of its own colonists. In spite of reinforcements the place was abandoned, its last occupants falling victims to the Indians.

Thus (in 1601), with the beginning of the new century, America still awaited settlement. Then came Champlain, the Pilgrim Fathers and the Virginia Company, and a new era begins.

✦   ✦   ✦

Samuel de Champlain (1567-1635) shares with Jacques Cartier the highest honours in the annals of French Canada. To Cartier belongs priority of discovery and of the conception of empire. Champlain, indeed, was not born until thirty years after Cartier's discovery. But in length of service and in actual accomplishment there is no comparison. Cartier's voyages, passed and gone in eight years (1534-1542), left no settlement. Cartier knew nothing, except from hearsay, of what was beyond Hochelaga. Champlain's service, in and for New France, of which he became the first Governor, lasted in all thirty-three years. He made thirteen voyages from France to America and twelve from America to France. He explored North America from the Bay of Fundy to Lake Huron, from the navigation head of the Saguenay to the head of the lake which bears his name. He helped to establish Port Royal on Annapolis Basin, the first white settlement since the Norsemen, and his 'Habitation' of Quebec, established in 1608, with which begins New France, is the first settlement in Canada that lasted without eclipse. Where he had worked he died (1635) and found his last resting place.

The life-work of Champlain that covers these long years can be set down here only in the briefest résumé. He was born to

*N. Dionne,
'Champlain,'
"Makers of
Canada"*

*To and From
America*
*1599   1601
1603   1603
1604   1607
1608   1609
1610   1610
1611   1611
1612   1612
1613   1614
1615   1616
1617   1618
1620   1624
1625   1629
1635*

the sea—the son of a sea captain of Brouage on the Bay of Biscay; was a soldier under Henri Quatre, and a ship's captain on a two-years' voyage to Mexico and the West Indies (1599-1601). He wrote a *Brief Discourse* of this, and proposed a Panama canal. He was selected in 1603 by a nobleman who had a royal patent as captain of a voyage to Canada. He followed in Cartier's tracks, up the St. Lawrence and beyond Lachine. In the next year the patent passed to the Sieur de Monts, under whose authority Champlain surveyed the Atlantic coast from the Gulf of St. Lawrence to Cape Cod, and aided in founding a settlement (1604-5) at Port Royal on Annapolis Basin, an inlet from the Bay of Fundy.

This was the first establishment in Nova Scotia, sixteen years before the patent, given by James I to Sir William Alexander, altered its name from Indian-French Acadia. Port Royal was to share the vicissitudes of two centuries of peace and war, eclipse and resurrection, cession and retrocession, till its identity passed on to the 'Annapolis' of Queen Anne, hard-by its original site. But Champlain's faith was set inland, not on the coast. In a new voyage of 1608 he founded and named Quebec—a landmark in the geography of history of the New World. He penetrated inland, opened up the waterway of the Richelieu to the lake named after him; took sides, in a fatal hour, for the Hurons and Algonquins against the Iroquois, and thereby prejudiced, if he did not compromise, the ultimate destiny of New France. Still looking for a western ocean he searched the lakes and rivers of what was to be known as Upper Canada, reached as far as Lake Nippissing, descended thence to the Georgian Bay and was the first of the French, not perhaps to see, but at least to reveal to the world, the marvellous interior country of lake and river, of rolling hills and fertile valleys that lay embowered under the forests of Ontario. This, Champlain saw—the upper slopes of the Western Peninsula, the Lake Simcoe district and the long chain of intermingled lakes that lead again to the Trent River and Lake Ontario. Crossing the lake to where is now Oswego, Champlain again adventured himself in Indian war and repeated his earlier fatal error by an attack on a palisaded Onondaga (Iroquois) fort, a replica in kind of Hochelaga. He had yet to learn,

S. E. Dawson, "The Saint Lawrence," 1905

as Frontenac learned later, that to destroy an Indian stockade meant no more than to knock down the nest of angry wasps. The wasps remained. The Iroquois from now on blocked the westward path of French settlement. The promised land of the Lake Simcoe district—Champlain's own discovery—slept for two hundred years like the enchanted wood in the fairy story.

With the coming and going of the season that froze and reopened his highway, Champlain went back and forward across the sea, seeking in vain that full aid towards colonization and real settlement which he never found. His Quebec remained little more than an outpost in the wilderness. The merchants wanted trade, the priests conversion, the Crown empire. All this was but a frame without a picture. As beside the Puritan emigration ship and the cradle rocked in New England, it was nowhere.

Then came the brief war of France against Charles I, which for a moment snatched Quebec from its founder and sent him a prisoner to England. The peace of 1633 gave back to France its own, and Champlain returned to Quebec, to serve and to die in service. It remained for others to realize in part his ambitions, and for another nation to realize them to the full. Yet in his thirty-three years he had definitely set the imprint of his purpose on New France. The unknown wilderness assumed an outline. The empire of France in America had begun.

One pauses to view here and there in detail this shadowy outline of empire. There is much in it that carries down to our day, not as of antiquarian interest but as bearing upon the supreme and still unsolved problem of settlement in a new country. Here, for example, is the Port Royal of Champlain and his associates, built on the hillsides that border a beautiful inlet of the Bay of Fundy. This was indeed a lost paradise in a fertile and exuberant wilderness. Yet here was made apparent already, as the first scene in the drama of civilization in America, that problem of want in the midst of plenty, of nature's bounty and man's ineptitude, which remains its latest dilemma and its increasing paradox.

Here was Port Royal, a beautiful settlement in a great quadrangle of spacious houses of fragrant logs—kitchens, offices, and

Lescarbot,
"Histoire
de la
Nouvelle
France,"
1612
smoking chimneys, snug as comfort itself—embowered with gardens, gorged with fruit and fish, fowl and game. Here was reproduced something of the comfort and more than the plenty of old France. Not even the chefs of the Rue aux Ours could furnish such a table. Such plenty indeed was it, that the assembled gentlemen must needs cheer their winter leisure with huge daily feasts, served to the midday appetite of open-air men, and carried in huge platters shoulder high, with ceremony and songs, under the mock rivalry of a circulating stewardship of the Order of Good Cheer (L'ordre de Bon Temps). Let the winter snow blow! To them February was as merry as May. Add to that, a wit or two among them, a touch of letters, and, in especial, a

Lescarbot,
"Muse de
la Nouvelle
France"
merry fellow called Lescarbot, snatched from the law to grace the wilderness. In his clever verses and his odd conceits we salute across three hundred years our first Canadian humorist!

Here, then, one may well seem to see a Utopia, to be the first of many, a vision such as people from an old and crowded world have ever pictured in the country of a new. Here were all the easy gifts of nature and, as their supplement, the handsome profits of the trade in furs, the by-product of the fisheries rapidly becoming greater than the fisheries themselves.

Why was all this too bright to last? Why was it that the labour of associated men could not demand an easy and continuous sustenance from a nature all too willing? And if not for them, with their limited contrivances of three hundred years ago, why still not, with the inconceivable increase in our mechanical control? This, next to the destiny of the human soul, remains man's chiefest preoccupation.

For Port Royal the explanation is not far to seek. The surface was appearance, the reality was below. This was no real gathering of free men, united for a common welfare. In this as in the other settlements of New France a worn-out feudalism, almost at the breaking point in Europe, tried to reach out its hand for the New World. Here were 'gentlemen and simple' where nature decreed equality. Here were, as the workers, indentured servants, wifeless in a new country, with no stake of their own, their eyes

CHARLES W. JEFFERYS, R.C.A., TORONTO, ONT., 1941

" . . . *Port Royal, a beautiful settlement in a great quadrangle of*
spacious houses . . . "— PAGE 51

in the pauses of their toil set only on some village street in Brittany. Not thus can the roots of a nation be sunk in a new soil. And over it all hovered the favour or disfavour of a court across the ocean, that gave and withdrew charters, conferred and confiscated monopoly, and could break a settlement with a word, as Port Royal itself was broken. Add to this the intermittent ravage of disease, the plague that ignorance could not fight, and that submissive piety could only amplify. Add again that outside somewhere in the great emptiness of the woods were the savages, incomprehensible, unreconciled. As the last touch of a darkening picture, add to the end the intermittent ravages of European wars that fell upon American settlements in their infancy, reduced them to smoking ruin, or traded them to and fro as the prize of war. Not thus comes Utopia.

Even at the death of Champlain New France was little more than an outpost in the wilderness. He had replaced his earliest 'Habitation' by the solid Fort St. Louis, built on the rock of Quebec, and capable, so the English presently reported, of withstanding ten thousand men. Quebec was already the Gibraltar of America. David Kirke forced it to surrender (1629) only by starvation, though its garrison numbered only sixteen. Quebec at this time contained less than 100 souls in all, and beside it were only the posts at Tadoussac and Three Rivers.

Nor did the situation greatly change for a whole generation after Champlain (1635-1663). The colony had been placed under the charge of a Company of One Hundred Associates—merchants of the fur trade with a sprinkling of 'birth' to mark ambition. Over all was the fostering care of Cardinal Richelieu, determined, as Champlain had been, to make New France a settlement, not an outpost.

But New France was misguided from the first. It was indeed so sturdy a plant that it clung somehow to the rocks of the St. Lawrence through all hardships. But it lacked settlers. The Huguenots, defeated and exiled, would gladly have come but their entry was forbidden. Their energy and industry must seek another flag. Most Frenchmen were too comfortable at home to cross the seas. The French are not a migratory race; the British, an island people, blow easily over the sea; the French remain in their vineyards.

F. Parkman,
"Pioneers of
France,"
1865

In place of the people at large came the priests and the nuns, the martyrs and the virgins of the Canadian wilderness. New France here profited, so to speak, by the back-wash of repentance that goes with a dissolute court. Ladies of fashion redeemed their sins by subscribing funds for the salvation of the savages. "The fair votaries of the court," it has been cleverly said, "found it easier to win heaven for the heathen than to merit it for themselves." Thus it came about that the little group of Recollet Friars who first accompanied Champlain were supplemented after 1625 by an increasing band of Jesuits, whose Order will be forever associated with our history.

It was, in part at least, the influence of this religious crusade which led the colony of New France to advance, regardless of danger, into the interior. Soldiers, priests and nuns formed the main establishment of the advanced post, the Ville Marie that became Montreal, set up by the Sieur de Maisonneuve in 1642. Champlain had already marked out a site hard-by the vanished Hochelaga. But even the courage of that day long hesitated to occupy a spot so dangerous in its isolation, so direct in its challenge to the resentful savage. Here arose the fort and the palisaded hospital that preceded the walled town beside the river. Grim and lonely the place must have seemed, with the sounds of many waters at night, the uncanny stillness of the forest and the dread of the ambush of the savage—a place habitable only by courage and faith.

W. H. Moore,
"The Clash,"
1918

The soldiers of the Cross went farther still, beyond all help of their kinsmen. They planted missions (1634) in the far-off Huron country at the foot of Georgian Bay, which Champlain, as has been seen, had reached by way of the Ottawa and Lake Nipissing. From first to last, twenty-nine priests, with but a handful of soldiers, shared in the good work of the missions of Ste. Marie and St. Joseph. Each year they taught their peaceful Huron converts the good news of the gospel. Then came the ravaging Iroquois, like the Assyrian of old, and sword and flame swept away the missions. The names of Father Brébeuf and Father Lallemant, put to death by the savages with tortures beyond all description, were added to the roll of honour of New France. These deeds of blood rendered this beautiful district (the present County of Simcoe) for the time desolate, and closed it against settlement for two hundred years. The motor tourist of to-day, pausing a moment on its highway for refreshment, may see a sign pointing him to the 'Martyrs' Shrine' and with it to a whole chapter of our history.

Thus did the Iroquois, in their fierce rage for the conquest of their fellow savages, overwhelm the Hurons as they were presently to destroy the Eries and the Andastes. They led the way in that mutual destruction which proved the suicide of the Indian race. The time was one day to come when white men, superior in number and bettering their instructors in ferocity, were to round up the Indian bands, as General Anthony Wayne did in 1794, and make an end of them. Only those who have read too little of American history can shed tears for the Iroquois. *S. E. Morrison, "Oxford History of the United States," Vol. I*

Meantime, by a strange irony of history, the inroads of the Iroquois, and their central situation, kept empty and reserved for British colonization the best part of the claim of French Canada.

Of such events as those described is made the mosaic pattern of our pictured history. How slight a shift could change the picture. Montreal could easily have been similarly overwhelmed. Indian massacre ravaged around it as late as 1689 in the hideous tragedy of Lachine. Both Montreal and the Huron missions on the Wye could have lived secure had New France received sufficient settlers. But the associated traders who managed Canada had no wish for them. They wanted trade with the Indians for furs to sell in France for money, not farms and homesteads in the bush that brought in nothing. They wanted scouts and runners of the woods, and forts and posts where the rivers met— far away in forests—not the church-bells and the river street of a settled village. The priests and nuns could spread the gospel among the savages. A colony they could never make. The real colonists are children—a lesson which even yet we seem unable to learn in Canada. Thus grew French Canada, magnificent in its imperial outline, an empire while yet New England was a meeting house—but an empire, as it proved, of dreams.

Yet with royal government (1663) a great change came. Here was now the driving power of a rigorous administration on the spot—a Governor, a Bishop and a Council and an Intendant, the first appearance of the 'businessman' in government, and in those days a sort of fifth wheel to the coach to keep the others level. In nominal form the new Company of the West Indies for a time (1664-1674) controlled trade, land and administration in all French possessions from Canada to Florida. But in reality all such rights were exercised in Canada by the Crown. In France was the energetic government of the industrious, despotic Louis XIV, whose will it was that settlers should come over to New France.

There is a stretch of exactly half a century between the initiation of direct royal government in Canada in 1663 and the Treaty of Utrecht of 1713—the great landmark of American history with which appears on the map a British North America that was there to stay. The record is all scarred and disfigured with European war and Indian massacre. But through it we may trace the slow upbuilding of the life and growth of French Canada.

"Past Censuses of Canada," Vol. IV of Census of 1871

The new status of the royal province was marked by an energetic attempt at colonization. The population of New France in twelve years (1663-75) was more than trebled (2,500-7,832). The colonists were recruited by the shipload, sturdy people, chiefly from the sea-coast provinces of France. Of 2,500 newcomers as between 1600 and 1680, 481 were Normans, 108 from

S. A. Lortie, "L'Origine et le Parler des Canadiens Francais," 1904

Brittany, 357 from Poitou and 517 from other provinces on the Bay of Biscay. Those from inland included 378 from the Ile-de-France, in which is Paris. From first to last during the seventeenth century Normandy contributed about one-fifth of the settlers, Poitou about half as many. Presently there were sent ship-loads of women to be the mothers of New France. Marriage was enjoined, celibacy placed under a ban and bounties paid for early marriage and full cradles.

Settlement followed the plan necessitated by the environment. It began with forts and strong places established along the great river and its immediate tributaries—Quebec, Tadoussac, Three

CHARLES W. JEFFERYS, R.C.A., TORONTO, ONT., 1941

"The colonists were recruited by the shipload . . . sturdy people, chiefly from the sea-coast provinces of France"— PAGE 58

Rivers and Montreal. The posts were set strategically to command the waterways, as did Sorel (1665) at the mouth of the Richelieu, or Chambly, some sixty miles upstream and opposite to Montreal. Farthest and boldest in its establishment was Fort Frontenac (Cataraqui, Kingston), where the ascent of the river finds Lake Ontario. But this for a long time yet was not a true settlement but a precarious military post, conceived in the conquering spirit of its founder. For generations the habitation of peace ended for French Canada with Montreal and its adjacent islands, and with the sound of the church bells of Ste. Anne's, at the confluence of the St. Lawrence and the Ottawa. Beyond this was the bush, the fur trade, the Indian country and war.

New France was practically roadless. Except for such a military highway as that from Chambly to Montreal, roads were only of local service and small at that. Hence habitation clung to the waterways, with every house its landing, and all touching elbows for protection of the nearest fort. Thus were gradually filled the favoured stretches of the St. Lawrence—on the Island of Orleans, below and above Quebec, at and near Three Rivers, on and around the Island of Montreal as at Longueuil, Lachine and the Rivière des Prairies, and on the Richelieu beside Sorel, Chambly and St. Johns. The holdings all lay side by side along *"Vieux* the river, reaching back to the forest. The houses had the high- *Manoirs,* pitched roof, the dormer windows and, for the better ones, the *Vieilles* solid walls of stone, built on designs out of Old France in a *Maisons,"* country still without architects. Even the casual highway tourist *Quebec Gov't* of to-day can trace this imprint of the earliest settlement. It *Publication* contrasts with the rectangular roads and townships, laid out in disregard of nature, and the square-shaped farms that were to mark the British settlement of Upper Canada. The latter bears the stamp of peace; French Canada the imprint of war and danger, the mould in which it was cast. Both were to be later carried to our North-West; the pattern of French settlement marked the Red River and the Assiniboine, and found its end in the rebellion along the Saskatchewan. The Upper Canada pattern reached its glory, and its collapse, in the vast checker-board of the grain provinces. Each had its historic advantages. The British hundred acres of grain farm of Upper Canada might make a farmer's fortune, but the Frenchman on his river strip was harder to starve out.

The progress of settlement in New France was facilitated by the establishment of a feudal tenure of land (the seigniorial system) under which the proprietors were expected to bring out and establish a tenantry. Such grants are almost as old as the colony. Three of them antedate the Hundred Associates, the first (1623; Sault-au-Matelot beside Quebec) to Louis Hébert, head of the first settled family, that of Cap Tourmente to Guillaume de Caen (1624) and the first Jesuit grant (1626) on the River St. Charles. The Hundred Associates made grants generously, in all about sixty, but many were given to persons who never came to Canada, or to favoured individuals who left them unsettled and uncultivated. Nearly all were revoked later. But under royal government definite obligations of settlement and definite terms of tenure were imposed, and presently set forth as law. The system was copied from the varied feudal tenures of France. Religious bodies, holding in Frankalmoign, paid with their prayers only. For example, when the Hundred Associates gave grants to the Jesuits, the Order undertook to say Mass on the first Tuesday of each December for the souls of the directors of the company— a heavy obligation if it had been carried down in our history.

But the great mass of the tenures were those "en fief," otherwise "en seigneurie." The seigneur received his land on condition of clearing the forest, establishing settlers and paying certain dues to the Crown. On his inception, and on a royal accession to the throne, he must appear and swear fealty to the king, by deputy, at the Chateau de St. Louis in Quebec. This fealty passed on with the conquest and the last ceremony of homage was enacted as late as 1854, when the system was terminated by statute. Even this statute left a small yearly rental payable, and still payable to-day, to the heirs of seigneuries by such Quebec farmers (about one-third) as occupy former seigniorial land. In 1940 the Provincial government capitalized and bought out the remaining claims which stood at $180,000 a year. The farmers will repay the government in twenty years—or perhaps later.

W. B. Munro, "The Seigniorial System in Canada," 1907

"Arrêts de Marli," 1711

In return for his big service to the Crown the seigneur had the right to sub-let to smaller feudal magnates or direct to peasant farmers. He received rents and various pay in kind and services. Tenants who went fishing must pay their lord one fish in every eleven—words which speak volumes to the despairing angler of to-day. For both the seigneur and his vassals military service was the essence of the tenure. The law tried to make the seigneuries "contiguous," that is, all one piece of land and not in scattered parcels as often in Europe. But apart from this condition, there was no uniformity in size or shape, and even the boundaries were vague for lack of scientific survey. The largest of the seigneuries could compare with contemporary European principalities. That of Gobin, situated in the Gaspé Peninsula, *1690* was "ten leagues by twelve wide." The smallest were plots of a few acres. The Sulpician Order "Messieurs les Ecclésiastiques du Seminaire de St. Sulpice, établis à Montréal," received the magnificent grant of the island and its environs—a munificence which gave to the later crowded city the open breathing space and the old world prospect of the Priests' Farm. The same order received the seigneurie of the "Lac des Deux Montagnes" (1714).

A special case was seen in the grants to the officers and men of the Carignan-Salières regiment, disbanded in Canada in 1667. These lay along the frontier of the Richelieu, as the Roman 'colonia' guarded the Rhine. Among the historic and picturesque seigneuries of the families of the colony are those of Malbaie, or Murray Bay, below Quebec; the seigneurie of Monte Bello on the Ottawa, the former home of the Papineau family and now the marvel of the tourist; the seigneurie of Longueuil, joined with two others to make the barony granted in 1700 to the family of Le Moyne d'Iberville; the woodland seigneurie of St. Henri de Mascouche, some twenty-five miles north-west of Montreal, and many others of similar charm and historic interest.

The standing difficulty of the Crown was to enforce the bargain, to insist on residence, on clearance, on securing a settled tenantry. The temptations of the fur trade, the chances of gain and adventure, lured the men of New France to the wilderness as *coureurs de bois* and left agriculture neglected. It was reported to the king in Frontenac's time that 800 men of a total population

*Louis XIV
to
Frontenac,
April 20,
1681*

*F. Parkman,
"Count
Frontenac
and
New France,"
1877*

of 10,000 were absent without leave. These *coureurs de bois* became a source of alarm, an object of horror to the Crown. King Louis ordered them beaten and branded and, for a second offence, sent to the galleys for life. Meantime the Crown alternately multiplied the seigniorial holdings, or cut them off in despair.

A report made to the king in 1711 showed 91 seigneuries in all—mostly held by religious orders, especially the Jesuits. Retired officers held about twenty and a scattering of small ones belonged to the merchants. The report was discouraging. Few grants were made for twenty years, indeed none at all in the ten years 1717-27. The census of 1734 showed better results as to cleared land and settlement (a population of 37,716), and the grants were presently resumed and generously awarded till the conquest. The number of seigneuries, high and low, lay and religious, that passed under the British Crown was 218.

This foundation of the seigniorial system in Canada stands out as the only attempt at creating in America an hereditary class of distinction that has ever had even a partial measure of success. Any such attempt in the American provinces, later to be the United States, withered at its inception, as when the Province of Massachusetts (1636) refused the flattering proposal of Lord Saye and Sele and Lord Brook to emigrate, rank, status and all, to the colony. In British Canada, later on, the proposal of the Act of 1791 to "annex titles" was born dead. The attempt to create a country gentry under the same act by land grants and a church reserve of land, failed of its purpose. The gentry of Upper Canada kept turning back into ordinary people. It was apparent that gentlemen are born not made, or that they were made so long ago that the pattern is lost and there can be no new ones. Indeed, some years ago our Parliament (1936), in a final access of despair, advised the Crown of the impossibility of making hereditary gentlemen in Canada.

Even for New France it has been a matter of controversy whether on the whole the seigniorial system was of advantage. Its opponents claim that it made for an over-docile people, priest-ridden, untrained in freedom and submitting all too readily to authority. Yet at least it underlay the life of the colony; men fought and died under it. It lasted until 1854; it never bred rebellion and it left behind it, apart from the beauty of the seigniorial homes, a conservative love of a settled order of life. Moreover, being based on the idea that the Lord will provide, it tended to encourage that full cradle which became the mainstay of French Canada. The judgment passed on the seigniorial system depends on the eye of the judge. But it still remains to be seen whether land settlement, for which the free-land homestead system has gone bankrupt, may not be reconstructed in suitable places on a plan to borrow many features of co-operative effort from the old-time seigneurie.

The fur trade, as has been said, militated against the seigniorial system, against agriculture, and, in many ways against the best interests of the colony. This trade had arisen as a by-product of the coastal fisheries. At that day fur-bearing animals abounded even on the eastern coasts. It is related that the shipwrecked survivors of the settlement attempted by the Baron de Léry, were brought home from Sable Island and paraded before Henry IV (1603) as objects of interest and pity. They were unkempt, bearded, objects of horror, but clothed from head to foot in skins of seal and black fox, killed on the desolate island itself, to say nothing of a rich store of which their rescuers had robbed them. One may imagine what a wealth of fur the woodlands of the interior could then supply.

The Indians eagerly met the demands of the traders. Furs were brought down from every river route, the trade reaching farther and farther into the continent. For the French, Montreal became the great depot of the fur trade; for the English, Albany, the one time Dutch outpost, with access through the country of the Iroquois. For the English settlers the fur trade was a secondary and incidental matter. The mainstay of their life was agriculture, their exports, fish and tobacco. Hence the English let the trade come to them. The French went after it, establishing posts at such points on lakes and rivers as would meet, control and divert the traffic. The trade thus conjoined with the magnificent reach of exploration and empire which was the glory of French Canada. The English of New England, were individual men with their wives and children looking for a home in a new land, isolated in their very freedom. The French were the servants of the Crown

C. M. Knowles, "Economic Development of the Overseas British Empire," Vol. II, 1930

and the Cross, carrying a banner in the wilderness. Only on the sea do we find an English parallel for what the French did in North America. To them was due almost the whole disclosure of the inland continent.

'   '   '

Champlain himself had reached Lake Huron. The priests founded a mission on its upper waters at Mackinac (Michilimackinac); there was a Jesuit mission in 1640 at the Sault Ste. Marie. Jean Nicolet, a *coureur de bois* who lived among the Indians, first discovered Lake Michigan. The waterway and portage that leads thence by Green Bay to the Wisconsin and the Mississippi, was first traversed (1673) by Joliet, a trader, and Father Marquette, a Jesuit. They followed the great river 1,250 miles to the mouth of the Arkansas. Greysolon Du Lhut crossed Lake Superior and reached the Mississippi by the St. Croix. Father Hennepin, ascending the Mississippi, first saw the imposing falls of the upper river which he named after St. Anthony of Padua (1680). Greatest of all, not a mere pathfinder but an empire builder in his dreams, Cavelier de La Salle, who came to Canada in 1666, carried the sovereign claims of France from his seigneurie of La Chine to the Gulf of Mexico. His earlier journeys took him up the lakes, past Niagara and over the short and easy portages from Lake Erie to the Alleghany and the Ohio. He never desisted till he opened and explored this route, the greatest of the water highways, to the sea (1682). His twenty-one years of enterprise, culminating in his expedition by sea in 1684, ended in assassination (1687) in the wilderness.

(Sir) C. P. Lucas, "History of Canada," Part I, 1901

But the fur trade brought its own difficulties. It was from the first under royal licence and monopoly. But the illicit trade was as easy as it was tempting and the records show that at least one governor sought thereby to retrieve a broken fortune.

The fur trade found its way into regions beyond geographical knowledge. Two Huguenot traders, Pierre Esprit Radisson and Chouart des Groseilliers penetrated the unknown territory north of Lake Superior till they reached salt water. They brought sixty canoes of furs to Montreal. Punished as illicit traders, they offered their services to the English. From this was to follow the formation in 1670 of the Hudson's Bay Company.

CHARLES W. JEFFERYS, R.C.A., TORONTO, ONT., 1941

"... trade .... conjoined with the magnificent reach of exploration and empire ...."—PAGE 65

The trade grew of itself, increasing the use and demand for such valuable skins as those of the otter and beaver, an animal dying out in Europe. The beaver hat came in early in the sixteen hundreds and had a run of three hundred years. It is recorded that in one single season (1650) a hundred canoes loaded with beaver skins came down to Tadoussac. But the effect of the fur trade was to accelerate that wide extension of New France which was tending to make it little more than a vast web of claim and conquest spread over half a continent, based on a single central point of strength. Quebec gone, there would be nothing else.

L. and C. Knowles, "Economic Development of the British Overseas Empire," Vol. II, 1930

Through this mist of the past we can see what was and what might have been in New France. But the atmosphere is clouded with the smoke of perpetual war, the night sky lurid with the flames of raid and massacre. The story reads as one long record of conflict. To the struggle of civilization against savagery, is added that of British against French.

Kirke had taken Quebec (with one hundred people in it) in 1629. It was given back in 1632. But peace with England was followed by raids of the Iroquois and the massacre of the Huron missions. With royal government De Courcelles, and then Tracy, made vigorous war and ravaged the Mohawk country (1666). Then came the great Frontenac (first, 1672-1682) and built Fort Frontenac, burned out the Senecas and put fear into the savages. His successors La Barre and Denonville were weaker men. They fought, burned and ravaged (1683) but failed to conquer. The angered Iroquois descended the river in the summer of 1689. In the dead of night, in a heavy thunderstorm, they fell in hundreds on the outpost of La Chine. There followed the massacre which ranks high in the history of horror. Two hundred of the French settlers were butchered on the spot, with eighty soldiers who sought to defend them. One hundred and twenty were carried away for death by torture. Then came Frontenac again (1689-98), a saviour in distress, for the whole of French Canada was now in peril. The heroic episode of Madeleine de Verchères defending the fort (1692) marks the danger of the hour. Frontenac raided the Indian country, drove the Iroquois from the fur trade routes, re-established Fort Frontenac and laid waste the land of the Onondagas and the Oneidas.

F. Parkman, "Half Century of Conflict," 1892

But a new war with England, occasioned by the expulsion of the Stuarts, had already begun. It had only ended in the Peace of Ryswick in 1697, a year before Frontenac died at Quebec. The peace was just a breathing space. There followed Queen Anne's War, as American colonists called it, otherwise the war of the Spanish Succession (1701-1713), fought to decide whether the French king's grandson should be King of Spain. These two wars spread danger and dismay over New France and New England, with foray and massacre along their frontiers, the savages as attendant devils on both sides. They were signalized by the massacre of the Dutch at Schenectady (1690), by two unsuccessful attempts against Quebec (Phipps 1690, and Admiral Walker 1711), the capture of Port Royal by Phipps in 1690, its retrocession and its final capture in 1711, with innumerable raids and forays that brought little but misery and devastation, until Marlborough's victories in Europe brought to a world, weary with war, the compromise Treaty of Utrecht.

In America the French kept Canada and Cape Breton Island, but gave up Newfoundland, except for certain fishery rights, and abandoned all claim to the territory of Hudson Bay. With this treaty appears a permanent British North America, a substantial part of the area now called Canada.

"... an English ship (The Nonsuch) ... reached the mouth of a great
river flowing into James Bay"—PAGE 76

CHAPTER III

BRITISH AMERICA AND FRENCH CANADA
1713-1763

The Hudson's Bay Company — The French Exploration of the West—
Growth of French Canada — And of British America — King George's War,
1744-48 — Nova Scotia, Halifax and the Acadians — The Seven Years' War
and the Cession of Canada

FROM the arctic seas of Labrador the Hudson Strait, a channel 100 miles wide and 450 miles long, leads to the great inland sea of the Hudson Bay. The bay is roughly a vast circle, of a diameter of some six hundred miles, extended on the south-east 350 miles by the shallow and rocky James Bay. The bay never freezes, but its river mouths and harbours are beset with ice. The strait, leading to it, has stern, precipitous coasts of rock, between which drive violent tides reaching to thirty-five feet. The strait does not absolutely freeze over, but the moving ice of bergs and floes, both inside the strait and drifting in a flood a hundred miles across its mouth, preclude navigation, even under present-day conditions, from the end of October to the middle of June. In the historic days of sailing ships, safe entry and departure was from July 15 to October 1, a period of ten weeks.

Canada Year Book, 1940

The shores of the Hudson Bay, as apart from the strait and a few high bluffs towards Ungava, are everywhere low, mournful and desolate, with but small suggestion of wealth or life. On the north-west are the barren lands of slate and stone; west and south the low forests that struggle towards the shore and fail to reach it, and at the bottom end the marshes and shallows of James Bay. Only at the mouth of the Churchill River is there a good natural harbour (Fort Churchill); the other river mouths are open roadsteads with tortuous channels through the sand. Such was the land of desolation that till yesterday God seemed to have forgotten. Beside its hidden wealth of to-day all the vineyards of France are as nothing.

But the bay has also its unseen natural grandeur. An area of 1,379,160 square miles of land, almost one-quarter of our mainland continent north of Mexico, is drained by the great rivers that on every side pour into the bay. This watershed, that was to become the grant to the Company, reaches out westward to where the headwater streams of the Churchill and the Saskatchewan give place to those that run to the Mackenzie and the Arctic Ocean; south-west and south to where it divides the Saskatchewan from the Missouri and the Red River gathers the waters of Minnesota. From the south come the Severn, the Albany and the Moose and the rivers from the fabled Kingdom of Saguenay. This vast river system became the waterway of the fur trade for two centuries (1670-1869) of Company rule.

A. H. De Trémaudan, "The Hudson Bay Road," 1915

In discovery and exploration the bay is all British. The strait was discovered in the Cabot voyages but the bay, within, never really penetrated till Henry Hudson's voyage of 1610. Hudson's crew mutinied and set him adrift at the south end of the bay. Admiral Button, looking for Hudson, founded and named Port Nelson. Captains Fox and James, both carrying letters addressed to the Emperor of Japan, pretty well explored the coast and realized that Churchill harbour was not the passage to the South Sea. After that, the bay was let alone for half a century.

Douglas MacKay, "The Honourable Company," 1936

Now there was in New France a man of exception, Pierre Esprit Radisson. He spent many years living among the Indians, actually living with them, and he bettered their instruction in craft and ferocity. Fighting against the Mohawks, he had been captured and his torture at the stake begun, when he was seized and rescued by a squaw, who knew a man when she saw one. From then on, Radisson did not hesitate to join in burning his enemies at the stake, and to join, if his own language means what it seems to, in the cannibal feasts that were another variant of Indian pleasure. Radisson left a journal, written in what he understood to be English. No history book, diluted by a hundred repetitions, can match the crude reality of it.

Radisson and a lesser associate, his brother-in-law Chouart des Groseilliers, had wandered for years in the Lake Superior country. As already said, they had found their way to the James Bay. Radisson writes that they "came to the sea shore" where they found "an old house all demolished, battered with bullets." The Indians told them of white men being there and of "peculiarities of European." As to this Radisson remarks, "We know ourselves and what Europe is, therefore in vaine they tell us as for that." It has been thought possible that this old house had sheltered Henry Hudson.

When the officials of New France cheated Radisson and Groseilliers out of their furs, they went to France and appealed to the Crown. This proving vain, they decided to offer their services *1666* to England. By a stroke of good fortune they were put into touch with Prince Rupert, the cousin of King Charles II, who became thereby the patron saint of our North-West Territory. Many will agree that this remarkable man has not been assessed in our history at his true value. Born to arms and to adversity as one of the thirteen children of the exiled King of Bohemia, he served as a youth in the Thirty Years' War, was the chief military leader of the king's party of the English Civil War, and admiral at sea against the Commonwealth; and, in his riper age, a commanding figure at his cousin's court. Prince Rupert was not only a soldier but an art connoisseur, a scholar, an inventor and a scientist, one of the founders of the Royal Society of London. It is characteristic of the scholarship of the age that Prince *E. Warburton,* Rupert could do everything but spell, a thing no doubt to which *"Life of* *Prince Rupert,"* he was quite indifferent. In one and the same letter we find him *1849* spelling 'dog' in two different ways.

The prince's capable intellect perceived at once the value of Radisson's discovery that the fur country could be reached by sea. The sea route was ice-bound and arduous but shorter than even the voyage to Montreal, the mere starting point of the trade. It

substituted a summer voyage for a year in the wilderness. Rupert
1668 and an associated group of friends sent out Groseilliers, in an
English ship (*The Nonsuch*), to try out the plan. He reached the
mouth of a great river flowing into James Bay ('The Rupert,'
he called it) and from it returned with a rich cargo of furs.

On the strength of this success, Rupert and seventeen asso-
1670 ciates obtained from the king their incorporation as The Govern-
or and Company of Adventurers of England trading into Hudson's Bay. The charter thus granted to these 'undertakers,' as
it calls them, is a lengthy document, containing some six thousand five hundred words. It has all the relentless repetition of the
*Beckles
Willson,
"The Great
Company,"
1899,
Text of
Charter in
Appendix* language of the law. Where literary English would speak of
"waters," it says, "havens, bays, creeks, rivers, lakes and seas."
Where we should write, "points," it prefers, "places, seas, straits,
bays, ports, havens and territories." But it is worth all its words.
It is the most far-reaching commercial document in British his-
tory. The charter of the East India Company (1600) meant more
as wealth. But in their bearing on the reality of British empire,
the expansion of our race, there is no comparison between the two.

In sheer spaciousness the grant has never been equalled, except
by such fairyland dreams as the grant of Pope Alexander VI
dividing the New World half and half between Spain and
1662 Portugal; or the charter of Connecticut which was supposed to
dive under New York and Pennsylvania, come up to breathe
in Ohio, and go on somehow to the 'South Sea.' Inside the
bounds of fact and geography the Hudson's Bay grant has never
been equalled.

The charter creates a Company, with Governor, Deputy Governor, Committee and General Court, who are to be true and
absolute lords and proprietors of the territory granted, holding
it from the Crown as a part of the Manor of East Greenwich, in
the county of Kent, in free and common socage. The territory
covers what we would define in present-day English as the basin
of the Hudson Bay. Exception is made of land already possessed
or granted in the area (but there was none), and exception made
also of land already held by any Christain prince, a limitation
that vanished with the Treaty of Utrecht. The company are to
own the land, the fisheries, both inland and on the coast, all

mines ("gold, silver, gems, and precious stones") and to have the exclusive monopoly of trade.

They were given full jurisdiction, under the Crown, over the maintenance of law and order. They had the right to maintain ships of war, men and ammunition, to build forts and works of defence. They had the right to make peace or war, within the sphere of their operations, against any prince or people that were not Christians.

The whole of this magnificent territory is christened by the charter "Rupert's Land"—spelled thus in two words. The name has been ungratefully edged off our map, bit by bit, by the provinces and the territories. It has now been reduced—or elevated —to a purely spiritual meaning as a diocese of the Episcopal Church. A similar lack of historic sympathy has clipped the Company's Bay itself to the official 'Hudson Bay.'

But the charter went even beyond Rupert's Land. Where their own government ended the Company were to have the sole right of trade in all the "havens, bays, creeks, rivers, lakes and seas" into which they could find passage from their own area. This was later to mean that the Company could trade over the still unknown Rocky Mountains and into the still unsuspected British Columbia. This access to such "havens, bays and creeks" was to stand us in good stead; it was our first grasp on the Pacific. In recognition of the Crown the Charter calls on the Company to yield and pay yearly two elks and two black beavers "Whensoever we or our heirs shall happen to enter into the said countries, territories and regions."

The Associates subscribed £10,500 and commenced at once the series of voyages to the great bay from which their trade spread and multiplied. Within fifteen years the Company had established forts at Albany River, Hayes Island, Rupert's River, Port Nelson and New Severn. Their ships, at this time usually three, sailed from the Thames at the opening of June and went northabout round Scotland on their course to the strait. Caution and experience proved their best insurance. Only two were lost in 175 years. The cargoes consisted chiefly of guns, powder and shot, knives, hatchets, kettles, fishing nets, with glass beads to represent native luxury. The vessels were due to arrive home in October.

of.
Tribute to Prince of Wales, 1927:
King George VI, 1939

George Bryce, "The Remarkable History of the Hudson's Bay Company," 1900

J. A. J.
McKenna,
"The
Hudson Bay
Route,"
Canadian
Government,
1908

From the first the French disputed the Company's rights. Overland expeditions set up French forts. Even in nominal peace English forts were attacked and captured. King William's War (1689-97) witnessed the advent of a French fleet into the bay, commanded by Le Moyne d'Iberville, and his complete triumph over the English. The Treaty of Ryswick declared the west coast British and that of Utrecht surrendered this entire territory to Great Britain.   ,   ,   ,

While the English were thus pursuing solid commercial advantage in the Hudson Bay territory, with assets that multiplied ten to one in fifty years and paid by 1749 a 40 per cent dividend, the French were still pursuing dreams. Their lofty ambition still staked its claim across the unknown continent, still searched for the Spanish mines and the waterway to the Western Sea (*la Mer de l'Ouest*). From their new Louisiana, explorers reached the plains beside the Red River of Texas, the Arkansas and the Missouri. Le Sueur reached the prairie of upper Minnesota, black with buffalo. La Harpe and Bourgmont reached the plains that are now Kansas. Finally, in 1740, the two brothers Mallet ascended the River Platte, crossed the Colorado plains and reached Santa Fé on the headwaters of the Rio Grande.

L. and C.
Knowles,
"Economic
Development
of the
British
Overseas
Empire,"
Vol. II,
1930

These are forgotten names and exploits that proved futile. But very different is the fame that has enshrined in our history the expeditions of Varennes de La Vérendrye and his sons, whose explorations carried the first claim of the discovery of the Rocky Mountains in the United States, and in Canada the opening of the valley of the Saskatchewan.

,   ,   ,

La Vérendrye or, to give him his full name, Pierre Gaultier de Varennes, Sieur de La Vérendrye, born at Three Rivers (1685), was the son of a lieutenant of the disbanded Carignan-Salières regiment, who held a small seigneurie and with it the position of Governor of Three Rivers at a salary of 1200 francs ($240) a year. To this he added the usual profits, lawful and otherwise, of the fur trade.

From his youth, Varennes de La Vérendrye was trained to *1704* the woods and to war. He took part in the Deerfield Raid in

"*Among these Indians* . . . *came the Frenchmen, looking for the Western Sea*" — PAGE 82

CHARLES W. JEFFERYS, R.C.A., TORONTO, ONT., 1941

New England, went over to the war in Europe and was left for dead on the field of Malplaquet. On his return to Canada he *1709* resumed and followed for over twenty years the life of the woods and the pursuit of the fur trade. In the country north of Lake Superior he heard tales from the Indians of a great Western Sea of salt water. This fired his imagination, and to this search he dedicated the rest of his life. In it were associated his four sons.

La Vérendrye sought royal help in vain. The best he could obtain was the grant of liberal privileges in trade still to secure in territory still to find. On the strength of these pledges, with such fortune as he commanded and such aid as friends and associates could supply, La Vérendrye and his sons carried on their expeditions that spread over more than a decade. From Lake Superior they first struck north and west, opening up the route that later became the water and portage way to the Red River. They set up forts, so called, along the route—stockades with log blockhouses inside them. Fort St. Pierre on Rainy Lake, Fort St. Charles on the Lake of the Woods, Fort Bourbon on the east side of Lake Winnipeg marked a chain of communication from the lakes to the plains. A profitable fur trade was thus turned from the Hudson Bay to the Lakes. Other forts reached farther out—Fort Dauphin on Lake Manitoba, Fort Rouge, probably near-by the present Winnipeg. One of the sons set up a fort at the mouth of the Saskatchewan, and ascended that river to the Forks—the union of the north and south branches. The forts were not all continuously occupied. Lack of means forbade it.

Seven years were spent in these labours, these hardships and dangers. The eldest of La Vérendrye's sons was killed, with *1736* twenty companions, in a hideous massacre by the Sioux on an island in the Lake of the Woods. Nor had any success attended La Vérendrye's search for the Western Sea. It retreated as he pursued it. Indeed the Indians now told stories of tribes to the south, on the Missouri, who knew the way to the sea. Thither *L. Burpee,* turned La Vérendrye. With two sons and twenty men he left *"The Search* Fort la Reine in October, 1738, to enter on the first of the series *for the* *Western Sea,"* of journeys over the plains from the Assiniboine to the basin of *1908* the Missouri and of the Yellowstone, that ended in the claim to the discovery of the Rocky Mountains (1743).

* * *

One cannot but admire the extraordinary intrepidity of these French explorers of the great plains. Here was a new country beside whose emptiness, desolation and danger, New France seemed friendly and familiar. Here were no longer the bark canoe and the river in the forest. Here in a treeless landscape huge shallow streams ran in a devastating flood, or dried to rivulets among the stones. The prairie blossomed green and gay with flowers, or burned, arid and waterless, beneath the sultry sun; in winter the fierce blizzard drove its snow across the frozen plains, and cut to the heart of life unsheltered. Here were strange Indians, their speech unintelligible. They rode on horses, wild horses that had bred and multiplied on the plains since the Spaniards brought them to America. In place of the canoe of Canada were long poles dragged behind the horses, with tent skins strapped across them. The Indians, as in the east, were in perpetual war of ambush and butchery that never ended—the Sioux and the Snakes (the Shoshones) a terror even to their fellows. Thus did the Indians of the plains, like those of the woods, pursue their senseless intertribal slaughter that spelt the doom of their race. What they did with limited means on their small scale, Central Europe, with the accumulated resources of centuries, now does on a large.

Among these Indians, utterly in their power but fearless with the pride of race, came the Frenchmen, looking for the Western Sea.

* * *

"Journals and Letters of L'Vérendrye," L. Burpee, Ed. 1926

These journeyings of the Vérendryes were the task of years—start and return and reconnaissance alternating with forward progress. La Vérendrye himself shared only in the earliest advance. Breaking health compelled him to return to Fort La Reine in 1739. His two sons carried on the work. At length in 1743 they came in sight of the outskirts of the mountains, a range of snow-capped peaks, beyond which—just beyond which, they thought—must be the Western Sea. Most probably they had reached, so it was generally estimated later, the Big Horn Range of Wyoming, an eastern outskirt of the Rockies, and, if so, the sea was still eight hundred miles away. But in any case they could not reach it. They had no means to go on. The Indians, circling on their path of war, were bent elsewhere.

The Vérendryes found their way back across the plains. On their homeward journey they buried on a hillside beside the Missouri, after a fashion already established in New France, a leaden tablet stamped on one side with the arms of France and an inscription prepared ahead, with the names of the King and the Governor (De Beauharnois), dated MDCCXXXXI. On the other, roughly scratched, was the name "Chevalyer de L VR" and those of two companions. It is uncertain which son now bore this title. Beside the names is the date "le 30 de mars 1743." The tablet was discovered in 1913 by school children of South Dakota in a hill across the river from St. Pierre.

On the second of July of 1743 the Vérendryes joined their father at Fort la Reine. La Vérendrye now returned to New France. Success and honour came to him at last. He was given a command of troops. He received the Cross of the Order of St. Louis. He planned a new expedition to the West and sent out supplies from Montreal to his forts. The help of the Crown for a new attempt to discover the Western Sea seemed assured. Vérendrye planned this time to ascend the Saskatchewan. Fate intervened. On the eve of his approaching departure for the West, La Vérendrye died at Montreal (1749).

The sons of La Vérendrye tried in vain to obtain leave to take his place. At the end of their resources and overwhelmed with debt, they wrote a pathetic letter of appeal. This plea was denied. Another military leader, Legardeur de St. Pierre, was given the place and the profit. Leaving Montreal in 1750, he took the search for the Western Sea very easily, never getting farther than Manitoba. Not finding it there, he let it go at that and from Fort La Reine he sent out a young officer, Jean Baptiste Boucher, Sieur de Niverville, who made his way on foot in winter across Lake Winnipeg and up the Saskatchewan to Fort Paskoyac. In the spring of 1751 Niverville sent men up the Saskatchewan who built a stockade, Fort Jonquière, at the foot of the Rockies. Niverville followed them but seemed to lack the courage to cross the mountains. The fame he thus refused was left for Alexander Mackenzie to gather.

The brothers La Vérendrye died in poverty and oblivion. Nor had ill fate finished with them even in death. It remained for modern geographical investigation to cast doubt—the unkindest cut of all—on whether they had really reached the Rockies or gone no farther west than the Dakota hills.

"South Dakota Historical Collections," Vol. VII.

Meantime the search for the Western Sea was lost from sight in the advancing shadow of the final war that was to end New France.   ,   ,   ,

The Treaty of Utrecht of 1713 had proved as unstable as all others during the long struggle between France and England from Louis XIV to Napoleon. War broke out again in 1744 and raged with its usual accompaniment of raid and massacre till 1748. It was signalized by the spectacular capture of the great fort of Louisbourg, Cape Breton, by ships, levies and leaders from New England. The Peace of Aix-la-Chapelle restored to France Cape Breton and its fortress but it brought only a calm before the final storm.

1748

Meantime the growth of the British Colonies in America was deciding the issue of the war before it had begun. New France had grown, indeed, but rather in outline than in intensity. At the time of the Treaty of Utrecht New France (Canada) had a population of 18,974, which had increased to 21,424 in 1720 when the Jesuit Father Charlevoix visited and described the colony. The total was 42,701 in 1729 and on the eve of the conquest (1754) it had reached 55,000. After that the statistics falter, as we have no actual count and many wild conjectures. During the same time the Acadians in the ceded portion of Nova Scotia had reached 8,500, of whom, as will be seen, 6,000 were presently expelled. The Acadians on the 'mainland,' later to be called New Brunswick, numbered 4,300 before the expulsion from Nova Scotia and gained by it later on about 500 refugees. Ile Saint Jean (Prince Edward Island) had 3,000 French in 1755, and likewise gained about 500 refugee Acadians. The new establishment of Ile Royale (Cape Breton) had about 3,000 people in and hard-by its Louisbourg fortress. Thus the whole French

"Censuses of Canada, 1665-1871," being Vol. IV of Statistics of Canada, 1876

F.-X. de Charlevoix, "La Nouvelle France," 1744

1755

CHARLES W. JEFFERYS, R.C.A., TORONTO, ONT., 1941

"... no wanton cruelty ... nothing in their fate of the
concentration camp ..."—PAGE 94

population in what we now call Canada, which was about 16,500 at the opening of the century, had increased to 73,800 by 1754.

The growth of New France itself represented further new settlements on the pattern of the old, river farms that made up the seigneuries of the Island of Orleans and of both sides of the St. Lawrence, those beside Three Rivers and up the Richelieu as well as on the Yamaska and the St. Francis. Population increased on Montreal Island, on Jesus Island and in the adjacent Terrebonne as well as across the river at Longueuil, Boucherville, Varennes and Verchères. Quebec with a population of 8,967 remained the commercial entrepôt as well as the military centre. Montreal alone approached it. This had grown to be a walled town beside the river, occupying what is now the financial district, with the rivulet and marsh that we call Craig Street below it. A mile or so south-west was the Seminary of the Sulpicians, the Seigneurs of the Island, whose two fort towers still stand beside their College of Montreal. The Chemin de la Côte des Neiges wound past the Seminary through the woods and over the hill to St. Laurent and to the villages of the Rivière des Prairies. Hochelaga still lay buried under its new forest beside its brook, undisturbed. Outside of Quebec and Montreal only a few towns (Charlesbourg, Varennes, St. Vincent de Paul, etc.) reached a population of a thousand souls. Three Rivers had less. Other places were mere villages or seigneuries with nearby tenants.

The seigneuries themselves kept being subdivided under the law of equal inheritance till many were little more than farms. Indeed one must be careful to distinguish the status of these seigneurs from that of the *noblesse* of France—the real thing. Authorities agree that no nobles of the highest rank came to settle in New France. Even of the 218 seigneurs at the close of the régime, probably only a score or so were of what would be called *noblesse* in France. François Masères, Chief Justice after the conquest, gives twelve as the maximum. But Masères was a Huguenot and ill-disposed. But we British-Canadians need not worry over this lack of noble blood among the French. There is far less among us. Noble blood does not emigrate to a wilderness. A castle is good enough.

Under the peculiar conditions of settlement in New France

C. W. Colby, "Some Canadian Types of the old Régime," 1908

Cavendish Debates on the Quebec Bill, 1839

manufacture and urban growth were impossible. Resources went unused. Iron was successfully smelted in forges at Three Rivers after 1737, and salt pans were operated at Kamouraska in the war time of 1744 but vanished with the peace. Shipbuilding,

F. X. Garneau,
"Histoire du
Canada,"
1913

desired and encouraged by France, could and should have flourished. It started and failed. In 1732 ten vessels, from 40 to 100 tons, were built at Quebec. But inexperience with Canadian timber balked the opportunity. Agriculture, fishing and the fur trade were thus the sole economic basis of the colony and provided its exports. From France came all wines and liquors, pottery, ironware, clothing, as apart from homespun, and, of course, all luxuries. There was no commercial wealth.

Once and once only a queer commercial "boom" lighted up the horizon of the little colony, with a glimpse of things as yet

1716

two centuries away. The plant ginseng was discovered in the Canadian woods, a plant that the Chinese were seeking eagerly as a magic medicine. It was bought in Quebec for two francs a pound and sold in Canton for twenty-five. The Canadians rifling their woods for ginseng dreamed dreams that their descendants were to share in 1928. The ginseng sent to China in one year brought home 500,000 francs. Then these first dreams went the same way as the last. The Chinese found the Canadian root overdried. The boom ended.

Charlevoix, indeed was painfully impressed with what he calls the "very general poverty" of New France. Yet he admires the agreeable society and the purity of the language, preserved by its very isolation. At least the colony was spared the curse of negro slavery (with the slave trade)—now over-spreading the colonial world, turning the West Indies black, and calling down

Files of
Quebec
Gazette,
1762-83

Ida Greaves,
"The Negro
in Canada,"
McGill
Publication,
1930

time's vengeance on America for its iniquity. Slavery was not illegal in French Canada, neither before nor after the conquest. Slaves were bought and sold and advertised for sale under the British rule. But the French government considered the climate too cold for negro slavery and prohibited any regular importation.

Communication from first to last was almost entirely by water, irregular and uncertain. There was a postal service, by monopoly, after 1721. Carriage and freight was so little organized that prices in Montreal might be fifty per cent above those of

Quebec. Money and currency were from first to last in confusion. From the beginning French coins were rare. Settlers and traders used beaver-skins and other substitutes as currency. Colonial coins (stamped by the Company of 1670) failed to circulate. Colonial (official) paper money never bred confidence and quickly lost value. 'Card money' with royal arms and a signature was about as bad. The Intendant's "promise to pay" was worse than either. The curtain of the conquest fell on this hopeless confusion. After the conquest came 'business,' and the Scots.

There is to the sympathetic mind something pathetic in this commercial failure of New France, on which military failure was now to set the seal—the lofty ambitions of empire as opposed to the "very general poverty"; the spacious feudality of a seigneurie that dwindled to a bush farm beside a creek; the agreeable manners of a people with little other hospitality to offer. Above all one thinks of the situation of the plain people, asking nothing but peace and obscurity on their river farms. The environment of Maria Chapdelaine, that has touched the universal sympathy of to-day, was there two hundred years ago. We who have fallen heirs to all that was best in New France should value its memory at its real worth.

Yet New France was not to pass without a spirited effort. A new basis of French power in America, was sought in the attempt to make Louisiana and Cape Breton replace, as two ends of the chain of defence, the losses of the Treaty of Utrecht. Louisiana, claimed by La Salle in 1682, occupied with a fort by Le Moyne d'Iberville at Biloxi in 1699, begins in earnest with New Orleans, founded by his brother in 1718. Its fortunes link with those of Canada till the conquest.

Cape Breton Island, separated from the Nova Scotia peninsula by the mile-wide Gut of Canso, had hitherto been disregarded. Fishermen alone used its coasts. It was now rechristened as Ile *1720* Royale. The huge fortress of Louisbourg rose on its coast, and Acadian settlers were invited in. In the closing days of the French régime it had a population of 4,300, doubled perhaps in the fishing season.

Beside it was the Ile St. Jean, our Prince Edward, another

desert island of France. This beautiful island—one-sixth of the area of Holland, which supports nine million people—lay long empty. Its mild climate, its fertile soil, its beautiful woods and meadows, have been the subject of praise from Cartier to Judge Haliburton. Cartier said it needed nothing but the nightingales of France, little realizing that it had its own. Haliburton, but this was later, threw in along with fertility, the fairy gift of longevity for its people.

D. C. Harvey,
"The French
Régime
in Prince
Edward
Island,"
1926

But history passed it by. The Comte de St. Pierre obtained in 1719 a charter of colonization, but it led to nothing. A few Acadian French came over to settle. With the war their little settlement was overwhelmed and most of them expelled. The habitation, called Fort La Joie, lost its nightingale name in exchange for that of the wife of George III (Charlottetown) and the island presently exchanged the name of St. John, for that of Prince Edward, later the father of Queen Victoria, at that time in command of the British forces in Canada.

1798

It is easily understood, therefore, that the growth of New France, apart from its ambitious outline, was as nothing compared with the overwhelming comparative advance of the English colonies in population, wealth, trade and command of the sea. The wiser of the French could see the reason. "The English," wrote Raudot, the Intendant of 1706, "do not leave their homes as most of our people do. They till their ground, establish manufactories, open mines, build ships, etc.; and have never yet looked upon the fur trade as anything but a subordinate part of their commerce." The mere statistics of the population show the case overwhelmingly. As compared with the figures above, the English colonies ('British' after the union of 1707) increased between 1650 and 1700 from a population of 100,000 to 250,000, and by 1750 had grown to 1,370,000. Boston alone had as many inhabitants as Quebec and Montreal together; the best of the seigneuries would hardly compare with the great manor houses of the wealthy Dutch on the Hudson, each with its train of white servants and black slaves.

F. X. Garneau,
"Histoire du
Canada,"
1913

Nor had British power in America grown only with this expansion of the existing Atlantic provinces. A new province was deliberately created after the Peace of Aix-la-Chapelle with the

1748

foundation of Halifax. It was obviously impossible to retain and develop Nova Scotia as a British province unless it was populated by British settlers. Two means were adopted to secure this, the one as laudable as the other was deplorable. The foundation of Halifax carries as its reverse side the expulsion of the Acadian French.

A splendid site for the new settlement was found on Chebucto Harbour. Here in 1749 was deliberately founded—a process hitherto alien to British policy—the town of Halifax, so called after the First Lord of Trade. The government went vigorously to work in a hearty British fashion, not doing the thing by halves. Parliament voted £40,000. When that ran out they voted more and more. Annual grants to Nova Scotia went on till in all

THE HISTORIC MARITIMES 1534-1763

£415,000 was expended. The government sought first for army and navy veterans. They gave free passage, free grants of land, subsistence for a year. They landed 1,400 immigrants at the settlement in the first season. The town rose under the hammer and the saw. They hammered such a British temper into it that it never lost it. Haliburton says that "in a short time there were 3,760 '*adventurers*' with their families." He means settlers of sufficient spirit to settle. The word '*adventurers*,' like its fellow word '*undertakers*,' has lost its nobility since the charter of the Hudson's Bay Company.

Even at that, there was great hardship. Many people died of cold in the first winter. Food sold at what seemed famine prices, milk at a shilling a pint. Much of the ground about the settlement was stony. A garden proved to be a bed-rock. The settlers were, many of them, as ignorant of agriculture as old soldiers are apt to be.

J. Wilson, "A Genuine Narrative," London, c. 1751

To supplement their efforts, Lutheran Protestants were brought out from Germany and 'planted' at Lunenburg, southwest of Halifax in 1753. The governor reported them next year as "almost incredibly industrious." They planted potatoes, flax-seed brought from Germany and appeared, said the same report, "greatly attached to their farm lots." Thus passed British Nova Scotia its early struggle for existence. The Crown, to fill the measure of its good-will, granted to the colony an elective assembly like those of the Atlantic provinces, a privilege admitted thus as a sort of common law right of British settlers.

1758

But with the morning light of the rise of Halifax a dark shadow falls across our history. As the annals of New France run to their close there is added the tragic page of the expulsion of the Acadians. This unhappy episode of opening war was to call forth the denunciation of Edmund Burke, the solemn condemnation of the historian Bancroft, and to be immortalized in literature with Longfellow's *Evangeline*.

"Narrative and Critical History of America," J. Winsor, Ed. 1884-89

The facts are these. Until the establishment of Halifax, the English had various claims on Nova Scotia but practically no settlement in it. There was James I's patent of 1621 which gave it its name. There had been the repeated capture and restoration of Port Royal. But at the cession of the peninsula (Cape Breton was not included) the settlers were French only. They numbered some 8,000 and were situated chiefly at Minas Basin where the rich land, dyked back from the sea and crowned with orchards, gardens and meadows, offered the lost paradise of Longfellow's poem. Other settlements were at Beaubassin (Chignecto) and Cobequid, now Truro.

These people, under British jurisdiction since 1713, were commonly called in the British provinces the "neutral French." Their status was uncertain. It was generally understood that France had made a plea in their behalf that they should only take an oath of allegiance to Great Britain with a proviso exempting them from fighting against France. No such privilege had ever been formally ratified by the Crown. But most Acadians had considered this status of neutrality granted. In practice the oath had been at times demanded but for the most part disregarded. When the war began, in actual hostilities not by declaration, it was feared that the Acadians might fight for France. An unqualified oath submitted to them in July of 1755 was refused by the bulk of them. It was decided to remove them from the Nova Scotia peninsula.

Hence such justification as can be found for their expulsion must rest on the plea of military necessity. Burke sweeps it aside with characteristic majesty. "Upon pretences not worth a farthing," he says, "we did root out this poor, innocent, deserving people whom our utter inability to govern or to reconcile, gave us no right to extirpate." A fine denunciation, worthy of Cicero; yet it must be remembered that Burke was a politician just as Barabbas was a robber. Rhetoric for party's sake carries a heavy discount.

Francis Parkman, "Montcalm and Wolfe," 1884

But there can be no justification for the manner of the expulsion as apart from its necessity. It struck without warning. It confiscated all possessions without compensation. In cattle alone the Crown seized a value of twenty thousand pounds sterling. It broke the Acadians up in scattered groups. It kept no record of their fate, no easy means for their communication. In many cases, by inefficiency not by malice, it broke up individual families, separated and lost for ever.

"Archives of Canada," CX. 110-111

See Authorities cited by Winsor

The act was done by the decision of the Governor (Charles Lawrence) and the Council of the Province of Nova Scotia. Under their orders Colonel Winslow called the Acadians of Minas Basin into the church at Grand Pré, at three o'clock on September 4, 1755. There appeared, so Winslow himself reported, "four hundred and eighteen of their best men." He then informed them, that all their lands, cattle and other property were forfeit to the Crown. They might take away their ready money and such small personal possessions as the ships could accommodate. He put them under guard forthwith. Towards night the unhappy people "not having any provisions with them, pleading hunger, begged for bread." Thus began the sufferings of years.

Winslow's "Journal," 1755

Many weeks passed before the shipments could begin. About four thousand people were sent away that year and in all, during the war, about 6,500. They were distributed among the seaboard colonies. No proper record was kept of departures and destinations. It was intended in the first year to send 1,000 to Virginia, 500 each to North Carolina and Maryland, 300 each to Philadelphia and Connecticut and 200 to New York and to Boston. Later on, about 400 were sent to Georgia. No special provision was made for their maintenance beyond what local help might give and human charity dare not refuse. Their reception was varied. Virginia, with slaves enough, tried to send them back. In Philadelphia people with an eye to business proposed to *sell* them, but Quaker piety prevailed, and took the Acadians to its heart. Drawn towards their own race, about 365 reached Louisiana in 1765. Their descendants are still there, the 'Cajeans' of what used to be called the Attakapas district. A large number in the course of time wandered back home, not to their own burnt and ravaged settlements but to new settlements in New Brunswick.

It has been argued that the Acadians were priest-ridden, that many of their young men had joined the French and that more were bound to do so. Such argument is unworthy. They were priest-ridden only as simple people, gathered round their priest. If their young men had *not* tried to join the French they would have been poor young men indeed.

All that we can say is that there was at least no wanton cruelty. Winslow at the start spoke to them with sincere sympathy. There was nothing in their fate of the concentration camp, the brute cruelty, the secret police and the mass executions of to-day. Those who wept the world over for the Acadians in Longfellow's day, died in time to save themselves from deeper sorrow.

But at the time the fate of the Acadians was lost from sight, and the world was deaf to their cries in the new tumult of war. The great war that lost Canada to France (1756-1763) had already begun in deed though not in declaration when the Acadians were expelled. The eyes of all the world turned to the Ohio, to Fort Duquesne, and the disastrous defeat of General Braddock. The ears of the world first heard then the name of Braddock's colonial officer, Colonel George Washington. The war thundered on three continents. The triumph of Minden in *1759* Westphalia was matched by the splendour of Plassey in Bengal. *1757* British sea power proved supreme. Hawke's victory at Quiberon *1759* has been called the Trafalgar of the Seven Years' War. Boscawen's investment and capture of Louisbourg showed how power- *1758* less was the sea-girt fortress against the power that held the sea. The crowning tragedy was Quebec. The brilliant handling of Admiral Saunders' fleet put Wolfe in reach of the Plains of Abraham. Yet nothing but a fleet could have kept him there, even had he lived to fight again. Few casual readers recall that the spring of 1760 brought a second battle of the Plains of Abraham (April 27), in which the French were victorious. The appearance of a British fleet when the St. Lawrence opened in the spring turned the victory to dust. Montreal fell as falls an apple from a bough and with it all the river settlements and seigneuries that had been New France and all the vast dream of empire beyond. When the war passed, New France was gone —but not, so it was to prove, French Canada.

MEMORABLE DATES

1727
English built Fort Oswego

1731-43
Journeys of La Vérendrye

1744
King George's War

1748
Peace of Aix-la-Chapelle

1749
Halifax founded

1755
Expulsion of the Acadians

1756-63
The Seven Years' War

1759
Battle of the Plains of Abraham

1760
Capitulation of Montreal

1763
Peace of Paris

"There was no religious persecution"— PAGE 103

CHAPTER IV

THE FOUNDATION OF BRITISH CANADA
1763-1815

Cession of Canada—Pontiac's War—British Rule in Quebec —The Quebec Act of 1774—The American Revolution —The United Empire Loyalists — The Constitutional Act of 1791—Foundation of Upper Canada—Governor Simcoe —The War of 1812.

THE capitulation of Quebec and the renewed British command of the St. Lawrence, compelled the surrender of Montreal by the Marquis de Vaudreuil to General Amherst. This surrender included all of New France and its western outposts of which the principal were Detroit and Michilimackinac. Fighting on land ended except for the abortive Indian rising under Pontiac, a chief of the Ottawas. Pontiac thought he knew the difference between easy-going French traders who only wanted trade, and the incoming of a flood of English settlers who would take the Indians' land. The plan of his abortive rising was to seize the western posts and call to the French for help. Pontiac was one of the few Indians who ever showed a capacity for leadership but he hopelessly miscalculated the situation, the military power of Europeans in arms and the futility of Indian ambush and stealth against organized regiments and artillery. Foiled at Detroit, he carried fire and massacre to half a dozen isolated posts, then realized the situation and let himself be bought off into peace. A few years later he was stabbed to death

Sept. 20, 1759

Sept. 8, 1760

1763-4

F. Parkman, "The Conspiracy of Pontiac," 1851

by one of his own race, bribed by an English liquor trader—a forest version of the death of Caesar.

´   ´   ´

While the war lasted, Canada remained under the military government of the British armed forces. But the ratification of the Peace of Paris (February 10, 1763) was followed by a royal proclamation placing the new 'Province of Quebec' under civil government. Its boundaries were peculiar, to a large extent huge make-shift lines of direction running through wilderness country, hardly even explored and none of it surveyed. On the east the boundary was the St. John River of Labrador that enters the St. Lawrence opposite the west end of Anticosti. From the source of that river, wherever it might be, the line ran more or less south-west to a corner of Lake Nipissing, then south-east to the St. Lawrence (near Coteau), east across the foot of Lake Champlain and then along the height of land south of the St. Lawrence to the Baie des Chaleurs. This was meant in a rough-and-ready way to include the basins of the St. Lawrence (up to Coteau), and of the Ottawa, but to keep clear of the Hudson's Bay Company's territory, of that of the Atlantic provinces and of Nova Scotia, which now presumably began where Massachusetts ended, and which was given jurisdiction also over Cape Breton and Ile St. Jean (Prince Edward Island).

Such rough-and-ready boundaries in unsurveyed country were presently to give trouble and to breed the boundary disputes—Maine, Oregon, Alaska—that were to disfigure the relations of Canada with the United States. No one could foresee this, least of all at that happy moment when boundaries hardly seemed to matter. With the cession of Canada by France and that of Florida by Spain, almost the whole of the known continental North America from the Gulf of Mexico to the Arctic Ocean, was British. There was no other sovereignty than that of the Crown of Spain to which French Louisiana had been ceded. Spanish America thus began at New Orleans and extended vaguely to the missions of the California coast where the known geography of the Pacific ended. All the rest was British, extending likewise into the unknown. It seems vast even now. In the unexplored world of that day it must have seemed beyond

W. Houston, "Documents Illustrative of the Canadian Constitution," 1891

1762

imagination. Where the map ended poetry began with its 'broad savannahs,' reaching in "airy undulation far away," its 'snow capped mountains' and its 'hyper-boreal regions' where "fading gradually, life at length goes out." The occupation of such an immensity must have appeared both in space and time distant beyond words. Few could realize that in less than two mere centuries the globe would have shrunk to the stifled world we know, its occupants clamouring for space, clutching for resources, with escape nowhere. Nor did many realize that in the union and opportunity thus gained, and presently so carelessly thrown aside, was to lie two centuries later the chief, perhaps the sole, hope for the salvation of western civilization.

J. Thomson, "Seasons"— 'Winter,' 1726

Under the Proclamation of 1763 the government of Canada (now officially Quebec) consisted of a Governor and Council. Power was given to the Governor to call an elected assembly. The power was never used and was rescinded presently in the reorganization under the Quebec Act of 1774. It was what we now call a 'gesture' of goodwill and a grant of freedom to the 'King's New Subjects.' But it could not be put into practice. To grant the vote to Roman Catholics, excluded both in Great Britain and in the then existing Parliament of Ireland, would have offended British public opinion. To elect the Assembly on a Protestant vote only, would have put four hundred people in control of some sixty-five thousand. Moreover there was no demand among the French for a popular assembly and a citizens' franchise, things of which they knew and cared nothing. The only demand for an assembly came from the four or five hundred Protestants who would have controlled it. These were the new traders and merchants, mostly from the American provinces, who had moved up to French Canada, and especially to Montreal, when it became British. These people became the bane of the history of the hour. General Murray, the first Governor-General of Canada, called them in an official letter to the British Government "four hundred and fifty contemptible traders and sutlers," and spoke of them to the Board of Trade as "licensed fanatics." Governor Murray's attitude gave such offence to this British section that their influence procured his recall. But unfortunately Sir Guy Carleton (later Lord

Sir C. Lucas, "Canada" (1763-1812) 1909

Dorchester), the brother veteran who succeeded him, went at it almost as roundly. Not only the traders but the new British office-holders, who obtained their positions by home influence and fattened on new fees and unknown charges, called down his denunciation, as "cantoning upon the country and riding the people with desperate savagery."

These vexed quarrels occasioned by the incoming of an alien and favoured minority, fill the foreground of our Canadian annals of the period and colour it with a false light. The régime under which French Canada lived until the eve of the French Revolution was for the most part one of happy neglect, that accidental art of government most congenial to the British temperament. Not knowing what to do with Canada in this interim, the British Government did nothing in particular, and, like the House of Lords in the Gilbert and Sullivan song, did it rather well.

W. H. Lecky, "History of England in the Eighteenth Century," 1878-90 Vol. IV.

It was indeed a little difficult to know what to do. It was doubtful at first whether Canada would be retained. The acquisition of Florida opened the vista of a great sub-tropical empire, with Jamaica and Barbados already British, with Guadeloupe and perhaps Martinique and St. Lucia to be ceded in return for the restoration of Canada. A Mr. Burke—a cousin of his celebrated cousin Edmund—wrote an open letter to show that a "vast, barren and almost uninhabited country, lying in an inhospitable climate and with no commerce except that of furs and skins," could not be compared to a sugar island like Guadeloupe.

G. Bancroft, "History of the United States," 1834-76 Vol. I

Diplomacy, the kind that lives in the dark, suggested that it might be wiser to let France keep Canada, in order to keep the American provinces dependent. "England," said the French statesman Vergennes, "will soon repent of having removed the only check that keeps her colonies in awe," and the opinion was echoed in England. Benjamin Franklin, however, at that time in

1761

England, wrote his famous 'Canada Pamphlet,' so-called, to ridicule what he called the "visionary fear" that the colonies might combine against England. What he said makes sad reading. "Can it reasonably be supposed there is any danger of their uniting against their own nation, which protects and encourages them, with which they have so many connections and ties of blood, interest and affection, and which, it is well known, they all love much more than they love one another?" This was written only a few years before the Declaration of Independence. Worth quoting also, from its having been so often quoted, is the prophecy of the Swedish naturalist and traveller, Peter Kalm, made *before* the Seven Years' War—"The English government has reason to regard the French as the chief power which urges their colonies to submission."

Peter Kalm, "Travels in North America," 1748-49

The realization of these circumstances shows why it was that Canada was largely left alone and how fortunate was this neglect. There was no religious persecution. The provisions of the capitulations of Quebec and Montreal and the Proclamation of Civil Government all contained clauses granting freedom of worship for the Roman Catholic religion, "as far as the laws of England permit." The limitation could have meant anything or nothing; in practice it meant nothing. The French language was left undisturbed, not by law, but by common sense. There was no way for the 'business men' to teach English to seventy thousand new subjects. Indeed the other way; retiring British officers who bought seigneuries and settled with their disbanded soldiers in the province presently spoke French and gave us the 'Frasers' and 'Mackays' of to-day whose English speech has vanished. No guarantee was given for the French language, nor ever later by the Imperial Government till the British North America Act of 1867. It was merely let alone. On the other hand it was not possible to let the law alone, and much confusion resulted. The military government applied the English criminal law, and it was continued under civil government. This bred no discontent, for the penalties were milder than those of French law. But the civil law of New France, the old *coutume de Paris*, and the land laws of the seigniorial system would not fit alongside of the law of England and the English land tenure and laws of inheritance; 'English,' be it repeated, not 'British,' since the Scots law was another matter, understood only in Scotland. Round this legal dilemma focused much of the trouble with the new British community of traders. They contrived, as far as they could, the introduction of imprisonment for debt, a cup of misery still untasted by poverty in the wilderness. They and their imported officials introduced a high scale of fees, adjusted

1759-1760

1763

to the wealth of commercial England and spelling disaster in Canada; "expense, chicanery and confusion," wrote Carleton, "with a deluge of new laws unknown and unpublished."

Yet even at that it is a mistake to exaggerate the situation of French Canada at this period. For most of its French inhabitants life pursued a more even tenor now that war had passed, that Indian massacre was over and they could be let alone. It is true the incoming British had many advantages. When Vaudreuil went away, nearly three hundred civilians, as permitted by the capitulation, left for France. These included many French officials and *noblesse*. There were many seigneuries thrown on the market. The British, then and later, bought them freely. General Murray obtained the seigneurie of Malbaie (Murray Bay), General Burton that of Chambly, Simon McTavish became seigneur of Terrebonne and Sir Frederick Haldimand of Sorel. By 1774 the chief seigneuries were British.

The British also enjoyed from the start that control of capital which was soon to count in a world beginning to be industrialized. The British (presently Scottish) command of the commerce of Montreal, and control of the banking and transport and monetary power—all this was due not solely, perhaps not principally, to the native genius or acquired capacity of the English merchant and the Scottish banker, but to the initial opportunity of circumstance. Something also of the new situation was due to the different habits of urban townsfolk, merchant people like the incoming British and British Americans, and people of the land like the French. The conquest brought the printing press and a Quebec *Gazette*, in which, like the genie in the bottle-smoke, first appears "the advertiser," whose oyster was to be the world.

Yet mainly the people agreed. British officers and soldiers fraternized with their late opponents as honourable combatants were able to do in the days of honourable war. "The soldiers," wrote General Gage to his superior, General Amherst, as early as 1762, "live peaceably with the inhabitants and they reciprocally acquire an affection for each other."

In this period of quiet was laid the foundation of the mutual tolerance and co-operation of French and British in Canada. Such troubles as existed have, as said, falsely coloured this

"Lumber and shipbuilding sprang into life" — PAGE 107

ERNST NEUMANN, MONTREAL, P.Q., 1941

interim of uncertain destiny. It has been the peculiarity of our Canadian history that it is commonly presented in too lurid a light. Its opening chapters of adventure, danger, war and massacre carry forward a sort of storm and stress that no longer belongs. The annals leap from war to war till peace seems alien, and commonplace life beside the mark.

A certain mistaken school of British writers has looked upon the policy of this period as a fatal error, destined, in a homely phrase, to come home to roost. The country, it was claimed, should have been made British from the start. The French language should not have been tolerated, the Roman Catholic religion should have lost all government support. The French-Canadians, to use Lord Durham's phrase of 1839, should have been led away from "their vain hopes of nationality." The contrary opinion is the sound one. This period first showed the possibility of a united French and British Canada, and with it the British Empire that we have.

While French Canada remained under its somewhat uncertain destiny for ten years after the conquest, Nova Scotia was being opened up for settlement and was assuming its characteristic form of a British, in places a Scottish, province. A few settlers came to Pictou County in 1667; then, in 1772, a whole shipload of Highlanders, landing with kilts (forbidden in Scotland since Prince Charlie's rebellion), skean-dhu, and broadswords, the woods loud with the bag-pipes. Other Scots settled on the Gulf of St. Lawrence coast, later New Brunswick. Lumber and shipbuilding sprang into life. The great pines of Longfellow's 'forest primeval,' furnished masts for the British navy, 108 feet long, three feet through at the butt and worth £136 each. The Irish came also, 500 of them to Colchester in 1766 and others to Cumberland County, with Yorkshire Methodists to balance their exuberance. Cape Breton by 1765 had enough settlers to rank it as a county, with two members in the Halifax Assembly. Thus was set on maritime Canada the stamp it has never lost—its homeward look, its industry of the woods and the sea.

M. L. Hansen, "Mingling of the Canadian and American Peoples," 1940

1761

W. A. Carrothers, "Emigration from the British Isles," 1929

Meantime the uncertain status of French Canada was brought to a close by the Quebec Act of 1774. This aimed at the permanent

Sir H. Cavendish
"Debates"
(of 1774),
1839

retention of Canada under British sovereignty, with such full measure of recognition of the religion, the customs and the law of the French-Canadians as should secure allegiance. In spite of all denunciation it fulfilled its purpose. Rebuilt into the later statutes of 1791, 1840 and 1867, its principles are still the basis of our commonwealth. It preserved the French civil law and with it the criminal law of England; it gave freedom of worship to Roman Catholics and authorized the collection of the tithe on farm land from Roman Catholic holders. It preserved the existing seigniorial tenures, in large part now bought up by British proprietors. It took for granted the use of the French language in daily life and in the courts, making no attempt to

extend English beyond its necessary official sphere. It declared it inexpedient to call an assembly. The main government was to consist of a Governor and a Council.

One clause rapidly made history. The act extended the boundaries of Quebec to include all of the unsettled territory south and west of the Great Lakes between the Mississippi and the Ohio. Thus Chicago, then an unredeemed portage-place from Lake Michigan west, was in this way for a brief interval under the fostering care of the Roman Catholic Church. The intention most likely was to preserve Crown control over Indians and land grants for fear of a new Pontiac. But New England read into it tyranny and Popish idolatry.

To Canada the act was generosity itself, a bid for Canadian gratitude and support. It was needed. Events were moving rapidly. It was possible that Britain in keeping Canada might find little else to keep. The unhappy colonial quarrel that began over the war debts, was going from bad to worse. The attempt at taxation by the Stamp Act of 1765, by customs acts and the tax on tea, had brought a sudden union to the disunited provinces. Disaffection grew on argument in New England, bravado in the South and stupidity across the ocean. By the time of the Boston Tea Party (1773) the whole country was in a turmoil of disagreement, reaching for arms if only to secure them first, while the current of public life moved with increasing tumult as the waters move above unseen Niagara. The Quebec Act, intended as oil on the Canadian waters, came also as oil on the American flames. The pulpits of New England thundered with denunciation, the echo of which reached French Canada and was never forgotten. The Quebec Act, in taking away the 'North-West Territory' from the provinces, many of whose charters claimed parts of it, took away the promised land. Already the resources of the Ohio Valley had cast a spell over ambition. Hence the new boundary offended both against the soul and the body, religion and profit, and could not last. Probably no one meant it to. In any case there was no time to see what would have happened; as usual, something else did. The rush to seize arms led to Lexington and Concord, to Bunker Hill; from fighting to war, and from war to independence and the republic. The most

Sir G. O. Trevelyan, "History of the American Revolution," 1899-1905

1775

important chapter of the world's history, as we see it now, was here being written.   ,   ,   ,

The war of the American Revolution (1775-1783) was the last of the four great wars which had ravaged the frontiers of North America in the eighteenth century. In all they cover thirty-two years, one-third of the century. Apart from the bravery of the combatants, its annals make sad reading. The war came to a divided people. Resolute patriotism took arms against resolute allegiance, a new ideal against an old loyalty, a sudden angry struggle, undreamed of yesterday and feeding on its own anger. Even if the separation of America from Britain was manifest destiny, and the republic a nobler ideal than kingship, the separation might have waited yet a while. The parting might have been made in peace.

On Canada fell the first full impact of the blow. To bring the Canadians into the insurrection the Americans tried both force and persuasion. Force came first, with General Montgomery's invasion and his capture of the fort at St. Johns, which gave him undefended Montreal. Montgomery's occupation of the city is still recalled by the tablet on his headquarters, an old stone house on Rue Notre-Dame, buried in the financial district of Montreal. The Governor, Sir Guy Carleton, gathered his feeble forces into Quebec. Montgomery followed. He was joined by General Benedict Arnold, who had forced a way through the wilderness of the Kennebec. Montgomery was killed in a night *Dec. 31, 1775* attack outside the gates. He was not yet forty. His name endures, lauded by both sides. Arnold had not the luck to die in the snow. He lived to be the Judas Iscariot of America.

With invasion came to Montreal a mission of persuasion from Congress, Benjamin Franklin and two others, honest men in the uncomfortable role of foxes in a hen yard. Then came the spring opening of the river and a British fleet, and invasion and persuasion vanished together. Canada was out of the struggle. Sir Guy Carleton (later Lord Dorchester), the defender of Quebec, kept guard over Canada. From it General Burgoyne presently organized, with care, his defeat at Saratoga. Carleton was afterward criticized for not throwing the French-Canadians into the struggle. The truth is, they would have been hard to throw; not from lack of bravery but from lack of motive. They only wanted to be let alone, a plea that has lasted now nearly two centuries.

Sir C. Lucas, "History of Canada, 1763-1812," 1909

The war went its way. Each year it threw a deeper shadow on the prestige of Britain. From the time when Chatham rejoiced that America had resisted, the British themselves were divided as to the struggle. The shadow fell on British arms with Burgoyne's defeat, and then, for the first time since the Dutch War of Charles II, it fell on the British navy. The loss of the command of the sea along the American coast compelled Cornwallis's surrender. Nothing but Rodney's crowning victory over De Grasse in the West Indies helped to save the record of what naval historians have called 'the British navy in adversity.'

1782

W. N. James, "The British Navy in Adversity," 1926

In their quarrel with Great Britain over stamps and taxes the Americans had been united almost to a man. But no one as yet (the words are those of Benjamin Franklin) "talked of independence, drunk or sober." When the quarrel led to fighting, unity of opinion fell apart. Republican ideas fermented. Then came Tom Paine's pamphlet *The Crisis*, written in camp, advocating independence and read everywhere—a sudden light to slower minds, a trumpet call to lively patriotism. Then came the Declaration of Independence of July 4, 1776, and five years of actual warfare.

This War of Independence was not in the full sense a national uprising nor yet a civil war. John Adams himself said afterwards that in 1776 one-third of the people were Loyalists. Indeed a large number of Tories took up arms, perhaps 50,000 in all, of whom one-half were from the Province of New York. But it must be remembered that among these were such bodies as the King's Royal Regiment of the Province of New York, raised by Sir John Johnson from among a Mohawk Valley settlement of Highlanders who had arrived only in 1773. After the war they became part of our Scottish Glengarry settlement on the St. Lawrence. Johnson, who had succeeded his father, Sir William, the famous Superintendent-General of Indian Affairs, raised, among his retainers and refugees and from Canada, various irregular corps, among them the Royal Greens, infamous for

C. H. Van Tyne, "The Loyalists in the American Revolution," 1902

their savagery. Other corps of similar origin, but higher honour, were the Highlanders recruited in Boston while still British, and the regiments formed under British army protection, the Royal Fencible Americans, the Prince of Wales' Americans and the Queen's Rangers, at first of Connecticut, later under Colonel John Graves Simcoe with Howe at Philadelphia. After the war the British Government voted half pay to the officers of a score of such regiments. Evidently such corps were in large measure alien. Most Tories were content with doing nothing. But in areas held by the British—as the town of New York, as New Jersey, as most of settled Pennsylvania for the first of the war, and the country round New York itself till the very end—the Tories by royal favour fell heir to the houses and properties of dispossessed rebels. This meant a day of reckoning. The terms of peace expressly provided for the safety of the Tories against retaliation, confiscation and ill-treatment. But there was no way as yet to bind thirteen states to thirteen codes of honour.

J. Winsor,
"The Narrative
and
Critical History
of America,"
Vol. VI.

Retaliation began at once. Many Tories did not even wait for it. Indeed Tory refugees had been moving out during the war itself. When Howe evacuated Boston in 1776, about 900 Loyalists went in his ships to Halifax; 3,000 left Philadelphia with the British army in 1778. With the peace and the separation from Great Britain, the movement became an exodus; partly of people who were afraid to stay, but mainly of people who did not want to. The first destination was Nova Scotia, a place of easy access by sea, for the province extended then on both sides of the Bay of Fundy, joining the Maine district of Massachusetts. "Nova Scotia is the rage," reported the London *Chronicle*. A great 'spring fleet' of twenty ships went in 1783, and another in the autumn. They flooded into Nova Scotia, into the Annapolis Basin and into the new town, or camp, called Shelburne, till it presently contained 10,000 people, the largest British 'town' in America. The ebb-tide of the flood left it a village. For the

1784-1820

Loyalists found better homes in Prince Edward Island, to which went 600, and in Cape Breton with 400—temporarily made a province by itself but without an assembly—and found a veritable land of promise in the valley of the St. John in the empty western end of the province. A muster roll of Loyalists as early

FREDERICK H. VARLEY, A.R.C.A., VANCOUVER, B.C., 1941

" 'Nova Scotia is the rage,' reported the London Chronicle"—PAGE 112

as the summer of 1784 showed 28,347 in Nova Scotia. Of these 9,260 were on the St. John River and nearly 3,000 more in that vicinity, a fact which led to the separation of their settlements as the Province of New Brunswick. Certain later troubles of the province were laid in its cradle at its christening. Achilles, we are told, started life vulnerable in his heel, New Brunswick in its boundary. It fell heir at once to its share of the ambiguities of the Treaty of 1783 that vexed half a century. By this treaty the boundary of British North America at one end was "the north-west angle of Nova Scotia"—there isn't any—at the other, a line drawn west from the Lake of the Woods to meet the Mississippi —it never will. But these troubles still were in the future.

J. Hannay, "History of Acadia," 1879

Other Loyalists made their way to other British territory by land. At this time Quebec ended, as settlement, with Lake St. Francis. Above that was the river stretch of the St. Lawrence, the Great Lakes, Ontario, Erie and Huron, and the peninsula between. This territory, which corresponds in latitude to Southern France, is the garden, one of the gardens, of Canada. Access was now open to it. From the settlements of the Mohawk Valley, portage routes led to Niagara, to Oswego and to Ogdensburg and thence across the Lakes and the St. Lawrence. The Indian danger was gone. Indeed the Indians themselves were now 'Loyalists.' The migration of Mohawks with their chief Thayen-danega—in easier English, Joe Brant—gave us Brantford. By this route now came many Loyalists, settling at Niagara-on-the-Lake (Newark) even during the war.

J. W. Lydekker, "The Faithful Mohawks," 1938

Other Loyalists came to the new region by the sea—a year's journey for many of them—to Nova Scotia, up the St. Lawrence, wintering on the way, many at Sorel, then past Montreal in a stubborn ascent of the St. Lawrence to the settlements laid out along the river to the new Kingston. The British Government was generosity itself; it did not do anything by halves. It supplied transport, tools, implements, seeds and food for one year and for more if needed. It gave land with an ungrudging hand; two hundred acres went to each disbanded private soldier; two hundred to every farmer civilian; to officers, according to rank, up to five thousand acres.

Difficulties, of course, there were. The Loyalists showed a

tendency to keep moving round like lost sheep; speculators bought up their land, the "location tickets" foolishly being made transferable; some grumbled, being Americans, for 'town-meetings,' to run their own affairs; others had had enough of town meetings for ever. Another grievance was that the government at first shut them off from the excellent land, still empty and easy of access, in what we call the Eastern Townships of Quebec. It seemed too near the United States from which it had, and still has, no real boundary. Other new-comers, thousands of them, were not Loyalists at all—just incoming Americans tempted by good land.

Indeed it is important to remember that the Loyalist settlers themselves were most of them not British in the first-hand sense, but Americans. Many of them came of families already several generations in America. They differed in this from the generality of the settlers, British people from their own Isles, who came later in the great migration after the Napoleonic War. Now allegiance is one thing, culture another. These Americans, Loyalists and others, helped to give to the Province of Ontario that peculiar stamp of similarity to "the States" in speech and habit which its plainer people have always carried. From them comes the Thanksgiving Dinner of Massachusetts, half appetite, half religion, originating from a turkey-feed with the Indians in 1630. From them came the 'York'—the New York shilling, 12½ cents—which many of us still remember as current calculation. From their traditions came presently the school 'sections' and the spellers and the spelling bees, and the township. They spoke of their "dooty" and they "reckoned" and "guessed" and "calculated" and used all those American 'novelties' of speech which were old in East Anglia when the Pilgrim Fathers left it. Time was when the word 'Loyalist,' and the prouder 'U. E. Loyalist' were terms used as if in contrast to Yankee or American. We know better now. The word British-American has come again into its own.

H. L. Mencken, "The American Language," Chapter II, 1919

The difficulties described led naturally to a reorganization of government. The Constitutional Act of 1791 divided Canada into the two provinces of Upper and Lower Canada, with a Governor-General for all Canada and under him a Lieutenant-

Governor for Upper Canada. In each province was a Legislative Council appointed for life, with hereditary titles grantable, but never granted, by the Crown. In each was a popular Assembly elected on a property franchise. The Governor and his Council were thus set over against the people's Assembly, with neither in control. But it would have been hard to go further at the time. It was a half-way house, in which was made too long a sojourn. This later brought rebellion. But at first the new government in Upper Canada worked wonders. Colonel John Graves Simcoe, the veteran Commander of the Queen's Rangers, was appointed as first Lieutenant-Governor of Upper Canada. He arrived at Kingston July 1, 1792 and organized his Legislature at Newark (Niagara) in the same month. For over four years he governed the province and immensely influenced its future.

Simcoe was a notable man. He had a vision that looked a hundred years ahead, and that lingered also a hundred years behind. He could see in the sandbars and marshes of Toronto the mirage of a metropolis; his great military roads swept in his fancy east and west five hundred miles; he held the North in his hand and Niagara was his footstool. For him Upper Canada— so he told his Parliament—went, in its responsibilities, "infinitely beyond whatever, till this period, have distinguished any other colony." *"The Simcoe Papers," Ontario Historical Society, 40 Vols., 1923-6*

Yet to Simcoe, democrat meant scoundrel; dissenter, snivelling hypocrite; and without the Church of England morality would go under. But he was all for what he considered progress; he must have schools, and grammar schools; he looked forward to a college; he gathered in a printer to set up the *Upper Canada Gazette or American Oracle*; he collected three refugee clergymen of the establishment to make a church, and asked the Crown for a bishop. *April 13, 1793*

For government Simcoe wanted British government and he wanted it all; its established church, its hereditary titles, its forms, its feathers, its venerable humbugs; and nothing newer than Queen Anne.

On these terms Simcoe called his first Legislature together on September 17, 1792. It met in a frame building close by the village of Niagara (Newark) with uncleared bush all around. It numbered twenty-three men in all, seven councillors and six elected assembly-men. The councillors, hand picked, were gentlemen, but more than half the others were a rougher lot, "fellows of one table," that is fellows who ate with their servants, and hence,

Duncan C. Scott,
'John Graves
Simcoe'
in "Makers
of Canada"
1905

to Simcoe, disqualified for British government. But Simcoe's vision saw it all in the colours of the autumn woods; he read its future in the majesty of the lake and the broad sweep of the river. All that Ottawa now is, he saw it then. And he must have the pomp to match it. He threw in more circumstance in one afternoon than the Philadelphia Congress in eighteen years of its drab sessions. There were mounted guards, soldiers in brilliant scarlet uniforms, Queen's Rangers in rifle green, guns from the fort answered by guns from the sloops in the harbour. Within there was a sergeant-at-arms, a ready-made dais and a "speech from the throne"—old as Edward I, and younger than to-morrow. As background spectators for the scene, there were Indians in full paint and feathers, with scalps of dead enemies hanging in their belts, to show that England still had friends.

Simcoe moved his capital to a strategic position at Toronto (York from 1793 to 1834). He planned and commenced arteries of military roads, that turned to avenues of settlement. One that was called Yonge Street, much of it at first only a horsetrack, led through the bush and over the hills to Lake Simcoe and so down to the Georgian Bay. Its first purpose was, so to speak, to outflank the United States. In place of that it opened up as farm land the hills and valleys forgotten since the martyr's mission of Brébeuf.

Thus as Napoleon made France so did Simcoe make Upper Canada. The best remains. The worst is gone. He named its most beautiful lake in his father's memory. Time has transferred it to his own. Simcoe told his Parliament, when its first session ended, that it represented an "image and transcript of the British constitution." At least he did his best to make it so. The seeds he sowed were to come up later as harvest, and some of them as tares.

All this however came later. The unexpected outbreak of the French Revolution and the twenty-three years of war that followed, called a halt to the natural development of British America. Immigration from abroad slackened. It would have failed altogether but for distress at home in Britain that drove unwilling settlers overseas. This was especially so with Scotland. The old Highlands of the clans were breaking up. Deer and sheep paid better than tenantry. Highland 'clearances' gave Canada some of its best. Reports showed that in 1802 above 3,400 people left Scotland; estimates claim that the West Highlands and the Islands lost a quarter of their population. Most notable in this period was Lord Selkirk's colonization of Prince Edward Island and on the Red River, as discussed later. To Upper Canada also came the immigration organized by Colonel Thomas Talbot on Lake Erie. But all this was held back by war in Europe, and presently stopped dead by war in Canada. Similarly, all through this period, trade moved among the alarms of war, over-quickened here and obliterated there, with certainty nowhere. Meantime legislation, as it has since the days of Tacitus, fell asleep in a country under arms.

W. A. Carrothers, "Emigration from the British Isles," 1929

Most unfortunate of all were the quarrels of Britain and America over maritime rights that culminated in the deplorable and fruitless war of 1812. Of the 80,000 people of the Upper Canada of that day, most were still 'American,' 35,000 representing Loyalists and their families, 25,000 later American settlers, and only 20,000 directly from the British Isles. Few hearts were in the war; many in secret hoped for republican victory. *Per contra*, in Massachusetts the war seemed wanton wickedness. Governor Caleb Strong by proclamation (July 26, 1812) called for a public fast for a wrong committed "against the nation from which we are descended."

"Niles Weekly Register," Aug. 1, 1812

Only the bravery of the combatants redeems the memory of the fruitless struggle. It is all a past echo now. The incursions across the St. Lawrence, the spectacular fights above the gorge of Niagara, the battle of the summer evening and night among the leaves of Lundy's Lane, the fury that committed to the flames the frame houses of York and the crude beginnings of Washington, the guns that thundered over Lake Erie, never to be heard again—all of this is now but the mist and echo of the past. The monuments that indicate for the tourist of to-day the site of these inroads and these combats, mark only a soil on which the seeds of dissension have long since sprung up as flowers.

When the war closed with the Treaty of Ghent, British America looked out, as did Europe, on a changed and changing world. War seemed dead; peace enthroned. The new economic life of liberated industry moved in a flood, sweeping the seven seas. The Great Peace, as it presently began to be called, rested on the new ideals of liberty, democratic justice, equal rights and equal trade for all; it had behind it the new power of the machine, the new organization of finance and the magic aid of science. It seemed to many at the time that it must last for ever. It should have. Some day it will.

"The emigrant ship . . . . was the world's symbol of peace and progress . . ."
—PAGE 124

CHAPTER V

THE MIDDLE PERIOD:
SHIPS, COLONIES, COMMERCE—1815-1867

Emigration and the Victorian Age—Upper Canada —The North-West and the Selkirk Settlement —The Rebellion of 1837—Lord Durham and the Union of the Canadas—Responsible Government—Maritime Progress — American Boundaries and Reciprocity —The Civil War—Provincial Deadlock—Confederation.

THE age that we now call Victorian began in reality before Queen Victoria was born. Under this name we think of the era during which England became the workshop of the world, Britain the mistress of the peaceful seas; the era of free trade and the rainbow visions that went with it; of the expectation of universal, perpetual peace that inspired the Great Exhibition and its Crystal Palace of 1851; and above all, the era of the literature of Scott and Dickens, Carlyle and Tennyson and the rising science of Darwin and Huxley.

It would have seemed the brightest age in all history but for the dark shadows behind it; the new poverty brought by the new wealth; the new liberty of people free to starve and of others free to let them do it; the stones in place of bread; the festering slum, the cry of the children in the factories, the *Song of the Shirt*, and starvation under its new name of the survival of the fittest. Seen thus, the new pauperism of the nineteenth century makes the rude plenty of the fourteenth century seem a golden

Spenser Walpole, "History of England from 1815," 1886

age, and a plain meal at sunset in a log cabin a very glimpse of paradise.

But in spite of all, this Victorian Age was an age of hope; such as was never before; such as is gone now, or at least is eclipsed beyond present vision. In this age of hope people could see poverty, want and war only as the last dark clouds of a night that was breaking into morning.

We cannot understand our Canadian history without an appreciation of this background in the mother-country. After 1815, we exchanged war for peace, political for economic life, conquest for commerce. The war was no sooner ended by the Settlement of *1815* Vienna than a great migration poured forth from the British Isles. In those forgotten days immigration fell like Portia's mercy as a double blessing, on him that gave and him that took. The emigrant ship, crowded and dirty and triumphant, was the world's symbol of peace and progress—the dirtier and the poorer the more welcome. At times cholera and scurvy swept the ships and turned the ocean transit into a horror, as witness Mrs. *Mrs. Traill,* Traill's account of the cholera in Canada in the year 1832. But *"The* *Backwoods of* mainly migration meant more hands to work, more chance of *Canada," 1836* prosperity for all. Time was to show that even in a new country prosperity comes not in leaps and bounds but in rises and falls, and that bad times are as hard to exorcise in the bush as on the Bourse.

But at first the current ran strong. Migration no longer meant the wanderings of adventure, the flight of refugees towards shelter or of pilgrims to the ecstasy of the wilderness. It was now the outgoing of people from a crowded mother-country to new homes. It assumed proportions never seen before. In colonial days in America no exact count of migration was kept. Settlement indeed was mainly effected by a first mass movement, as to Massachusetts in 1629-30, and then by slow infiltration. Perhaps, at the best, 3,000 British settlers came to colonial America in an ordinary year. But in the five years after Waterloo 98,000 British went overseas. Twenty years later the immigrants of five years (1835-9) numbered 280,000, and for 1850-54 as many as 1,639,000. Here began the still unsolved problem of empty land and willing men, the jig-saw puzzle over which the economists mumble algebra. It is not only still unsolved but grows more difficult with each new complexity of civilization. At this time not only was British North America little more than a mere outline and a frame for future settlement, but Australia and New Zealand lay entirely open. A certain tide of the new migration went therefore to Australia where New South Wales was opening into respectability with other sheep than its original black ones. The migration of free people to Australia reached 15,000 in the year 1840.

W. A. Carrothers, "Emigration from the British Isles," 1929

But the main outflow of migration came to British America, and overwhelmingly to Canada. In the twenty years 1815-34, 403,000 British settlers went to British America as against 269,000 to the United States. Into Upper Canada they poured in a steady stream. The steamboat now began to multiply the movement. The steamship was originally the child, and presently the main support, of inland waters, beginning where sail ended. With the St. Lawrence canals that began in 1821 the steamboat came into its own. Even for the ocean voyage steam joined forces with sail with the Cunard Company of 1839. Hence immigrants now came direct from the old country up the St. Lawrence to the Lake Ontario settlements and marked out all the lake-shore counties from Kingston to Niagara. From Toronto, Yonge Street took them northward to Lake Simcoe, and Dundas Street westward to the valleys of the Grand River and the Thames. Along Lake Erie was spread the settlement that marked the enterprise of Colonel Thomas Talbot. With a grant of 5,000 acres he had begun actual colonization in 1809. His operations were checked by the war of 1812, his flour-mills and saw-mills burnt in American inroads, he himself at the front, or looking for it. But with peace Talbot went on. The Government gave him grants of land, the original 5,000 acres and then more and more. Admiral Fisher once said "There is nothing like favouritism." He meant there is nothing like having the power to advance a good man. In Canada the Crown still had it. Talbot brought out settlers in thousands. His Talbot Road went all along the Lake Erie shore. Before the Rebellion broke in 1837 Talbot claimed to have had 50,000 people settled on 650,000 acres of land, and all of it good.

M. L. Hansen, "The Mingling of the Canadian and American Peoples," 1940

Anna Jameson, "Winter Studies and Summer Rambles in Canada," 1838

He is the Thomas, if not the saint, whose name is preserved in the chief city of his making. Many, perhaps most, of Talbot's settlers were Americans from New York and Pennsylvania and helped to balance the larger influx of purely British stock.

Of these other people a great many were settled by the old Canada Company, chartered by John Galt in 1826. It was an enterprise possible only when one and the same authority could control the outgoing and incoming of migration, its financial support, the grant of land and the conditions of settlement. In our eagerness not to give too much of this power to anybody, we have taken it all from everybody. Westminster, Ottawa and Winnipeg must now all act together before a sparrow can light in Manitoba. None do.

It was different then. John Galt was a Scot, a typical Scot, for he combined a literary culture with good works and a keen sense of business. His culture has enriched the literature of migration with those haunting verses that convey all the wistful affection of the exile.

> *From the lone shieling on the misty Island,*
> *Mountains divide us and the waste of seas.*
> *But still the blood is true, the heart is Highland,*
> *And in our dreams we see the Hebrides.*

But John Galt's Canada Company did more than dream. They subscribed money and bought land from the Crown, nearly 2,500,000 acres in the Western Peninsula. Their payments ran to £20,000 a year but the Government accepted the building of roads, schools, churches and bridges as part of the price. They advanced land and money to settlers and looked ahead for the return, forward and upward. They put 4,500 people into the Huron district. They founded Galt and Goderich and Stratford. Most notable of all is the story of their foundation of Guelph. Galt and his friends stood on a summer evening, on a forest slope, all dripping from a day of rain. There they felled a huge maple to mark the selected site of the town. This done, they passed around whisky and drank the health of the whole Royal Family. Patriotism could go no further.

J. W. Aberdeen,
"John Galt,"
1936

For a time it looked as if this tide of migration might also flood into the North-West, thus anticipating history by half a century. After the Treaty of Utrecht had confirmed their territorial rights, the Hudson's Bay Company went forward undisturbed with their enterprise. It is true that French traders from Montreal, especially after Vérendrye, drew away a certain share of the fur trade by way of the lakes. But the main territory around the bay, known and unknown, was still theirs. Their ships came and went. Their sagacious policy promoted exploration to find new fields. The Company's agent, Samuel Hearne, made three successive journeys westward from the Churchill across the treeless ground of slate and stone and flattened river valleys—the Barren Grounds of Canada. These are 'lands forlorn,' in summer carpeted with grass and humming with a myriad insects, with wide lakes, a glare of day that hardly knows sunset, fast rivers that cannot linger, and in winter the starlit desolation of arctic snow. Thus Hearne made his way to the Coppermine River and to the sea over mineral wealth still waiting.

1713

G. Bryce,
"Remarkable
History of the
Hudson's Bay
Company,"
1900

S. Hearne,
"Journey from
Fort Prince
of Wales,"
1795

Douglas,
"Lands
Forlorn,"
1914

There was still, of course, with each recurring war, the danger of French attack by sea. It was to meet this that the Company had built, at the Churchill post, Fort Prince of Wales, a great stone fortress at the mouth of the river, three hundred by three hundred feet, its walls thirty feet thick—and twenty years in the building. It was a veritable European castle among the Canadian rocks. Yet when La Pérouse's warships ravaged the bay in 1782 Samuel Hearne, its Governor, could do nothing but surrender. La Pérouse demolished what he could of the great fort, and burnt York Factory. He took care when he sailed, to leave supplies of food for his fugitive enemies. Such was war between gentlemen.

Meantime the cession of Canada transferred to British traders the overland route from the St. Lawrence to the fur country. This meant trouble. There began a vigorous opposition of independent traders, determined and energetic men, caring nothing for the Company's rights, their eyes on present profit, with no time to reckon in centuries. These presently joined together into the North-West Company. They traded out of Montreal, Beaver Hall their headquarters and their 'wintering partners,' on Lake

Superior. In this new rivalry the two companies bid against one another for Indian trade, to the detriment of both. The older settled routes were broken, the trade disturbed. Fire-water out-bid red blankets and kettles. The path of peace was abandoned for the ways of violence, and the North-West fur trade threatened for a time to degenerate into anarchy.

Alexander Mackenzie, "Voyages from Montreal," 1801

In these annals of rivalry and ill-will one brighter page is illumined by the record of the voyages of Alexander Mackenzie which helped to give to Great Britain its future British Columbia. In the service of the North-West Company, Mackenzie ascended the valley of the Saskatchewan to the farthest reach of French exploration. He passed from the Saskatchewan to the Peace, and thence descended the river that bears his name. This was no barren ground, no land forlorn. From the Athabaska River and the Great Slave Lake forest and fertile soil run onward till the last stunted willows end only at the arctic coast. Here in the streams and marshes of the river delta the sea-tide that

July, 1789

swamped Mackenzie's tents, told him that he had reached the ocean. His next journey was more momentous still. From the Saskatchewan he again crossed to the Peace, and from its head-waters reached and descended the mountain streams that swelled into rivers to the Pacific. He reached its shores. One of the memorials of our history is his inscription on a sea-side rock: "Alexander Mackenzie, from Canada by land, 22nd July, 1793. Latitude 52° 20′ 48″ N."

Unpublished Memoir of Mackenzie Family quoted in 'Alexander Mackenzie,' "Makers of Canada," also Sir D. Barton, "Bernadotte and Napoleon," 1921

With this connects a strange by-path of history. Among those who read Mackenzie's *Voyages* was Napoleon. It was Napoleon's dream of conquest to 'get behind' the English—from Ireland, from Egypt, from India. We have it from Bernadotte, when King of Sweden, that Napoleon had planned a 'campaign of Canada,' by an ascent of the Mississippi from the French colony of Louisiana and thence an inroad from the north-west. General Bernadotte was to be made Governor of Louisiana to carry out the plan. Information was needed. Smugglers brought over Mackenzie's *Voyages*, which had been published in London in 1801. The book was translated into French, and one or two copies sumptuously bound. Napoleon had one still at St. Helena. The sale of Louisiana in 1803 forestalled the adventure.

FREDERICK H. VARLEY, A.R.C.A., VANCOUVER, B.C., 1941

"Thither he brought his Highland colonists . . . the journey was of a year, summer to summer . . ."— PAGE 131

Midway into this struggle of the rival companies of the north-west, was thrust the new Red River Colony founded by Lord Selkirk. This was a young Scottish nobleman whose eager sympathies were enlisted for the unhappy Highlanders, now dispossessed by the 'clearances.' He had heard from Montreal traders of the fertility of the North-West, the rich alluvial soil laid down by its rivers during uncounted centuries. The Hudson's Bay Company, nothing if not canny, had seen no reason to talk about this. Selkirk had already planted with some success a colony of about eight hundred Highlanders in Prince Edward Island. But the field was too small. He now (1811) bought from the Hudson's Bay Company a vast tract of 116,000 square miles in the North-West. This practically covered all the basin of the Red River and its tributaries. It is only fair to those who sought to destroy the colony to question the right of one man, an absentee, by the mere power of money, to acquire such ownership, no matter how elevated his motives. Thither he brought his Highland colonists in successive shiploads, by way of the Hudson Bay, the Nelson River, Norway House and Lake Winnipeg. The journey was of a year, summer to summer, the settlers frozen in for one winter.

Chester Martin, "Lord Selkirk's Work in Canada," 1916

The colony never had a chance to prosper. Of necessity the huge grant of land, with full ownership and rights of rule, excited the jealousy and presently the open hostility of the North-Westers, already in the field. The attempt was first made to coax the settlers from their holdings. Then came open ill-treatment and violence. A North-West factor wrote to a fellow official of "commencing open warfare with the Red River Colony." This ended in an attack and massacre of Governor Semple of the Hudson's Bay Company and twenty-one of his men. Selkirk coming out in 1817 could get no redress. Influence was too strong. He himself raised a force of ex-soldiers, by virtue of his powers as a magistrate, to arrest the guilty. The only result was a warrant from Upper Canada for his own arrest. Selkirk went home to die of a broken heart. Injustice triumphed. The two rival companies were united and lived happy ever after. The Red River Colony survived as best it might, waiting for to-morrow.

1816

The opening era of peaceful settlement in Upper Canada, as

described above, was presently shattered by the Rebellion of
1837. Nor had it all been sunshine, nor mellow evening after the
rain as at Guelph. There were great hardships. These were the
days of pioneer settlement, and life was rough. Experience was
already showing that the large grants of a thousand acres could
not create a manorial society. They broke into the smaller holdings of independent farm families, each living for itself with
but little outside commerce. These were the days of subsistence
farming, of home-spun clothes and home-made furniture. Food
was plentiful but comforts few and luxuries nowhere. Some of the
simplest things, beneath thought with us to-day, were hard to
get. Salt in the Talbot settlement was worth twelve dollars a
bushel. Settlers 'toted' it on their backs through the bush. Yet

Emily Weaver,
"Counties of
Ontario,"
1913

one must not hold too much by such gloomy and disillusioned
pictures as that given in Mrs. Moodie's *Roughing it in the Bush.*
In the life of pioneer hardship there is at least the stimulus that
goes with being on one's own, the 'magic of property,' if only
of a bush farm. To many people one hour of factory labour
seems longer than the longest day on one's own place.

But worse perhaps than hardship was the ill-adjustment that
brought 'bad times' even in the wilderness, that peculiar starvation in the midst of plenty that is the ghost behind the scenes of

Lord Durham's
Report,
Methuen
Edition, 1902
pp. 150-1

the promised land. Lord Durham's Report was to give a full
account of these hardships of Upper Canada, and the unhappy
contrast with better luck across the border. "On the American
side all is activity and bustle. . . . On the British side of the
line, with the exception of a few favoured spots, all seems waste
and desolate."

On this hard ground ill weeds grew apace. Hardship helped
to make the Rebellion of 1837. But more powerful perhaps were
the angers that go with 'class,' the indignation of plain people
against others claiming superiority. Such angers have followed
our British history. John Ball, the Kentish rebel priest of 1381,
called poverty to revolt with the slogan, "When Adam delved
and Eva span, who was then the gentleman?" The world asks
it still. And it was asked, and went unanswered, in the bush
settlements of Upper Canada. Simcoe's aristocracy was ill-cast.
It had no crusade behind it. Aristocracy must begin as a thousand

years old. Simcoe's established church with its reserve of one-eighth of all the land as allotted, was worse still. Surveyed but not yet apportioned, not used, the church land blocked settlement.

When the Napoleonic Wars ended, Simcoe was long since gone, *1796: died 1806* but the system, good and bad, was still there. Appointments and offices and emoluments went overwhelmingly to a favoured class. The little capital at York hatched out an aristocracy, and inside it a group of office holders called a 'family compact.' The family relationship was really small. The term was probably at first a joke, meant to be amusing in its absurdity, comparing this little coterie to the great Bourbon Family Compact of France and Spain, then still within memory. The Bourbons forgotten, the joke stands all alone, misinterpreted as in earnest.

Was there much real grievance? The Assembly could not control the public funds; could not control the public lands. As the population grew apace, this seemed all the greater hardship. There were 77,000 people in Upper Canada just before the War *"Censuses of* of 1812; 150,000 in 1824 and at the outbreak of rebellion 400,000. *Canada," 1876* But even at that, there are limits to the principle of self-government, especially in a new country with a handful of settlers and boundless resources. Who could hand over half a million square miles, ten times all England, to 400,000 settlers and throw in a fleet and army to guard it? What they needed as yet was not different government but better government.

The quarrel as between Governor and Assembly went from bad to worse, its course too intricate to follow here. It culminated in the outbreak of 1837. The rebels mustered and drilled around the farms all through the summer of that year. There were plenty of old soldiers in those days to show them how. The malcontents argued on the platforms and in the end they found a leader to their heart in William Lyon Mackenzie, a Scot, arrived in 1820, editing the *Colonial Advocate*, as honest as daylight, and as uncompromising as the Westminster Catechism. With him were many who would go half way, to the edge of rebellion and back; and others, men of sterner mettle, like Samuel Lount and Peter Matthews, who would go the whole way, and ultimately went it. The American rebels, Washington, Franklin and the rest, thought they were staging a demonstration under arms; it turned into war and independence. Were the rebels of Upper Canada in 1837 staging a demonstration? Very likely many did not know.

The upshot was a straggling gathering up Yonge Street, its intention to seize Toronto. It hesitated, missed its moment and was lost. Armed force gathered against the rebels. The explosion proved a damp squib. The rebels dispersed and were hunted as fugitives. Lount and Matthews were executed at Toronto. The boys of Upper Canada College had a half-holiday to see the execution. Mackenzie escaped to the United States to live eleven years in the shadow and to return home forgiven—and forgotten.

W. Kingsford, "History of Canada," 10 Vols., 1887-97

Several books have been written to show that the Upper-Canadian rebellion was a storm in a tea cup. It was more probably a tea cup in a storm. The storm of radicalism that shook all Europe in the eighteen-thirties, and brought down a throne in France, these winds of the new gospel of individual rights swept also the woods and fields of Canada. The sense of injustice bites harder than hardship. Indeed most of what hardship there was came from nature, not man.

Nor was rebellion in Upper Canada a real rising of the people. For every dozen rebels there were a dozen 'Tories.' As the rebels gathered above Toronto, the word went round the back settlements, and half-pay officers, ex-soldiers of Wellington's armies, took down their muskets and were off in pursuit of them. To these settlers their life might indeed be hard, but would be no softer with a mock republic in Toronto at the mercy of the United States.

F. P. Hett, "Georgina," 1939

Mrs. Traill, "The Backwoods of Canada"

Some of us now living can remember surviving 'rebels' of the Ontario countryside; old men, still 'Grits' unalterable, or 'Tories' immovable, the sinking fires of life banked over their earlier flame of the Radical ideal of reform or the Tory loyalty to order. These contrasted ideals, like twin circulating stars, have ever since held our political life within its orbit.

In French Canada the case was different. French it had remained. The census of 1844 showed for Lower Canada a population of 697,000 of whom 524,000 were French. But the English-speaking minority were mainly included in the 40,000 odd of the

Eastern Townships, the 31,000 English-speaking people of Montreal (out of 65,000) and the 18,000 (including 7,000 Irish) of the 45,000 total of Quebec. Outside of these areas English was practically a foreign language.

The Eastern Townships had been opened to British settlement, after 1796, with the British land system. The district became and remained, till yesterday, the counterpart of Upper Canada, settled from the same class of people with the same culture. The village of Sutton, Ontario, born fast asleep in 1819, has its counterpart in the drowsiness of Sutton, Quebec, both drawing on the perennial slumber of Sutton in Hampshire. Apart from the Townships the province was French, its population increasing by cradlefuls.

Here, as in Upper Canada, the Assembly found itself unable to control. Here, as in Upper Canada, only more so, were sinecure offices, often held by absentees, and profits and emoluments for the favoured. But every other discontent was here merged in the larger hostility of nationality. Those in control were British, those below were French. If Upper Canada was carried forward on the winds of European radicalism, so was Lower Canada swept by the new winds of nationalism that were remaking the Europe of the nineteenth century. Lord Durham's phrase "two nations warring in the bosom of single state," summarized the whole situation. The rest was nothing, or at least was all derivative from this. Hence when rebellion came, it struck harder. The stubborn fights along the Richelieu (St. Charles, St. Denis), the stubborn defence of St. Eustache were broken only by solid military force. When the Lower-Canadian rebellion flared out again, in inroads from the States next year, Sir John Colborne struck it ruthlessly down. The rebels left fifty dead on the field at Odelltown.

When rebellion in Upper Canada had collapsed, the British Government sent out Lord Durham to find out what the rebellions were about. Durham was at once an impassioned liberal and an autocrat. He saved the rebels' lives with a general amnesty for all and a special banishment for twenty-four of them. The action was disallowed and Durham called home. In place of it Sir John Colborne's military court hanged twelve rebels at

'The Patriotes of '37,' Alfred D. Decelles, in "Chronicles of Canada," 1916

Nov. 9, 1838

Montreal and sent three score of others to convict settlements in Australia. This changed rebellion to martyrdom. The French-Canadians called their lost comrades 'the patriots,' and the English later on discovered that they were.

Lord Durham's "Report on Canada," 1839

But Durham's importance in our history lies elsewhere. He presented to the Crown his famous *Report*, a state document matchless in style, penetrating in its analysis but feeble in its conclusion. Durham was a typical aristocratic liberal, determined to administer the new liberal freedom as medicine is administered to schoolboys. His *Report* shows a marvellous insight into the past; for the future his vision was the direct gaze of a bat in the daylight. What was needed in Canada, he urged, was to obliterate French nationalism. This was to be done by submerging it under British freedom, like a kitten in a water barrel. Unite the province, he said, with a single government with one legislature, with free votes for all, and the French will be voted out of "their vain hopes of nationality." Durham did not live to see his system in operation. Strangely enough his premature death was followed by that of Governor Sydenham (1841), Governor Bagot (1843), both in Canada, and of Governor Metcalfe, called home to earthly honours that came too late (1846).

J. L. Morrison, "British Supremacy and Canadian Self Government," 1919

But the system went into effect. The Act of Union of 1840 (in force, 1841), joined the two Canadas into the Province of Canada with a single elected legislature, and with English its language of record. The united government began life in the new capital of Kingston where French nationality was to commence its vanishing act. In place of that the opposite happened. There began that peculiar balance of nationalities which has held the French and English together ever since by keeping them sufficiently apart. Durham's very 'freedom' was made the means of survival. French members under Louis Hippolyte LaFontaine joined with the English under Robert Baldwin to outvote all classes of Tories and claim the government. Sir Charles Bagot considered that this 'responsible government' was implicit in the Act of Union. He thus put in control a group of men some of whom had been rebels or half way to it. The news shook Tory England. The aged Duke of Wellington was reported 'thunderstruck.' Old men often hear thunder in the evening.

Troubled years followed. Bagot held to the new freedom, but died. Metcalfe would have trampled it under, but died. There seemed a spell on Canada. Lord Elgin broke it. He was Durham's son-in-law, there to fulfil his work. He recognized responsible government and set the seal on it by refusing to disallow the Rebellion's Losses Bill of 1849. Tory Montreal mobbed him out of town, but his pelted carriage in its flight had passed a milestone of British history.

The principle of responsible government once conceded to Canada could not be withheld from the Maritime Provinces. Here, however, were no great grievances nor extreme hardships. Such difficulties as there were arose out of the ill-adjustment of economic life, the over-dominance of the timber trade that hindered agriculture and the lack of both credit and cash that hindered every kind of enterprise.

For years timber was king. When Napoleon closed the Baltic he made the fortune of British-American lumber. Before the Great War of 1793 colonial timber only supplied one per cent of the British market; in 1824 it supplied three-quarters of it. Lumber camps, the precursors of farm settlement, opened and spread through Upper Canada and New Brunswick. The eye of history can see in the old pine stumps of our pastures the Napoleonic decrees and the Treaty of Tilsit. Logs went down the *1807* spring drive on the rivers to gather into huge rafts, a quarter of a mile long, on Lake Ontario, to break again over the rapids, re-form below Montreal and so on to Quebec. Throughout the Maritimes logs for timber gathered in every port. To Britain went square timber, masts, staves, puncheons and barrels. Even after the Napoleonic War the customs preference over the Baltic *L. C. A.* countries gave the trade its lead. The preference, under the free *Knowles,* trade impulse, was reduced in 1843 and vanished in 1860. Its *"Economic* *Development* loss was to be a part of the sorrows of the Maritime Provinces. *of the British*

But the tears were not yet. Lumber was the base of Maritime *Overseas* *Empire,"* life, for export and for shipbuilding. Nova Scotia shipbuilding *Vol. II, 1928* seemed likely to conquer the world. In 1846 the province had 2,583 vessels as against 604 of Canada. "Nova Scotia," wrote Sir Edmund Head, when Governor of New Brunswick in 1852, "is destined to be one of the largest ship-owning countries in the world. She owns now nearly one-third as much tonnage as France." Nova Scotia ships filled the West Indian trade. One great advantage was that shipbuilding could be carried on as a sort of domestic industry. A sea-side farmer could cut trees on his farm and, with the help of his sons, build a ship and rig it, load it with wood off the farm, sail to Boston, sell the wood and load up for the West Indies. It seems like a dream. Little did they realize that the demon of machinery, which will not tolerate Utopia, was waiting with the iron ship, the doom of Nova Scotia.

F. W. Wallace,
"Wooden Ships
and
Iron Men."

Even at that, the highest year of wooden shipbuilding in the province was 1870, and in the Great War of 1914 the wooden ship heard the familiar echoes and came back. This earlier progress of the Maritimes is reflected in the fact that for forty years after the Loyalist migration the Maritime Provinces had a larger population than Upper Canada. Thus in 1824 Nova Scotia had 81,000 people, New Brunswick 74,000, Prince Edward Island over 24,000, and Upper Canada only 150,000.

This, unhappily, is only one side of the sea-side picture. It shows rather what might have happened than what did. Progress proved one-sided and unstable. Shipbuilding side-tracked agriculture. Many immigrants knew nothing of farm life. Many knew nothing and cared less. A farmer seemed a poor drudge beside the axe-men of the woods and shipyards. Nova Scotia fed on New York flour, and exchanged barrels of salt mackerel for New England pork. The Nemesis came when the St. Lawrence canals opened. Settlers flocked up the river to the farms of Upper Canada. In the long run the farm beat the forest and the sea, as it always has. Even sailors dream of farms.

In this Maritime environment there was no room for the heroic politics of a larger scene. Nor was there ground for it. The trouble was not with evil government but with muddled government. This showed for example in the hopeless lack of any proper money of exchange, bad coins mixing with worse paper and store-credit being swapped for uncut logs and unborn cattle. This cramped all business and checked advance. There was, too, as in Upper Canada, the same division of class and of opinion as between Reformers and Tories. There was the same over-privilege of the Anglican Church and the same favours to a favoured

STANLEY ROYLE, R.B.A., R.C.A., SACKVILLE, N.B., 1941

"Logs went down the spring drive on the rivers . . . ."—PAGE 137

class. Hence arose the same demand for responsible government, its Nova Scotia champion being Joseph Howe. He was the people's voice, his "Twelve Resolutions" of 1836, their Petition of Right. Yet Howe was at the same time the voice of empire, one of the first, advocating British-American union, hearing already the "whistle of the steam engine in the Rocky Mountains," and dreaming of a federation of all the Britains. Lord Glenelg, the Colonial Secretary, had refused Howe's responsible government flat, as only proper for a "metropolitan" government. But Canadian rebellion, and responsible government in Canada, threw it as a ripe apple into the Maritime lap. From there it passed around the Empire. It reached its highest flight in 1893, with the gift of responsible government to Western Australia. This put 50,000 people in control of 975,000 square miles of land and all its resources. This was imbecility, but being inspired, its inspiration pardons it.

J. W. Longley, 'Joseph Howe,' "Makers of Canada," 1926

Such was the setting that accompanied responsible government in Canada as between 1840 and 1849. But the next decade was to prove the new united government as unworkable as the old. Responsible government was unworkable because it had to work a double shift. To make it work there must be a majority in the Assembly for the Government, but it must mean also a majority as of French and as of English. On this turned the vexed politics of the eighteen-fifties. Here were Tories mainly entrenched in Upper Canada (Canada West) but with an annex of 'Blues' in Canada East. Here were Liberals, the name imported to replace the 'Reformers' of Rebellion times, and with them an advanced wing (the Grits), radical ahead of time, who were men of "clear grit," a country metaphor that can be understood by turning a grindstone for a couple of hours. In Lower Canada were 'Liberals' also, an orthodox party strongly supporting the Church, and a group of 'Reds' following the European radicalism of the epoch. Among these must be found a parliamentary majority. It could not have been done but for the skill of the new leader, Mr. John A. Macdonald of Kingston, who could control two factions at a time as easily as a circus rider goes round on two horses. He did it by having no principle —or rather by being content with one—the allegiance of a

Sir John, 1867 C. Dent, "The Last Forty Years," 1881

contented people under the British Crown. Of such things as free trade versus protection, of abstract principles of economics, he never cared a farthing. "A British subject I was born, a British subject I will die"—the words are those of his last remembered address, still far away. No one was asking him to die, but as a tariff argument it "beat all." With this and with the easy intercourse of good nature, he led his fellow men for a half century. Macdonald therefore was able to create a 'Liberal-Conservative' party in 1854, its very name a scandal to nicer conscience.

Macdonald managed to keep government going in his ins-and-outs of office. He gave Roman Catholic schools to Upper Canada by the French vote, and militia to Lower Canada by the English vote. His opponents, such as the famous George Brown of the *Globe*, as straight as a figure in Euclid and about as attractive, denounced Macdonald's politics and viewed his shifts and turns as embodied sin. But without Macdonald, the collapse of government would only have come all the sooner. The province had had a dozen ministries, original or reconstructed, as between responsible government in 1848 and George Brown's resignation in 1865. In the last three years there were four ministries and two general elections.

Difficulties were enhanced by vexed American relations. In those unhappy days the monarchy and the republic had not learned to live side by side as steady as the Lion and the Unicorn. A large part of the history of the by-gone Province of Canada (1841-1867) turned on the unsettled relations of British North America and the United States. The boundary disputes that arose out of the ambiguous Treaty of 1783, dividing unexplored territory, vexed its opening years and almost precipitated war. The Ashburton Treaty of 1842 settled at last, by a compromise, the boundary between Maine and New Brunswick. The original

James White, "Boundary Disputes and Treaties" (Canada and Its Provinces) 1910

treaty of 1783 had turned on "the north-west angle of Nova Scotia"—and there wasn't any. So the whole thing became a riddle of the Sphinx. Lord Ashburton and Daniel Webster divided the territory as between friends. That either party got cheated is just a legend. Ashburton and Webster, being friends, sat discussing the clauses, since the weather was warm, "in their shirt-sleeves." This gave history the same kind of offence as when Lord Elgin presently made the Reciprocity Treaty of 1854 by "floating it through on champagne." Yet what better way to make treaties? Made thus they lasted. Champagne and shirt sleeves proved better than "blood and iron."

There followed the more acute crisis over Oregon. The Oregon territory in reality had no boundary. It was just a name. It must end north at the lowest reach of Russian America (latitude fifty-four, forty) and end south at the top reach of Spanish America (Mexico). Britain and America both claimed it. For a time the shout of "fifty-four forty or fight," almost precipitated war. Garrisons were increased. Lord Cathcart, one of Wellington's men, came out as Governor. In the Washington House of Representatives it was proposed that the American Eagle should

Congressional Globe, June 24, 1846

stick his claws in the nose of the British Lion and make him spout blood like a whale. Common sense ended the quarrel in a compromise. Looking at the map we can still weep over the sweeping elbow of the Columbia River, where it leaves us. But even without it British Columbia is an empire.

Far more important in its after-effects was the famous Elgin-Marcy Treaty of 1854. Here the disputes were real, the issues vital. There had been a background of ill-feeling for nearly twenty years. Many Americans had sympathized with the Rebellion of 1837. They would have liked Canada to "come in." Even when the Rebellion was suppressed, there was an aftermath of veiled hostility along the Niagara that led to the seizure and destruction, beside Navy Island, of the rebel steamer *Caroline*, which went over the Falls in flames—or didn't. History and legend dispute.

More far-reaching was the contrast of what seemed American progress with Canadian stagnation. This was the America of the "roaring forties," of the all-fired energy of the great epic of movement to the Middle West; the America of the canal boats, and the river steamers and the banks that both blew up, boom towns that vanished and log cabins that were to turn into cathedrals; swamps and cane-brakes where the voices of the springtime frogs sang a greeting to the civilization that was to turn them into park and meadow. This was the America that Charles Dickens saw, or rather, failed to see. Dickens could shout with fun over the scrambles of life in England, could roar with Mrs. Gamp over bad gin and worse English, but in the vast glory of this new birth of America, he saw nothing but vulgarity, tobacco spitting and river ague.

M. Minnigerode, "The Fabulous Forties," 1924

Such were the times. As such did they react on men. To many Canadians this shouting prosperity of the republic, exuberant even in its alternating success and failure, seemed to mean that there was a new price to pay for their British allegiance. They were shut out of this rising market. They watched from across a river, as people watch a fair and trudge home supperless. Even men who had none of the rebel in them began to think of 'joining the States.' Small blame if they did. Much British opinion leaned the same way. The free trade school already saw the

Empire floating asunder on a milk-and-water ocean of universal peace and brotherhood. It is not to be wondered that such circumstances and opinions presently led to an Annexation Manifesto, put forth in Montreal in 1849 and signed with names only to be mentioned in a whisper. It seemed manifest destiny for Canada to fall into the arms of Uncle Sam, except for a lingering doubt whether Uncle Sam was quite a man to be trusted.

Allin & Jones, "Annexation and Reciprocity," 1912

Lord Elgin found a better way. His treaty was negotiated in 1854 with Mr. Marcy, the Secretary of State. Elgin was all airs and elegance and affability; Marcy a grim, old veteran of war and politics. These extremes met and made a treaty that turned the track of history. The treaty set up free trade across the border in a long list of natural products. It gave mutual freedom of navigation on Lake Michigan and the St. Lawrence. It went into effect with instant benefits to both sides. Along with it there came to Upper Canada the war boom of the Russian war. Death in the Crimea meant life in Canada. Wheat rose to $2.50 a bushel. Settlers paid for their whole farms with three years' crops, paid all old mortgages and put on new ones. Look through Ontario with the eye to see and you will mark, in many old brick houses set behind straggled lilacs and broken hedges, the memories of the Elgin-Marcy Treaty and the Crimean War.

L. Oliphant, "Episodes in a Life of Adventure," 1887

Then came the American Civil War. In Canada the plain people were overwhelmingly for the North, and so too in the Maritimes. It is commonly estimated that at least 50,000 British-Americans fought in the Federal ranks. So, also, a certain number for the South. For the South also was British aristocratic sentiment—blind to the future and wanting America divided.

H. G. MacDonald, "Canadian Public Opinion on the American Civil War," 1926

Aristocratic circles in Canada, some of them, reflected back this moonlight. The South, too, sent its refugee rich to Upper Canada to build porticoed houses at Cobourg and to fill old-time hostelries in St. Catharines. Canada thus was made a base for Southern plotting, if only in a barroom, and once or twice of actual raiding.

The war threw everything out of gear. An American naval captain seized two Southerners from the British steamer *Trent*, and nearly precipitated war. With this came the realization that if war should come, Canada was in a way defenceless. In winter it was frozen in. Even its Governor must drive, as Bagot did, through the snows of New York State. Until then the question of better communication, of a railroad from Canada to Nova Scotia, had elicited only feeble interest in England. The union of the scattered parts of British North America had not seemed a matter of moment. Proposals of general union went back indeed as far as Chief Justice Smith's ideas of 1790 and to Durham's Report, and had recently found vigorous utterance from Joseph Howe. Such ideas remained mere oratory till the American Civil War precipitated the union of British North America.

The moment was indeed ripe. The four Maritime Provinces—Newfoundland being one—were already discussing the obvious advantage and common sense of union among themselves, as commonwealths all alike in kinship and common interest. For the Maritime Provinces Canada was far away. All their interest was across the sea and in that peculiar sympathy and converse with New England that had descended from the time of the Loyalists. Boston with Harvard College was still, if not the intellectual capital, at least the Mecca of the Provinces.

Nor was this all. Government in Canada (the united province) had proved unworkable. It could not even find a capital where to lay its head. From Kingston it had gone to Montreal. The Tory riot of 1849 lost Montreal its place. The capital ambulated, turn about, from Quebec to Toronto every three years, from all French, to all British. This would not do. Common agreement settled on Bytown up the Ottawa. It was named from Colonel *1825-1832* By, the engineer of the Rideau Canal which was built as a water route to evade the American frontier. Renamed Ottawa, it became the seat of government in 1864. It had the merit of scenic beauty and solitude. No enemy from the States would find it.

Nothing worked right as between Canada East and Canada West—neither school, nor church, nor militia. With old troubles gone, new ones came. The Clergy Reserves of Upper Canada *1854* had been handed over to education. The seigniorial tenures of Lower Canada were terminated, except for holders who preferred, as some did till the year 1940, to pay their annual rent.

But to separate utterly the two Canadas proved impossible in an age when the steamboat and the canal and the railway were turning wagon-ways into through traffic and a market town to a metropolis. The canals on the St. Lawrence offered a completed route by 1850. Railways spread like a running grapevine over Upper Canada. The year 1856 saw a Grand Trunk that joined Montreal to Toronto, led inland to Chicago and outwards to the sea.

In 1864 government practically collapsed. No one could get a majority. "Deadlock," said Goldwin Smith, "made Confederation." Worse still, the Reciprocity Treaty was running out, denounced by the Americans. They claimed that the new protective tariff made by Canada in 1858-59, to shelter its infant industries, broke the spirit of the Treaty. Moreover, as the Civil War in the States drew to its close there was talk, mostly Irish talk, of shifting the war to Canada to take vengeance for the wrongs of Ireland.

It was time for men of good will to get together. Even George Brown was willing to pretend to be friends with Macdonald. The British Government, as eager to salvage a dissolving Empire as it had once been to let it dissolve, offered every help, a railway to the sea, and the whole expanse of the Hudson's Bay Company's territory as a royal gift all ready for the new christening. The gift of the territory was not discussed with the Métis halfbreeds who lived there. So it came about, just as the Civil War across the border drew to its close, that the Quebec Conference—whose members were later to be called the Fathers of Confederation—gathered to create the Dominion of Canada.

Memorandum of Sir Edward Head, 1857, Colonial Office Papers and Canadian Hist. Review, Dec., 1935

O. Skelton, "The Railway Builders" (Chronicles of Canada), 1916

Goldwin Smith, "Canada and the Canadian Question," 1891

Oct., 1864

MEMORABLE DATES

1774
Quebec Act

1783
Treaty of Versailles

1784
United Empire Loyalists

1791
Constitutional Act

1812-15
War with the United States

1837
Canadian Rebellion

1840
Act of Union

1842
Ashburton Treaty (Oregon 1846)

1854
Reciprocity Treaty

1867
Confederation

Upper Canada College, Toronto, 1829-1877. " . . . the red-brick Government House flew its flag, and over the way the red-brick Upper Canada College set itself to make scholars and gentlemen . . ." —PAGE 155

CHAPTER VI

THE NEW DOMINION STRUGGLING INTO LIFE
1867-1878

*The Making of Confederation—Canada at Confederation—Meeting of Par-
liament—Nova Scotia and Repeal—The Red River Rebellion—Admission of
Manitoba—British Columbia enters Confederation—Prince Edward Island
—The United States, Reciprocity and the Washington Treaty—The Pacific
Scandal and the Fall of the Government—The Liberal Government, Hard
Times and the Election of 1878.*

THE stages by which the Dominion of Canada was formed
stand as follows. A Conference was held at Charlottetown
to discuss the union of the four Maritime Provinces. Delegates arrived from Canada inviting the Conference to adjourn
to Quebec to discuss the wider union of all British North
America. The Quebec Conference met in October of 1864. These
were the Fathers of Confederation, known in the familiar picture
by Robert Harris. Their formal dress of bygone fashion, their
wide Prince Albert coats and flowing side whiskers, lend them a
certain air of distinction, not to say antiquity. Of the total
thirty-three Fathers the most remembered names are those of
John A. Macdonald, George Brown, Etienne Taché, Georges
Etienne Cartier, all from Canada. From Canada also was D'Arcy
McGee, the 'lost leader' of the Fenian movement, who was to
pay for his conversion with his life. From Nova Scotia came Dr.
Charles Tupper of Amherst, a veritable maker of Canada, who
was to represent Cumberland County at Halifax and at Ottawa

Sept. 7, 1864

*W. P. M.
Kennedy
"Constitution
of Canada,"
1922*

*Sir G. Bourinot,
"Constitutional
History of
Canada,"
(List of
Members,
1901)*

for thirty-two years. He was Joseph Howe's great rival in a province that never had room for both of them. Howe, being out of office, had no share in either Conference. For New Brunswick was Leonard Tilley and for 'The Island' J. H. Gray, the Prime Minister. From Newfoundland came Ambrose Shea and Frederick Carter, two Fathers who deserted their offspring in its cradle and never came back.

The Convention drew up the seventy-two Resolutions which became the basis of our present constitution. These were submitted to the Legislature of Canada and called forth, in the famous Confederation Debates, a record of the public opinion of the day. Such opposition as there was arose chiefly from French-Canadian fear of absorption, or reflected Christopher Dunkin's melancholy prophecy that Canada was too sectional for unity. The two Houses joined in an address asking the Crown for an Act of Parliament.

Feb. 3-March 14, 1865

"Confederation Debates" 1865

If Canada had been alone concerned, that would have been the end. But federation, as things stood, had no chance in the Maritimes. Newfoundland ran away from it. Prince Edward Island petitioned the Crown against it. New Brunswick held an election on the issue and snowed it under, Tilley's government with it. In Nova Scotia, public opinion, roused by Joseph Howe, ran wild against the plan. Tupper did not even attempt a general election. It seemed in 1865 that federation had been strangled in its cradle. Nor is the reason far to seek. To the Maritimes, Canada was another place. People used the word in that sense for forty years after Confederation. Union with Canada meant to them French rule for British people. In taking away their power over customs duties it would take all their revenue. It meant, they felt sure, a protective tariff, high prices for Canadian manufactures and British goods shut out. Their market was going. Reciprocity was running out. The wooden ship was foundering, flag up. The shades of night were falling, and the night was called Confederation.

1865

Then came destiny and altered everything. The Civil War in America ended virtually at Appomattox. As its echoes ceased, the new tumult of Fenianism was heard across the border; men drilling in thousands, unimpeded, the Washington government

April 9, 1865

looking the other way. There was to be invasion, and with it a Republic of Canada to avenge the wrongs of Ireland. The invasion came, its raids across the border meeting an inglorious end. But with invasion the hearts of the Loyalists stirred again within their grandchildren. A second election (1866) carried Confederation through in New Brunswick. In Nova Scotia the government, right or wrong, grasped firmly the nettle of difficulty, and passed a legislative vote for union without asking sanction from the people.

G. Denison "Soldiering in Canada," 1900

A delegation from the Province of Canada had gone to London in 1865. A new delegation, Canadian and Maritime, was sent over in the autumn of 1866. The famous Westminster Palace Conference arranged better terms, larger subsidies for the Maritimes. It was agreed all round—except by the people in the North-West—to throw in the North-West into the bargain. The plan of union left an open place for British Columbia, for Prince Edward Island and for Newfoundland. This gave it that continental aspect which overcame and still overcomes, to the view of common sense, all local and minor divergences. As beside this ideal an independent Red River and the shadow republic of to-day in Laurentia, are just nowhere.

Dec. 4, 1866

In those days the only method of procedure to alter the constitution of the British American Provinces was by an imperial statute. Strangely enough it is the only method to-day. We cannot ourselves amend our constitution. The British North America Act of 1867, having no amending clause, locked the door of the past and threw away the key. The lock could only be picked by the imperial locksmith. Our new Westminster Statute of 1931 goes further. It throws away the other key. Amendment of Dominion and Provincial relations, if ever done, can only be done now by pretending that the British Parliament has a power which this statute expressly says it has not. That, however, offers no great difficulty for people with what is called the British genius for government. We have lived for centuries on just such fictions and obsolescences. Compare the Chiltern Hundreds and the Keeper of the Swans.

All that, however, was not yet. The British North America Act of 1867 still reserved very real power to the Imperial Government.

A. B. Keith,
"Responsible
Government
in the
Dominions,"
1912

The Governor-General could of his own initiative reserve Canadian bills. The supreme military command rested with Great Britain. Imperial garrisons were in Canada till 1871 and naval establishments at Halifax and Esquimalt till 1903. Foreign relations and diplomacy were in imperial hands. One by one all these powers faded out, or were explicitly wiped out or forgotten. The Westminster Statute only stated a fact.

Such was the union of the Dominion of Canada which was to embrace when it was complete over three and a half million square miles, an area larger than Europe. But apart from its great size it was, in early Confederation days, little more than an outline. The far greater part of it and much of the best of it was trackless, almost unoccupied and unused. The Maritime Provinces with 767,000 people offered a fairly compact block of settlement, although the interior of New Brunswick was still mostly forest. From New Brunswick the wilderness reached to the French-Canadian settlements on the St. Lawrence at Rimouski. Westward the occupied country ran all along the St. Lawrence and for some distance up the Ottawa. From the St. Lawrence, settlement continued along the north side of Lake Ontario, reaching at most a hundred miles inland. Thence it spread all over the Western Peninsula to Lake Erie and Lake Huron. But except for the Eastern Townships of Quebec and the Western Peninsula of Ontario, there was no 'depth' to occupied Canada. "The country," wrote Governor Sir Edmund Head, "is all frontier." Everywhere the bush was close at hand and where the lumber-shanties ended, forest and outcropping rock, broken with innumerable lakes, a maze of islands and a rush of rivers, went on for ever to the north.

Of the ports and cities of Canada at Confederation, Nova Scotia could boast of Halifax, with 29,000 people, already a place of world renown, a naval and military station, with all that goes with a seat of government and a college town. On The Island, Charlottetown was an old-world seaport, like an old-fashioned child, with a Government House, visits of naval ships and the romance of the tall white schooners of the West Indian trade. For New Brunswick, larger and with great forests and valley farms and the open seaport of Saint John, prosperity seemed already around the corner—of the Bay of Fundy. Quebec, its population 59,000 in 1871, had lost its priority in shipping and commerce to Montreal. The improvement of the river channel, together with the opening of the St. Lawrence canals, was turning Montreal into a seaport metropolis. It was superior in situation to New York, but the grip of the ice condemned it to alternating death and resurrection.

In Upper Canada, henceforth Ontario, Toronto was a commodious capital city of 60,000 inhabitants. Its streets were embowered in leaves above which rose the many spires of the churches. Its wooden slum district was herded into the centre and, like poverty itself, forgotten. Where the leaves ended a sort of park land began and in it stood the University of Toronto, secular and scientific, but housed in Norman architecture of beauty unsurpassed. To the west, more rural but less beautiful with earthly beauty, was Trinity College, founded in protest against the existence of secular Toronto. But down below, along the water-front, was a business district, built like a bit of London, all of a sky-line and with cobblestones rattling with cabs. The new railways sliced off, as everywhere in Ontario, the shore line, vilified with ash-heaps and refuse. All over Canada between the vanishing beauty of nature and the later beauty of civic adornment, there extended this belt of tin cans and litter.

Just above the railway lines rose the red-brick Parliament buildings, the red-brick Government House flew its flag, and over the way the red-brick Upper Canada College set itself to make scholars and gentlemen as good as real ones. Guarding the harbour entrance was the Old Fort, its frame barracks of the same old pattern and roof-slope that had already gone round the Empire, its ramparts crumbling but its ponderous old guns in embrasures still looking feebly dangerous. The tone of society was English at the top but the barber shops spoke American. There was profound peace and order and on Sunday all bells and Sunday-best. It seems, as most places do, a pleasant place in retrospect. At least it was cheap. The chair at Toronto that Professor Huxley tried in vain to get, carried a salary of £400 and meant an ample living.

1871

A. N. Bethune, "Memoir of John Strachan," 1870

H. Scadding, "Toronto of Old," 1873

1829

From the business district the shops ran for half a mile up Yonge Street and, beyond that, Yonge Street ran thirty-five miles to Holland Landing where water communication began. It had a tavern to every mile and plenty of grain wagons to keep them busy. The main railway ran through from Montreal to Sarnia-Chicago. But from the half-dozen little railway stations of the Toronto of early Confederation days, there radiated, like the fingers of a hand, half a dozen little railways with various gauges, reaching out north to the lumber woods—Huntsville, Coboconk, Haliburton—and north and west to the lake ports of Lake Huron and the Georgian Bay. Along the stations of these railway lines the horse and buggy and the lumber-wagon took up the traffic. General stores, each a post-office, with a near-by blacksmith shop, arose at the cross-roads, and if there was also a river with a waterfall, there appeared a sawmill and a grist-mill, and presently, as the farms multiplied, a village. Then the village became a little town, with not one but rival stores, a drug store, a local paper and a cricket club. In it were four churches and three taverns. One church was of the Church of England, one Presbyterian, while the Roman Catholics, Methodists and Baptists divided the other two. On the map of Ontario Protestantism was everywhere, but Roman Catholicism ran in zig-zags. The three taverns were one Grit, and one Tory and one neither. Many things in Ontario ran like that in threes, with the post-office and the mail stage alternating as the prize of victory in elections. The cricket club is now just a memory, gone long ago. Thus the little Ontario town grew till the maples planted in its streets overtopped it and it fell asleep and grew no more. It is strange this, and peculiar to our country, the aspect of a town grown from infancy to old age within a human lifetime.

But other towns had better luck. To them fell the new factories of the protective tariff that after 1858 began to turn out ploughs and implements, boots and shoes, cloth and cottons and furniture. They grew bigger than town-size, cut down the maples on the main street, put in a horse-car from the 'depot' to the 'business section'—and then stuck dead again as cities. Even in 1880 London, Ontario, had a population of only 19,000, St. Thomas of 8,000, and Hamilton of 35,000. The ten western

*O. Skelton,
'The Railway
Builders,'
"Chronicles of
Canada,"
1916*

lakeport towns extended all the way from Kincardine to Parry
Sound, each waiting to become the main outlet of the North-West,
living on the lumber trade and the excursion business meanwhile,
till in many of them the cedar piles rotted and the wharves sagged
with weariness of waiting. None ever became the outlet. Each
is waiting again now, seventy years later, to be the ocean port
of the inland sea-way.

Beyond the Muskoka district Canada went on indefinitely *Rev. Geo. M.*
north and west. There were fishing harbours on the Georgian Bay *Grant,*
and beside Manitoulin Island, and a settlement where Lake *"Ocean to*
Superior has its outlet at the Sault Ste. Marie. Inland was nothing *Ocean,"*
but trading posts here and there and the Red River settlement of *1873*

ONTARIO
AT
CONFEDERATION

Approx. Scale of Miles

Assiniboia. This district covered roughly a circle of a fifty-mile radius around the Hudson's Bay Company's Fort Garry at the junction of the Red and the Assiniboine. Winnipeg—the word means dirty water—was the name for a random collection of saloons and shacks down the road from the fort. More respectable was the French-Canadian village of St. Boniface, across the river, its stone cathedral marking it as a bishopric, and containing some *1871* 750 souls as against the soulless 250 of Winnipeg. On the plains was Regina, still a 'pile of bones,' buffalo bones, and called so, and beyond it the various Company posts of the Saskatchewan and Mackenzie Valleys. Edmonton appears as the Edmonton House, established in 1795. There was no Calgary. Nor was there any town Vancouver. Beyond the Rockies British Columbia was to be reached only by sea, round the Horn or by way of the Panama Isthmus. After 1869 the Union Pacific Railway and a steamer from San Francisco supplied a more rapid transit. In British Columbia were, in 1871, some 25,000 Indians and 10,000 whites.

To group all these fragments, these solitudes, into one great Dominion, to join it with a continental railroad, to embrace it all in one jurisdiction by law and order, seemed to many people a task beyond endeavour. Thus, in the days of Jefferson's Louisi-
1803 ana Purchase of 900,000 square miles, had seemed the western
J. B. McMaster, prairies to the people of the United States. The Roman poet
"History of the Virgil said proudly—think what a task it has been establishing
People of the Rome as a nation! We may well say the same of Canada.
United States,"
Vol. II, 1885 Yet the task was begun. The British North America Act
A. P. Cockburn, became law in March, 1867, and went into force on July 1,
"Political 1867. Lord Monck was appointed Governor-General. John A.
Annals of Macdonald, now fittingly Sir John, was appointed to summon a
Canada," ministry, purposely drawn from both sides of politics. Georges
1905 Etienne Cartier became his chief support among the French.
Sir Georges, But Macdonald in the opening years of Confederation himself
1868 guided the policy of Canada. Opposition fell into the hands of Alexander Mackenzie, an unflinching Canadian Scot, self-made and not to be made over again, and of Edward Blake, a man of cultivated intellect and Roman dignity, about as genial as a Latin grammar. Beside the easy-going jocularity of Sir John A., they were, for Canadian politics, nowhere. A large part of the

first session was devoted to legislation organizing the departments of government and initiating a system of finance. These were largely matters of routine. But the difficulties of the new government began in its very cradle. Its life opened with the conflict of Dominion and Provinces which has ever since vexed the Canadian union. Of the nineteen members from Nova Scotia all except Dr. Charles Tupper went to Ottawa only to protest against being there.

Well might the members sit in protest. These were indeed hard times for the Maritime Provinces and especially for Nova Scotia. The termination of Reciprocity had lost the American market. Wooden shipbuilding was obviously moving to its decline. Confederation had destroyed revenue and dislocated finance. There seemed no remedy but in repeal, in renewed relations with the States and renewed access to British trade. This repeal movement fills the early years of Confederation and centres round the name of Joseph Howe. From his past views and his imperial ideals, Howe should logically have been the maker of Confederation. As has been said, he was out of office and had no part in either the Charlottetown or the Quebec Conference. The task fell to his opponent, Tupper, a man less genial but of greater strength. Howe bitterly opposed the plan, not of Confederation in general, but of what he called "the Quebec scheme," which, he said, "utterly sacrificed the interests of the Maritime Provinces." He was sent to London with two others, at the expense of his sympathizers (Howe had no money) to oppose the plan. After Confederation was adopted, Howe for a time led the agitation for repeal. Then silence fell upon him. Sir John Macdonald was consulting him, in correspondence and in conference, about better financial terms—for Nova Scotia and for himself. The better terms for Nova Scotia were granted in the increased subsidies of 1868. It was then learned that Howe was to join Macdonald's cabinet at Ottawa. Following this ministerial appointment Howe stood, by constitutional custom, for election to Parliament. A fierce contest followed in the County of Hants. Howe was elected and repeal shattered. Till the government fell, Howe remained in the cabinet, his untrained hand learning to play second fiddle, with no applause. His four

*J. W. Longley,
'Joseph Howe,'
"Makers of
Canada,"
1904*

1866

years in the Dominion cabinet were, in the words of a biographer, "the least glorious of his career." For over a generation Nova Scotia people went on discussing whether Joseph Howe was a lost leader, bought and sold, or a great patriot, honest enough to admit error. In the long retrospect of to-day, those who should know most, think best of him.

The dissatisfaction felt in Nova Scotia was shared in all the Maritime Provinces. In part it was due to the nature of the new federation. The British North America Act had left the existing provinces practically unaltered in their constitutions. But it superimposed a federal government made up of a Governor-General, an elected House of Commons, an appointed Senate and a responsible Cabinet. The essence of the Act lay in the distribution of power. The intention was to place the main authority firmly in the centre. The privileges of minorities as to religion and schools were safeguarded. The French language was made equal with English in the Dominion administration and in Quebec, and in any province which wished it so. But there provincial autonomy was meant to end. The union was made in full view of the object lesson of the American Republic, thrown into civil war over States' rights. The statute gave all legislative power to the Federal Government except over matters expressly reserved to the provinces; power to levy any kind of taxes, to make any and every regulation of commerce, of money and banking, and to disallow any provincial statute it proposed to disallow. Nothing was clearer in intent; nothing has proved more fallacious in its issue. The lean kine were to eat up the fat. The feeble provinces of 1867, apparently denuded of revenue and devoid of all but meagre and necessary power, were to be changed by altered circumstances and by judicial interpretation into the autonomous units of seventy years later, a sort of heptarchy whose members control the whole public domain and vast revenues from sources unknown at Confederation.

All that, however, was to come later. For a time the Provinces felt themselves overshadowed by the Dominion and no longer in control of their own home and patrimony. But once in, there was no way out. Nova Scotia appealed in vain to

A. H. F. Lefroy, "Legislative Power in Canada," 1897

B.N.A. Act, s. 91

Westminster for repeal. For at least a generation the Maritime people felt that Confederation was like the lion's den in the Latin fable—no foot-tracks led out of it. Newfoundland seemed to be the wise fox who had noted this in time.

Queen Victoria's reign began in Canada with the Canadian Rebellion. The Dominion of Canada began its rule in the North-West with the Red River Rebellion. Both came from the same cause. The queen knew nothing of Canada and Canada knew nothing of the North-West. The troubles on the Red River arose essentially from the fact that the time had come when the North-West must wake out of its two-hundred-years' sleep. It could not remain a fur-trade preserve. The world needed it. Civilization began to throw its advancing shadow on the rich land of the west and the shadow at its first touch struck chill. For years before Confederation the British Government had been considering the reorganization of the Hudson's Bay Company, the restriction of its activity to trade and the resumption of its land and sovereignty. The question of an overland telegraph to Europe loomed large before the underwater cable of 1866 made it unnecessary. A first cable had been laid in 1858. Queen Victoria and President Buchanan exchanged congratulations. Then silence fell. There was no cable through the Civil War and its absence was an object lesson. If a submarine cable was not feasible, then a land telegraph must reach Europe from America by way of Alaska and Siberia. On the map of north-west British Columbia may still be found the name Telegraph Creek beside the Stikine River. It is not so much a name as an epitaph. A new cable was laid by the Great Eastern in 1866. By 1869 there were three. Telegraph Creek was all in. But in the early sixties the overland telegraph project seemed certain of execution.

Sir E. Walkin, "Canada and the States," 1887

So the Hudson's Bay Company's sovereignty had to end. High finance, buying up its shares through a syndicate, with government approval, was busy in London with that peculiar air of wickedness that high finance always wears. The loyal servants of the Company in North America grew apprehensive. Till now the profits of the Company had been handled on that grand old maritime system of something for everybody—a

D. MacKay, "The Honourable Company," 1936

system that came down from the Saxon Vikings and obtains still with prize money, salvage, and the spoils of the sea. The 'wintering partners,' as the factors and traders were called, received 40 per cent of the Company's profits which meant at this time, over and above all cost of living, about £800 sterling each year for the factors (there were fifteen), and £400 for each of the thirty-seven traders. When retired, a factor kept an interest worth in all over £3,000. Clerks received salaries of about £100 a year but stood in line for promotion to traders. Boatmen and labourers were on wages, but with living and old-age assured. All this was now to be reorganized on 'business lines.' It seemed that the good old times would end. Until this period the proprietors in London used to sign their letters to Rupert's Land, "Your loving friends." Would the new International Finance Society of London do that?

When the Hudson's Bay officers in North America learned of the proposed changes they felt as if they had been bought and sold. Hence their peculiar attitude of inactivity—one must not say apathy—towards the proposed transfer to Canada that was to consolidate the change, and their failure to oppose the protests of the half-breeds who had been their servants and associates for a lifetime. These Métis half-breeds formed the larger half of the people of Assiniboia (5,757 out of 11,500). They were attached to Company rule, looking to its paternal care of their interest. They were Roman Catholics, speaking French and seeing in their French cathedral-village of St. Boniface the abiding shelter of their religion and language. Not without hope were some people, both there and in old Canada, that this nucleus might grow to a French North-West and guarantee for ever the racial duality of Canada, or even restore the racial dominance of the French-Canadians. This frustrated vision, presently to be clouded and lost in the mass migration that followed, added a touch of bitterness to the attitude of the French-Canadians towards the Dominion in the West. They had lost French Canada over again.

But there were other settlers, especially newcomers from Ontario, whose view was entirely different. These people wanted the end of Company rule, the ownership of the land and the full status of citizens, not the tutelage accorded to a subordinate

"Agents and surveyors had been sent to the Red River country . . ."
—PAGE 165

class. They welcomed the proposed transfer as the beginning of a provincial freedom. Their demands were voiced in their *Nor'-Wester*, the first local paper of the plains.

The Confederation of Canada had given the British government just the chance needed. The transfer of the North-West to Canada would escape the seeming bad faith of taking back rights once given. The price arranged (£300,000) and the liberal land grant which went with it could satisfy the claims of both shareholders and faithful servants. The transfer would solidify British North America from sea to sea, and dissipate the American ambitions that might repeat the quarrel over Oregon. A British statute authorized the surrender to the Crown of the Company's rights concerned, and a Canadian statute provided for temporary government of Rupert's Land and the North-West Territories. The transfer was all set for December 1, 1869.

30 and 31 Victoria, c. 105

32 and 33, Victoria, c. 33

But when the date came transfer was not possible. Trouble had begun. Agents and surveyors had been sent to the Red River country in the autumn of 1869. The people on the spot watched them mark out square township lines that seemed to disregard the river-lots of the actual occupiers and obliterate the squatters' rights on the plains. To the half-breed Métis and to many of the old-time Red River Scots, Canada seemed as distant and alien as it had to the Maritime people. There was at once protest, meetings, anger.

G. Stanley, "Birth of Western Canada," 1936

It is generally agreed now that up to this point the protest was warranted, the anger justified. The government of Canada had been guilty at least of gross neglect. In reality all that the protesting settlers wanted—their own land, their own church, school and language, their own right of government—was presently granted under the Manitoba Act of 1870. Nor had any one wanted to take it away. But suppression came first and explanation after.

G. Denison, "Soldiering in Canada," 1901

Meantime the disaffected had found a leader in Louis Riel, a cracked visionary who had enough megalomania for two rebellions and not enough capacity for one. That Louis Riel ever wanted to fight anybody is very doubtful. His idea of a rebellion, as amply appeared fifteen years later, was taken from the rhetoric class of a secondary college. It meant talk, oratory and then a settlement and the award of a prize with applause. But his leadership dragged him on. Of those who might best have held him back, Archbishop Taché, the beloved prelate of the North-West, was absent in Rome. The Hudson's Bay Governor, William MacTavish, was old and mortally ill. Riel and his armed Métis seized Fort Garry unopposed. They held MacTavish as a prisoner. They hoisted a flag that combined a French *fleur de lys* with an Irish shamrock, a gesture to Fenianism over the American border. Riel set up a provisional government but neither then nor later explicitly repudiated the sovereignty of the queen. Meantime the opposing Canadians and British, led by Colonel Dennis of the survey party and Major Boulton, rallied under arms to the Stone Fort, Lower Fort Garry, twenty miles down the river, and called for volunteers. Riel seized a group of these volunteers in Winnipeg, and held them prisoners. Among them was an Irishman, Thomas Scott, a man reckless and fearless, jeering at Riel with the contempt of a brave man for a coward. Thus stood affairs on the Red River Settlement as the winter of 1869 closed in. Riel and his adherents in Fort Garry fed fat and waxed strong on Hudson's Bay food and supplies. But there was no disorder.

Meantime the new Commissioner and Lieutenant-Governor from Canada, the Hon. William McDougall, arrived at the Minnesota border seeking entry. He expected to 'take over' on December 1, 1869. The date had been postponed at Ottawa on news of trouble. McDougall didn't know this and in what followed played the part of a sort of comic relief, alternately entering Assiniboia and being chased back to Minnesota, and issuing proclamations on his own from across the border.

McDougall mattered not a rush. The man of the hour was coming. Here first appears on the public scene of our history that man of iron, Donald Smith. He was sent to Fort Garry by Sir John A. Macdonald as a special commissioner for information and advice. We commonly associate his fame with the West. He never saw it till now in his fiftieth year. Donald Smith had come to Canada in 1838; had served the Hudson's Bay Company for six years on the St. Lawrence north shore—the land which Jacques Cartier allotted to Cain. He had served the Company for twenty further years in Labrador. Even in that desolation

Sir Donald, 1886, Lord Strathcona, 1897

Beckles Willson, "Life of Lord Strathcona," 1915

his energy, his instinct for trade, his capacity for saving and management, impressed all who saw him. In 1868 the Company made him Resident Governor at Montreal.

Smith went by rail to St. Paul, then six hundred miles by sleigh to Fort Garry. He arrived just as the year ran out. Riel kept him under arrest at the Fort. Smith, being a Scot, said nothing. He gathered information as he could. Riel's vacillating mind was now this now that. In three weeks he let his prisoner address the citizens, a thousand of them, at the safe temperature of 20 below zero. They were persuaded to elect a convention. French ancestry woke within them. They drew up a Bill of Rights. They arranged for a delegation to Ottawa. They liberated the Fort Garry prisoners.

Dec. 27, 1869

Up to this time no harm had been done, only one life—of an escaping prisoner—had been taken and that by a sort of accident. A new provisional government was organized, asking nothing better than full provincial status. But Louis Riel now shifted from majesty to murder and that changed everything.

What happened was this. The Canadian and English party, mustering at Portage la Prairie, made an unsuccessful march on Winnipeg. They were too few to fight. Riel gathered in forty-eight as prisoners. Major Boulton was ordered for immediate execution but Riel's nerve, under Smith's warning, failed. Thomas Scott, liberated before, had been retaken. He struck at a guard, defied Riel and swore to kill him when free. Riel's council condemned Scott to death. He was put against a wall of Fort Garry, where a firing squad shot him half dead. Someone with a revolver finished him. A hundred and fifty people looked on. A story runs that later he stirred again in his coffin in the Fort, and was again despatched. This was plain, brutal murder. That was all Ontario knew or ever wanted to know about Louis Riel. That was the reason for the singular satisfaction in the province at his execution in 1885. Till this moment Ontario cared little about the Red River troubles. It was now lashed to a fury of anger. The 'delegates' arriving from the West were arrested for the murder, then released for want of cause.

S. Steele, "Forty Years in Canada," 1915

Meantime a strange calm settled over Fort Garry. There was no more violence. Sir John A. Macdonald at Ottawa knew exactly what he wanted—to get the outbreak in the palm of his hand and then close it. Till he could have force, he spoke Fort Garry fair. Parliament drew up and adopted the Manitoba Act for provincial government as of July 15, 1870. But Riel's delegates had no part in it.

At Macdonald's request the Imperial Government organized a Red River Expedition under Colonel Garnet Wolseley. In it were 400 Regulars, and 800 Canadian militiamen, mostly of Ontario. It was announced as gently as if the men were missionaries. They were to guarantee peace. But the Ontario militia at least knew exactly what they meant to do to Riel. Their route lay by way of the Lakes and the Lake of the Woods portages. The story of this expedition reads like an Odyssey of shout and song and feats of strength. With them were Crimean veterans of the past like Wolseley himself, and soldiers of the future— Captain Redvers Buller, a giant in strength, an ideal soldier whose fame was later on to be eclipsed by the Tugela disaster. There were Canadian soldiers of the future, too, such as young Sam Steele, the famous Major-General of the Great War. The

Expedition reached its goal but the rebels had long since received news of its coming and had vanished to their homes. They had nothing to stay for. Wolseley's own advance message assured them of amnesty. They knew already that the Manitoba Act

granted them full provincial government. Riel stayed awhile with the idea of a formal reception of Wolseley. Then he thought better of it and vanished over the border.

The Government, as said, had already adopted the Manitoba Act which guaranteed the Roman Catholic religion and schools in almost, but unfortunately not quite, the same words as those of the B.N.A. Act. This was to make it a lawyer's harvest when the Manitoba School Question convulsed Canada twenty years later.

Meantime the province began its life inside its 'postage stamp' boundaries of 1870. Donald Smith had become the man of destiny of the West. Chief Commissioner of the Hudson's Bay Company in Canada, he refused the new Lieutenant-Governorship of Manitoba. He had seen enough of small puddles. He was elected in 1871 and re-elected 1872 and 1878 to the Ottawa House of Commons, becoming a master of politics. When he had too few votes in a riding he made a temporary move of Hudson's Bay half-breeds out of another. For this he was unseated in 1879. But his vision for some time was elsewhere than on politics. If the North-West was to be opened, he proposed to open it himself. His foresight saw already the approaching Manitoba boom and the coming of a Pacific railway.

With the end of the Red River troubles and the organization of Manitoba, settlers began moving in by way of the Minnesota Railway to St. Paul and the stage and river-steamers beyond, and presently (1880) by rail from Minnesota clear to Manitoba itself. The occupation of the land was facilitated by the Homestead Act of 1872, modelled on the United States legislation of 1862 which was rapidly filling the American west. Meantime new surveys struck out across the plains, looking for the railway *G. Grant, "From Ocean to Ocean," 1873* route to the Pacific that was to consolidate the union. The stage was all set for the Manitoba Boom.

The admission of Manitoba to the Dominion was followed in 1871 by that of British Columbia. This magnificent province of 366,000 square miles in extent, with its happy climate, immense resources and its Pacific outlook, is an empire in itself. Yet for three centuries it lay all unknown to the world while Europe struggled for America. The Spaniards coasted its shores as far back as 1774. Later they made landings at Nootka Sound. Even before that, Russian whalers and explorers descended the upper west coast of America. British knowledge of the Pacific coast begins with Captain Cook's voyage of 1778 along its shores to the Behring Strait. Captain Vancouver followed in 1792, dis- *E. S. Meany, "Vancouver's Discovery of Puget Sound," 1907* covering the entry to Puget Sound. Alexander Mackenzie came overland to the Pacific in 1793. Simon Fraser, another North-Wester, followed, established Fort George just over the divide, and in 1786 a fort on the river that bears his name. David Thompson descended the upper Columbia in 1811. When the fur trade was consolidated the Hudson's Bay Company made the Pacific slope their Western District. Their chief representative was James Douglas, whose long career fills the annals of the *Sir James, 1863* Pacific till Confederation.

The stockaded Fort Vancouver on the Columbia was the original centre of the trade. Other traders found their way from England round the Horn. The independence of the United States after 1783 brought American traders. The ship *Columbia* sailing out of Boston found the mouth of a great river, south of Puget Sound, and gave its name to it. The *Columbia* sailed home by way of China, traversing fifty thousand miles of sea. At Boston they struck medals for it. Lewis and Clark made their way overland in 1805-6 from the Missouri down the Columbia to the sea. John Jacob Astor founded his Pacific Fur Company in 1811. The Americans called the whole country by the vague Indian name of Oregon. The Hudson's Bay Company traders, mostly Scottish, unable to use 'Nova Scotia' twice, called their part of it New Caledonia. The Spanish claims had been extinguished by a convention of 1794. The Russian boundary was settled by a treaty of 1825.

1792

R. H. Coats and R. E. Gosnell, 'Sir James Douglas,' "Makers of Canada," 1908

But as between American and British claims, Oregon was no man's land. The Hudson's Bay Company set up their forts on the inland rivers, Yale and Berens on the Fraser and, later on, Fort Simpson on the northern coast. After 1843 their chief centre was Victoria on Vancouver Island, beside it presently Esquimalt. The situation of Victoria rapidly advanced it over all other points. At this time the trade in furs and supplies went in part around the Horn. From the inland posts the 'brigades' wound their long way over the Rockies and the plains to Norway House. The need of supplies led the Company to set up farms around Victoria, to build mills and tanneries and even to mine the Vancouver Island coal. Thus originated the Fort Nanaimo of 1852. American settlers began to come in over the mountains. Missionaries brought their little flocks. As the Oregon dispute grew, what we now call 'propaganda' joined with missionary zeal to bring in American settlers. When the treaty boundary line was drawn (1846) some of these were converted into British. But till the days of gold the fur trade was still above all, and life as quiet and undisturbed as in the Spanish missions to the south. Gold in California brought a burst of activity to Victoria, the sole harbour of supply beyond San Francisco. To promote settlement the British Government turned over Vancouver Island to the Hudson's Bay Company, whose own original jurisdiction was

A. G. Brown, "British Columbia," 1912

HAL ROSS PERRIGARD, A.R.C.A., MONTREAL, P.Q., 1941

"Then came the discovery of gold and quickened the pace of life"— PAGE 173

only to the Rockies. They were to pay a rent of seven shillings every first of January, to bring out settlers, provide for law and order and sell land on a ten per cent commission. Under these auspices settlers came in. Victoria was laid out in streets in 1852. Things moved slowly, but they moved. The town had 300 souls in 1855 and Nanaimo 125. To these were added the 1,700 Indians of the island, docile and accepting Christianity with pleasure.

Then came the discovery of gold and quickened the pace of life. The first findings were on the coast and on the Queen Charlotte Islands. These proved of no great value but presently the *1856* gold on the Fraser River brought a rush of miners to the 'diggings.' Victoria shared in the glory of its Australian cousin. In one season twenty-five thousand miners landed, took on supplies and went on through. Two hundred buildings went up in six months. Town lots sold at a thousand dollars a foot frontage. Prices and profits rushed up, with flour at thirty dollars a barrel. Then the boom broke and the diggers came floating back on the ebb-tide. The mining was not poor man's gold, loose in shallow rivers. It had to wait for capital and machinery. But the ebb-tide at least freshened growth.

Vancouver Island was reorganized as a British colony in 1856. Douglas was its Governor, and presently it had an elected Assembly. A little later the island settlements were grouped as another colony. With them began the name British Columbia, *J. M. Gibbon,* suggested in a letter from the queen. The French, in compliment *"Steel of* to Scotland, had taken 'New Caledonia' for their future convict *Empire,"* island. Columbia, the queen noted, was used by itself for the *1935* United States "in poetry." The capital was laid out at New Westminster, James Douglas the governor also of this second colony. A detachment of Royal Engineers was sent out from England under Colonel Richard Moody to make surveys, construct roads and preserve the peace. A representative legislature was called in 1864. As a matter of common sense the colonies of the island and the mainland united as British Columbia in 1866 with Sir James Douglas as governor.

It was in these circumstances that the proposal of Confederation with Canada found the people of British Columbia. They were half-hearted about it. Some, it is said, even dreamed of union with the States. Others, of Victoria, were British enough to want to be left alone. But Macdonald's pledge to start a Pacific railway in two years and finish it in ten, carried the day. The province saw a vision of Pacific steamers, of cargoes of silk, of ocean ports facing a new world, in other words a vision of exactly what happened—only later on. As it was, seven years passed with nothing of a railway except a railway scandal. When Lord Dufferin visited the province in 1876 his carriage was confronted with an arch carrying the legend *Carnarvon Terms or Separation*. The tactful governor had it altered to "*or Reparation*." But the grievance remained.

After British Columbia followed Prince Edward Island. The Island up till that time had on the whole done well. Its original French settlers, its Loyalists and Lord Selkirk's Highlanders had been followed by a more or less steady influx of immigration. It had 24,000 people in 1822, 62,000 in 1848, and by this time (1871) the population was 94,000. The ill-advised system of the grant of its public land to a few score of favoured proprietors had left a perennial dispute as between landlords and tenants. The Island suffered also from the difficulty of access in winter. Moreover, it had shared the railway mania of the period and had a toy railway on its hands. It looked back on its first refusal of Confederation and decided, like the Scottish old maid in the song, that it had been 'daft to refuse.' By the purchase of its railway, a liberal subsidy, the extinction of the proprietors' claims and help across the Northumberland Strait, the Island was coaxed in (1873). Later repentance came too late.

With each year the discontent in the Maritimes and the demand from British Columbia for secession, was weakening Macdonald's hold on power. Nor had his government gained much prestige from its dealings with the United States. It had proved impossible to renew Reciprocity. The famous Washington Treaty of 1871, which settled the *Alabama Claims* and therewith laid down laws of neutrality, remained as a monument of international law, while international law remained a monument. But it was settled, so Macdonald said, "no matter at what cost to Canada." The United States moreover refused to consider any payment for Fenian damages.

Macdonald was sustained in the election of 1872. But it is *Sir J. Pope,*
"Sir John doubtful if his government could have carried on long. In any *Macdonald,"*
case it had no chance to. Its unhappy attempt to initiate a *Vol. II,* Pacific railroad brought it to disgrace and disaster. It was felt *1894*
that the Dominion could not itself finance the road. The govern-
ment invited company support with a land grant, and, finding *G. Denison,*
two rival companies, invited subscriptions to its party funds. *"Soldiering*
in Canada" This was dramatically revealed in Parliament. Subscription to
funds as a tribute of admiration is one thing, as a *quid pro quo*
another. Conservatives fell away. In particular the defection of
Donald Smith, the new power in the West, hit Macdonald hard.
He did not say, gently *"Et tu Brute."* He said he "could lick *Canadian*
that man Smith quicker than hell could frizzle a feather." The *Hansard*
government resigned.

The Liberal government organized by Alexander Mackenzie
in 1873 fell heir to ill-fortune. It has often been observed that
British governments naturally alternate in office while governments in Canada tend to strike root and stay. Mackenzie had no
chance. The general panic of 1873 broke as he took office, leaving
Canada stranded in the ebb-tide of six years of depression. Mortgages fell on the Ontario farms like snowflakes. Public revenue
dwindled and deficit was inevitable. Seen in retrospect the
Government, for all its honesty and goodwill, went into a decline
in its infancy.

The public finance of Canada at Confederation was on a
modest scale. The whole expenditure of 1868 was only $13,-
486,000. Duties were still moderate, the Income Tax undreamed
of. The public debt, assumed from the provinces, stood at
$75,000,000 in 1867 and had risen to only $100,000,000 in 1873.
But even on this scale the government failed to carry on. Budget
deficits of over a million a year looked like impending disaster.
Nor had the public policy of the administration called forth
enthusiasm. A new pilgrimage to Washington for Reciprocity
fell flat with a United States Senate refusal of 1874. The Pacific
railway problem was like a ghost behind the scene. British
Columbia bubbled with secession. Macdonald had offered a
Pacific railway as easily as a juggler would take a rabbit out of
a hat. Mackenzie stood appalled at the cost. His plain honesty

could not see how to pay for it. The whole project seemed to many fantastic. A Pacific railway, said Edward Blake, the Minister of Justice, would never pay for the axle grease of its locomotives; or if he didn't say it, people said he said it. So the government undertook to crawl across the West, in and out of the water, like a duck.

On this rail-and-water route they spent over $37,000,000. Of this $28,000,000 went on the construction of 710 miles of railway, built or building; $200,000 for a meaningless Rainy Lake Canal, and over $3,000,000 on endless surveys—and they were still nowhere. But they had at least such credit as came from the completion of the Intercolonial Railway in 1876. To keep far from American danger it wound its course the longest way round, like a person hugging the wall to avoid a spectre. It was understood that on these terms it could hardly be expected to pay. The understanding proved correct.

As the allotted life of Parliament ran out, Mackenzie called an election in the bright after-harvest of the autumn of 1878. Macdonald and his party were out with a big new idea, noisy as a circus parade and comprehensive as a circus tent. This was the 'National Policy'—Canada for the Canadians, and something for everybody—in its own words, as expressed in Macdonald's motion to the House of Commons in 1878:—

"The welfare of Canada requires the adoption of a National Policy which, by a judicious readjustment of the tariff, will benefit and foster the agricultural, the mining, the manufacturing, and the other interests of the Dominion." The fight was as between 'do-somethings' and 'do-nothings'. The issue was never doubtful. The result gave the Conservatives a majority of eighty-six and eighteen years of power.

"... *through* ... *rock and gorge and forest*"—PAGE 184

CHAPTER VII

BETTER TIMES
1879-1896

Administration of Sir John A. Macdonald—The National Policy—The Canadian Pacific Railway—The Manitoba Boom—The North-West Rebellion—Unrestricted Reciprocity and the Election of 1891—Manufacture and the Growth of Cities—The Manitoba School Question—Fall of Conservative Government.

THE Conservative administration entered upon office in October, 1878, and was destined to hold it for almost eighteen years. The opening of the new régime coincided with the departure of Lord Dufferin and the advent as Governor-General of the Marquis of Lorne, whose wife, the Princess Louise, a daughter of Queen Victoria, now became the châtelaine of Rideau Hall. This seemed specially fitting to Conservative politics as a mark of what was called in those days the "loyalty" of Canada to "England." Both words are now out of fashion. "Loyalty" is called "co-operation" and England must not be named without Scotland.

Macdonald himself chiefly guided the course of policy till his death in 1891 but he had as his right arm Dr. Charles Tupper. *Sir Charles, 1879* Etienne Cartier was gone but Hector Langevin helped to hold *d. 1873* the Blues to the party. Yet it was Macdonald's own peculiar gift to keep the party united. He held the Orangemen of Ontario by his allegiance to Queen and Empire, and he held the French-Canadians by keeping faith with church and nationality. The

E. B. Biggar,
"Anecdotal
Life of
Sir John
Macdonald,"
1891

Sir Joseph Pope,
'The Day of
Sir John
Macdonald'
"Chronicles of
Canada,"
1915

rank and file of his countryside followers he held with cigars, jokes—specially selected—by the geniality of his visits to their taverns and town halls, and by the little compliments treasured, repeated, and remembered to garrulous old age. This is democracy. While Macdonald lived union remained; Macdonald gone, the party melted asunder.

On the opposition side Edward Blake became the leader. With him was presently Wilfrid Laurier who had already sat in the Parliament of 1872 and in Mackenzie's ministry. Laurier was a French-Canadian country-town lawyer and editor, educated at L'Assomption College with a final touch of McGill. He had no start or influence beyond his own ability and background. But he had somehow contrived to take on the gracious manner of an old-world statesman, the rounded English of a British orator and the moral pose of a British Liberal. Many will agree that in intellectual power he was outranked by such of his colleagues as

Sir William
1902

Jan. 19. 1941

William Mulock, the later Chief Justice of Ontario, whom Canada congratulates, as this page is written, on his ninety-seventh birthday, as the most eminent and respected of our citizens. But as compared with Mulock's higher talent, Laurier was fortunate in his greater availability. He was a French-Canadian who had somehow turned into a British institution; a 'moderate protectionist' who yet received the Cobden medal, an ardent imperialist except as to who should pay the bill, and with it all, courteous and undisturbed, a gentleman. His appearance in one of the carriages of state at the Queen's Diamond Jubilee of 1897 seemed to put, if not a crown, at least a silk hat on imperial unity. In a sense Laurier was the gifted child of good fortune, floating on a wave of prosperity. Macdonald dominated Canadian politics; Laurier presided over them.

The first task of the new government was to put into effect

Canadian
Hansard,
March 14, 1879

the new National Policy. Mr. Tilley's budget of March 14, 1879, brought on the new tariff. The peculiar point of it was not the height of the duties on imported manufactures, (although they ran to 30 per cent), but in the avowed purpose of favouring the

Sir Richard
Cartwright,
"Reminiscences,"
1912

home producer. This, to Liberal opponents of the school of Sir Richard Cartwright, the financier in opposition, and to British observers was like an open confession of sin. We must recall the

tone of the times. The triumph of British free trade had given
to that policy not only the endorsation of statesmen and economists, but a sort of peculiar and irritating sanctity. Speakers
deplored colonial protection in Victoria (Australia) and in
Canada as due to colonial ignorance and colonial crookedness.
A leading English economist, Sir Robert Giffen, declared in 1881 *Sir R. Giffen,*
that in a few years the last of the protectionists would be extinct. *Essays,*
The truth was the other way. Within a generation a Cobdenite *1879-84*
—free trade for everybody everywhere in everything—was only
to be found in a museum.

But Macdonald cared nothing for theory. His party pleaded
the swamping of the Canadian market by slaughtered American
goods. Even as theory, they could plead John Stuart Mill's
unlucky admission that protection was in place in a new country
for a short time on behalf of an appropriate industry. This
'infant industry' argument lasted till the huge infants rolled off
their mother's lap. They had to be picked up as too big to
abandon, and the argument altered to suit. But the real claim
to the National Policy was that there was such a lot of it, in
fact something in it for everybody—farmers, fishers, woods-
men as well as manufacturers—whether they needed it or not.
The legend gives us a picture of Sir John A. sitting in the famous
old Red Parlour of a Toronto hotel, handing out tariff favours as
freely as cigars. The result showed that protection was there to
stay. No later government removed it. The Liberals denounced
it as evil, from their opposition of 1879 till their Ottawa Conference of 1893. British writers, whether Conservative or Liberal,
still deplored it. A brilliant London journalist, visiting Canada, *E. Porritt,*
presently wrote of "Sixty Years of Protection in Canada" as *"Sixty Years*
who should say, sixty years of sin. Even the protected manu- *of Protection*
facturers carried, if not an uneasy conscience, at least a special *in Canada,"*
willingness to subscribe to all charities, as medieval robbers *1908*
knelt at the altars of the saints.

Yet protection, whereby came home manufacture, proved part
of the economic life of the country. With it came greater urban
concentration, and quickened intellectual life. Art and science
clung on protection, as parasites on a bear, or let us say, more
fittingly, as mistletoe on oak. Let it be granted that tariff

protection had its evil side, that it gave new opportunity for job-bery, for doubtful fortunes, for wider divergence than ever between worth and wealth. But at least these advantages did not hold from generation to generation as landed privilege had done. Fortunes that the relaxing hand of the dead could not carry away went to colleges and hospitals. The consumer lost out; but the consumer in Canada was dead, or survived only in the British settlers living on money from 'home.' The typical Cana-dian viewed himself as a producer, thinking in terms of earnings not of costs. The system became part of the complex of our life. No one could tell that fifty years later it would degenerate into the hopeless aberration of the economic nationalism that has helped to destroy Europe.

The one exception that the government made in their pro-tective policy was their continued quest for American Reci-procity. This became for twenty years the Holy Grail, so to speak, of Canadian politics. Mark Twain, in his description of the Knights of King Arthur's Court, explains with illuminating irreverence that every little while the "boys went grailing." So they did from Canada as, for example, George Brown in 1874 and, for this new government, Sir John Rose. It was all in vain. Each new light in the south that called out a pilgrimage proved a will-o'-the-wisp over a marsh of difficulty.

With the new impetus of the National Policy was associated the forward drive for a Pacific railway. This enterprise, initiated with the charter of 1881 and completed with the famous gold spike driven by Donald Smith at Craigellachie, B.C., on November 7, 1885, was one of the greatest triumphs of our history. The United States had opened its first transcontinental railway in 1869. But it did not do so till there were nearly three-quarters of a million people on its Pacific coast and over six million in the States and Territories between the Mississippi and the moun-tains. We commenced ours with only 24,000 white people in British Columbia; with Winnipeg a town of 7,985 inhabitants; Regina a pile of bones; Calgary not on the map, and on all the plains little but the forts of the fur trade and the tepees of wandering Indians.

The story of the Canadian Pacific Railway has been too well

O. Skelton,
'The Railway
Builders'
"Chronicles of
Canada,"
1916

told to need detailed repetition here. The Company was organized under a Canadian Act of Parliament of February 15, 1881, on terms of what appears at first sight princely generosity. It was to receive a cash subsidy of $25,000,000, payable as construction proceeded, and a land grant of 25,000,000 acres. The land was to be selected out of what was called the Fertile Belt of the North-West, meaning roughly the valley of the North Saskatchewan, as opposed to the country farther south and west through which the main line of the railway was to pass and which was at that time still regarded as largely desert. The company was to receive a large measure of tax exemption, free import of construction materials and a protection, for twenty years, against competition in a north and south direction. It received the ramshackle assets left over from previous failure, including 710 miles of road constructed or under construction. The sum total sounds colossal. As beside the work to be done it was hopelessly inadequate.

The making of the road is indeed a fascinating story, or rather it is three fascinating stories. There is first of all the gathering of the capital that initiated the company. It was put together by an adventurous and indomitable group of men, Donald Smith, George Stephen, Richard Angus and their associates, who found it, so to speak, lying across the map of Minnesota. It consisted of a half-made railroad which had fallen back into the possession of a group of Dutch bondholders, to whom it owed over $20,000,000, and into the occupation of vast annual flocks of grasshoppers which were eating everything in the country except the iron rails. The Canadian group bought out the Dutch, it is often said, for a song, yet it was a song that touched the highest note the Bank of Montreal could sing ($6,780,000). Then the grasshoppers went away, and in their place came immigrants, settlers, goods and chattels and more and more settlers—till the Canadian syndicate hardly knew what to do with their money. A shrewd associate said to Sir John A., "Take their money while they still have it." And that was how the Canadian Pacific Railway, as finance, came into being.

As construction, as road building, the story sounds even better. Under the driving power of William Van Horne they drove the

O. Skelton,
'Railway
Builders'
"Chronicles of
Canada,"
1916

railway over the plains, carrying its own sleepers, rails, plates over the ones just laid—at the rate of two, three and even three and a half miles a day—once as much as twenty miles in three days. They hoisted it on trestle bridges and filled it in before it could fall. At the other end they bought up Mr. Donald

1883

McIntyre's Canada Central Railway that took them west from Montreal to Callender on Lake Nipissing, and from there they drilled, filled, blasted and bridged their way through the Lake

J. M. Gibbon,
"Steel of
Empire,"
1935

Superior wilderness. Even to-day the winter traveller through that still region of rock and gorge and forest may marvel at their enterprise. Riel's rebellion gave a transport business that helped out the half-made Superior section. The same year saw it completed. At the same time they laid out a terminal town on the Pacific and called it Vancouver. Then came the final day

1885

when Donald Smith drove a gold spike, as already said, right into the heart of the Rockies, and ended them.

Best of all, though less realized, is the national aspect of the enterprise and the credit due above all to Sir John A. Macdonald. His was the firm insistence, in spite of all technical opinion, that the railway must be all Canadian, must at any cost pierce the wilderness. That it must also, and that it did later, go west via the United States (Chicago-Minnesota) was another matter. It had to be Canadian first. To the same credit belongs the unending help given by the Government over and above the contract, the final generous assistance that meant salvation on the verge of disaster. The story is one to give us confidence that all the later difficulties that threaten our present transportation with disaster, may be met and overcome with the same spirit.

The definite initiation of the Canadian Pacific Railway enterprise naturally stimulated the movement into the West and brought the striking episode of the 'Winnipeg Boom' of the opening eighties. The policy of what is called Homestead Settlement

S. Leacock,
"My Discovery
of the West,"
1937

had been adopted some years before in a statute of 1872. It was copied from the American Homestead Law of 1862, which was rapidly filling the Mississippi Valley.

The system gave to each settler 160 acres, a so-called quarter-section, of land. He must live and work on it for at least three months a year. It became his very own after three years. His sons living at home could each have an adjacent 160 acres. He could, under the original pre-emption law, reserve for his purchase as much more. In his mind's eye the settler's farm already reached farther than his mind's eye could. But in the earlier years of the system the North-West still seemed far away, and even dangerous. Settlers in the seventies went from Ontario not to go west but to get out of Ontario. The mortgages turned out the sons of the farms as cruelly as they ever did a Highland clearance. But with better knowledge passed from farm to farm and with rail communication after 1880 from Minnesota into Winnipeg, the prospect changed. It was discovered that Manitoba—still pronounced properly with a bah at the end of it—meant 'God's country,' and with that the prairie turned into the promised land, and the exodus began.

The homestead system developed a great appeal. In other systems of colonization—a lord of the manor, a privileged company, or the Wakefield endless chain of hired man and proprietor that was tried out in New Zealand—the settlers began in service *1837* or in debt. The homestead man came as his own boss, living *R. Garnett,* perhaps in a house made of sods, surviving as best he could on *"Life of* paid winter work. Each crop lifted him forward as the waves *Edward Gibbon* *Wakefield,"* lift a swimmer through the surf. He saw himself already lord of *1898* a bonanza farm, reaching beyond the horizon, bending with golden grain that fell with a sigh beneath the knife of the binder. He saw himself in winter affluence on the portico of a California hotel. It was a picture that called forth while it lasted all the best impulse of individual effort. It is all gone now. There is no land left and no insatiable market for its unified crop. We must turn back to the forgotten pages of history and pick up again manorial and company migration where we left it. But the independent homestead in early prairie days appeared in the sunrise. It drew colonists from all over the Empire, Scottish farmers from Midlothian, appalled at Manitoba methods, Cockneys who didn't know 'Haw!' from 'Gee!' remittance men, and Oxford graduates with a little Latin still for use in barrooms.

Since Winnipeg is the gateway of the West, the channel of *W. J. Healy,* supply, the emporium of import and the market for land sites, *"Winnipeg's* *Early Days,"* the Winnipeg Boom followed as an inevitable consequence. The *1927*

G. Ham,
"Reminiscences
of a
Raconteur"

town became a babel of tongues, a clatter of hammers. The real-estate man rode on the wind, the genius of the hour. Prices were high but didn't matter. There was work at high pay for everybody. Life on Main and Portage was a round of drinks, a roar of good fellowship, a merry-go-round of sudden fortune.

On the uplift of such a boom, a new town anywhere, a San Francisco, a Carson City, turns into a magic Bagdad—especially a place as small and as new as Winnipeg. Life in a boom town takes on an intensity, a focus not known elsewhere. It has no past. It has no elsewhere. It is all here and now, like the world into which each infant is born. In the light of such a rebirth, people see one another better. Everybody becomes a 'remarkable man'—as he is—a 'hell of a good fellow'. And why not? It is a half-caught vision of what life might be all the time.

The boom broke. The fortunes vanished. The good fellows turned back into ordinary people, many of them turning slowly to down-at-heel survivals, glad of a treat across the bar. The Oxford men got jobs in a livery stable. The Cockneys went away, looking for a war, and the boom was over. When it was done bankers and economists explained it all away as an over-expansion of credit. The opinion may be hazarded that this is nonsense. The boom is the reality, the collapse the accident. The town of Winnipeg, with only 8,000 people in 1881 and all the North-West behind it, need not have broken. The proof is that it has now well over 200,000 and the Prairie Provinces two million and a half. Nothing was wrong except our inability to handle so much that was right. Some day, when peace comes, real peace, there will be another boom beside which the Manitoba Boom was only a whisper.

G. Stanley,
"The Birth of
Western
Canada,"
1936

This expansion into the North-West brought with it, as an unforeseen and unnecessary consequence, the North-West Rebellion of 1885. Expansion of settlement meant, of course, a certain further restriction of Indian nomad life. In Canada, as in the States, railways and buffalo could not share a bed. Nor could they both have 'corridors.' The open plain must be exchanged for the closed reservation. For the half-breeds, also,

W. J. PHILLIPS, R.C.A., WINNIPEG, MAN., 1941

"*At the same time they laid out a terminal town on the Pacific
and called it Vancouver*"—PAGE 184

the new settlement must break the pattern of their old-time life, their side-by-side holdings on the river and the isolation of their language and speech. But there could have been many compensations and more civility. A cigar goes a long way, even with an Indian. But the government, as before, acted with culpable indifference. Surveys were run along the Saskatchewan, newcomers appeared, dispossession seemed imminent, with little if any attempt to explain it. All through the summer of 1884 the Saskatchewan country murmured with discontent. The murmurs grew to loud protest. Meetings were held. The settlers sent over to the States for Louis Riel, living in exile in Montana. Riel had spent the last few years alternately between school-teaching and going partly crazy, a thing quite intelligible to the profession. But to choose him as a leader was the worst choice that could have been made. His very name infuriated Ontario. This time they must fight. For Ontario that one name, Riel, blocked all consideration of real grievances.

G. Denison, "Struggle for Imperial Unity," 1909

The prairie country had been since 1873 under the surveillance of the North-West Mounted Police, whose name now fills and thrills the movie world. But at this time the world knew little of their arduous life, the patrol of the plains, the control of the desperado, the winter life in the wooden-shack barracks at 20 below zero. The exploits of these Riders of the Plains remained untold. A poet could write:—

They need no sculptured monument, no panoply of stone,
To blazon to a curious world the deeds that they have done.
But the prairie flower blows softly and the scented rose-bud trains
Its wealth of summer beauty o'er the Riders of the Plains.

The police well knew what rebellion in the North-West could mean. The danger was not of the half-breeds; they were too few. The danger was of an all-Indian rising, a last wild attempt to exterminate the Whites. The Indians of the West of fifty years ago were not like the humble quarter-breeds of the Ontario reservations, gratified with a red shirt and drunk on one drink of whisky. These latter had long since sold out savagery at ten dollars a year. But look in any illustrated book at the pictured faces of such full-blooded braves as Imasees, son of **Big Bear**,

S. Steele, "Forty Years in Canada," 1915

and you may reconstruct again the terror of bygone centuries and understand the vain warnings of the police.

All through the winter in the West the half-breeds organized and collected arms, unheeded. The Indians gathered near to the isolated posts on the North Saskatchewan, as wolves approach their prey. With the spring there came the clash of an armed column, made up of police and settler volunteers, met and heavily outnumbered by a gathering of several hundred half-breeds. There was a fierce fight, brave enough on both sides, with Louis Riel standing by, praying before a crucifix. The police left nine dead and hauled their wounded to Fort Carleton. Thus came the Rebellion, as sudden to Canada as the onrush of a March blizzard.

Duck Lake, March 26, 1885

There followed the hurried call to arms of the militia—there were no 'regulars' now—the trainloads of volunteers made up in Toronto, each man to carry with him three days' food of his own, the shouting crowds at the Union Station, with K. Company from 'Varsity' as a part of the Queen's Own. The boys of Upper Canada College had a worthier half holiday this time than when they went to see Lount and Matthews hanged in 1838.

There followed the railroad journey westward—broken by the unfinished gap of railroad north of Lake Superior; the gathering in Winnipeg and the campaign on the plains of the Saskatchewan. There was the fierce fight at Fish Creek, the attack on Poundmaker's Reservation at Cut Knife and in May the final three-days' assault on the rifle pits at Batoche that broke the back of the Rebellion. There followed rapidly the recapture of the outposts, where Indian massacre had degraded the Indian's cause, and then the round up of Big Bear, far to the north, and the execution of his guilty followers. It remained to deal with Louis Riel. The advance of the soldiers had struck apprehension to his heart. He had no spirit for the fight at Batoche, and was captured miles away, near Prince Albert. A surviving artillery man of the Winnipeg Field Battery told the writer of this book the other day of seeing Riel brought in by two mounted police, "a little insignificant, bearded man, shabby in rough homespun." His execution at Regina on November 7, 1885, seemed to Ontario the justly deserved fate of a murderer.

H. A. Kennedy, "The Book of the West," 1925

V. LaChance, 'Diary of Francis Dickens,' "Queen's University Bulletin," 1930

A. Guy Ross, Jan. 31, 1941

The close of the Rebellion marked the end of the old North-West. It seemed to change with strange rapidity. If not in the twinkling of an eye, at least in the twinkling of a decade it all seemed gone. The buffalo grounds had become the grain farms. Long lines of steel kept crawling across the prairies. The Indian tepee gave place to the frame house of the homestead, and the stockaded fort to the grain elevator. The Indian brave and the buffalo rider before long were known only in the Calgary Stampede and in the films of the moving pictures. This rapid change in the panorama of the West was due to the impetus of settlement given by the completion of the Canadian Pacific Railway, the rapid extension of its branches, and the influx of homestead settlers taking up land.

But as the 1880's drew to a close, public interest in Canada turned away from the West to revert to the everlasting question of the tariff and our relations with the States. The Conservatives had won the two elections of 1882 and 1887 with no great difficulty. The issue turned on endorsing their forward policy. The Liberals had little to offer but the cold negations of free trade and their bill-board appeal, equally negative, *"Has the National Policy made you rich?"* All through this period Canadian militant politics were illustrated and enlivened by the genius of J. W. Bengough whose cartoons in his weekly *Grip* became a national feature, never attempted before, never achieved since. This tendency to turn our politics into fun we share with the Americans. Its influence for good has been incalculable. This is a digression, but the memory of Bengough is worth it.

As the decade closed, the Liberals embarked on the 'whole hog' policy of Unrestricted Reciprocity, with two years of agitation as a new election approached. Its appeal was to lie in its uncompromising thoroughness. It was to remove all tariffs as against the States. This was a declaration of war on manufacturers, except such as could survive in the continental market. But for the farmers, and for the Maritime fish and lumber men, it was meant to restore the sunshine of the lost paradise of the Reciprocity of the sixties. The new movement had behind it the powerful support of the illustrious Goldwin Smith, then living

Goldwin Smith "Canada and the Canadian Question," 1891

A. Haultain,
"Goldwin Smith,
His Life and
Opinions,"
1913

in Toronto, an Oxford scholar of such eminence that he could agree with no one but himself, who found England too English and the United States too American. His participation in the foundation of Cornell University (after the Civil War) he had abandoned, still in the heat of the day. He now lived in retirement in his Toronto Grange, the patronizing patron of Canadian culture. His independent fortune heightened the independence of his mind, but narrowed its outlook. His biographer tells us how Goldwin Smith stood one day at his drawing-room window, overlooking the grounds of the Grange, musing on the reported strikes and violence at Cripple Creek. "Why can't people be content," he murmured, "with what they have?" Why not? He himself, in property and investments, had close to a million.

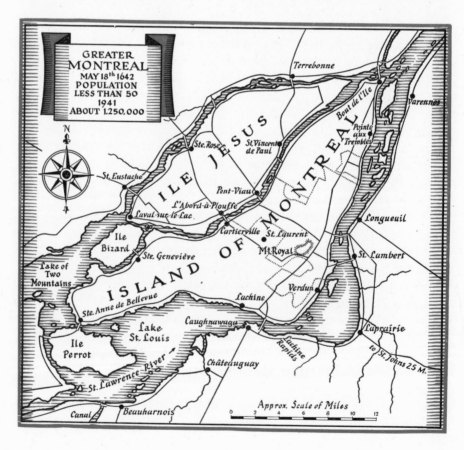

To enlighten the Ontario farmers Goldwin Smith established his *Farmers Weekly Sun*. But it is hard to convert farmers from a Victorian drawing-room. The sunlight of the *Weekly Sun* was feeble beside the coal-oil and naphtha of the Conservative hustings. Price's Corners repudiated Oxford.

In any case unrestricted reciprocity was doomed from the start. It meant too much or too little. If complete, it meant that either the United States must give up protection, an impossible supposition, or there must be only one tariff for both countries, tight as marriage, and made at Washington. Intellectuals like Mr. Blake and Mr. Edgar might juggle with schemes for entry of British imports without exit. It was too complicated for plain people to whom "unrestricted" meant all or nothing. Then came *Sir Joseph Pope,* the disclosure that a section, only a section, of the advocates of *"The Day of* Reciprocity meant it just that way, full tariff union and annexa- *Sir John* tion. The cause was lost. Macdonald knew then that he had only *Macdonald,"* to wave the flag at it—at "the veiled treason" that opposed him. *1915* Here belong the words of his last election address, already *Feb. 7, 1891* quoted, "A British subject I was born, a British subject I will die." He spoke only too truly. The election was carried (March 5) and Macdonald died June 6, 1891.

For a moment the election was a triumph and a jubilee, a new mandate of power. But with Macdonald's death the Fates began to cut the threads of Conservative destiny. Already the first ominous signs showed commercial depression approaching. Canada as an export country imports its hard times. We have no choice. The break of the European market brings to our North-West disaster that spreads throughout the Dominion. It was this peculiar dependence on the outside world that brought to Canada the hard times of the opening nineties. Taking the country by itself it should not have been so. For this was the beginning of the new electrical age which expanded and intensified the life and activity of the cities. Electric light, that was first seen in London, 1878, began now to illuminate Canada. Its unsightly cedar poles added a new touch of ugliness to the streets. But life received a new wakefulness from the arc lamp and the electric bulb. The uphill agony of the street-car horse

ended in euthanasia. Electric cars ran in Montreal in 1892 and
in the same year in Toronto. The telephone appeared in Montreal in 1879. It had 282 subscribers in 1879 and soon a myriad.
Now appears the commuter, a half-urban, half-rural being,
whirled in and out in his suburban train. Here begins the passing
of the single city house with its back garden and garden wall,
its one plum tree, its square of grass, a little *rus in urbe*. In
place of it appears the apartment house with its new cliff-
dwellers and its fountain hall with a rubber tree and goldfish,
art compensating for vanished nature. The visible sign of the
age is the growth of Montreal from its 100,000 people at Confederation to its 328,000 of the opening century; of Toronto,
similarly, from a little more than 50,000 to more than 200,000.
At Confederation 80 per cent of the Canadian people lived in
the country or in country villages, but by 1901 the rural population was only 62 per cent, that had fallen to 50 per cent when
the Great War ended. Already, at the time referred to here, the
rural sections of the country began to be invaded with a skirmish
line of golf clubs, summer cottages and, later, overrun and
obliterated by the motor-car and the radio. These last changes
came later but the beginning was already there, the handwriting
on the wall—of the farmer's barn—in the early nineties.

But it did not need the oncoming of hard times to destroy the
J. S. Ewart, Conservative régime. The Manitoba School Question had
"Manitoba doomed it already. Read by an outsider in a book, the Manitoba
School School Question sounds like a lawyer's lullaby, about as interest-
Question," ing as a Privy Council decision on the sanitary authority of the
1894 City of London. The reality was very different. The question
was bitter in its intensity. The political life of Canada, then and
to-day, moves on ground beneath which are the ashes of the
fires of two centuries ago, of French against English, of Roman
Catholic against Protestant. They can still be fanned to a flame;
they might still precipitate a conflagration. Hence arises our ever-
familiar warning to one another not to "raise the race cry." This
to us is like "raising the devil" in the Middle Ages. The devil of
race and the devil of language and the devil of religion all appear
in the smoke together. The Conservative party in an evil hour
raised the devil. It happened thus: Manitoba had started life in

HAL ROSS PERRIGARD, A.R.C.A., MONTREAL, P.Q., 1941

"Life received a new wakefulness from the arc lamp and the electric bulb..."
—PAGE 193

1870 as a bilingual province. It had of its own authority set up bilingual schools, and separate schools for Roman Catholics. But the influx of English-speaking and non-Catholic settlers into Manitoba in the twenty years 1870-1890 had entirely altered the environment. French was practically gone. Manitoba spoke what it understood to be English. The Roman Catholics were only 20,000 in a population of 150,000. The province undertook to pass a new School Act, abolishing the separate schools. At once the fat was in the fire, or rather in the law courts, when a Mr. Barrett entered suit against the City of Winnipeg for taxing him for non-Catholic schools.

J. S. Willison, "Sir Wilfrid Laurier and the Liberal Party," 1903

1890

The separate school system had been instituted in the former Province of Canada, and passed on in 1867 to Ontario and Quebec, where it still exists. The British North America Act guarantees it for Ontario and Quebec against provincial interference. Whether this guarantee extended to Manitoba under the terms of the (Canadian) Manitoba Act of 1870, and the Imperial Act of 1871 which validated it, was a complicated matter of legal interpretation. But the further question rose as to whether the people of Manitoba would stand for interference from the courts or from the Dominion, whether their new School Act of 1890 was valid or not. The cry arose, "Hands off Manitoba," and all over Canada the ashes of old angers broke into flame. The government was in a dilemma. To oppose Manitoba would lose the Protestant vote, at least the Orange part of it, but it would gain the Catholic blue and the Irish green. The only hope was that the flood of argument would spread from court to court, from appeal to appeal, to die away at last in the Privy Council as a desert river runs to nothing in the sand. The opposite happened. Public interest grew with each appeal; the torrent ran to a tidal wave.

The party began to waver. The death of Sir John Thompson, the Roman Catholic prime minister, had followed close on that of Macdonald. His successor, Sir Mackenzie Bowell, a Protestant, carried on as best he might. Then came the Pickwickian decision of the Privy Council, namely, that Manitoba had full power to make the Act, and the Dominion Government full power to unmake it. This last was under what was called the 'remedial

Feb., 1895

power,' and rests, for the curious, on Section 93, Clause 4, of
the British North America Act. On the strength of this the
Dominion Government first ordered Manitoba to alter its law
of 1890 and, on refusal, introduced a remedial bill to coerce the
Province. This was too much. The party was breaking on the
issue. Bowell was forced to resign. Sir Charles Tupper, brought
from his High Commissionership in London to be Prime Minister,
tried in vain to carry the bill. The Conservative majority had
melted away. An appeal to the country brought Sir Wilfrid
Laurier and the Liberals triumphantly to power.

The inquisitive might well ask what happened to the Manitoba
School Question. Few people could answer. Those most feverish
about it forgot it most easily. In reality it was all settled by
compromise within a year, inasmuch as compromise was possible. Though impossible as between Conservatives at Ottawa
and Liberals in Winnipeg, it was easy as soon as a Liberal
government in Winnipeg faced a Liberal government in Ottawa.
Laurier indeed as leader had not needed to do anything, except
do nothing. He called this "the lines of Torres Vedras," a doubtful compliment to Wellington's memory. The new act allowed
teaching in French—or in any other language—for a school of
so many pupils, and Roman Catholic teaching, or any Christian
teaching, after hours, without cost. Everybody lived happily,
not ever after, but at least till all sorts of odd languages multiplied like prairie chickens in Manitoba and presently had to go.

The incoming of Sir Wilfrid Laurier's ministry dates as from
1896. But it belongs really with the new century, for the first
eleven years of which it ruled over the smiling prosperity of
Canada. Its opening years ran parallel with the growing troubles
in South Africa and witnessed the episode of the South African
War. That tragic struggle needs no extended record here for its
terrible reality lay far away and outside the path of our history.
Canadian participation in it was on a wholly voluntary, indeed
on a competitive basis. For most who went, the war was a glad
adventure. Its cost was paid elsewhere. Canada knew little of
the fierce opposition to the war that was evinced by a large
section of the British people. Goldwin Smith and Mr. Henri
Bourassa fearlessly denounced the war. But for most Canadians

Feb., 1896

*Sir Charles
Tupper,
"Recollections
of Sixty Years
in Canada,"
1914*

June 23, 1896

*Sir Wilfrid,
1897*

the general principle of support to the mother country out-
weighed the argument in a particular case. At any rate the
generosity of the treatment of the conquered, the gift of free
government and the final union of two races on an equal footing
in South Africa, was altogether congenial to Canadian sympathy.
Nor can it be doubted that comradeship in arms in South Africa
was to aid towards the union of hearts in the life-and-death
struggle of later conflicts, still behind the veil.

MEMORABLE DATES

1869
Red River Rebellion

1870
Manitoba Enters the Dominion

1871
Treaty of Washington

1871
British Columbia enters the Dominion

1873
Liberal Government of Alexander Mackenzie

1873
Prince Edward Island enters the Dominion

1878
Conservative Government

1885
North-West Rebellion

1886
Canadian Pacific Railway opened across Canada

1896
Sir Wilfrid Laurier, Prime Minister

"Many came in caravans of prairie schooners—children, chattels and all" — PAGE 207

CHAPTER VIII

THE OPENING OF THE TWENTIETH
CENTURY — 1896-1914

The Lost World of International Peace — Halcyon Days in Canada: the Invasion of the West: the New Provinces — Oriental Immigration — Intellectual Life, Letters and Art — The Empire Question — Federation vs. Alliance — The United States, Alaska and Reciprocity — Election of 1911 — The Conservative Government — The German Peril — The Great War.

THOSE who can remember the opening of the present century will recall the discussion as to whether it began in 1900 or in 1901. The discussion will be renewed in the year 2000. But for Canada the century more properly began in 1896 with the turn of the tide of prosperity, the advent of the Liberal Government and the great influx of population into the North-West.

Sir Wilfrid Laurier was fortunate in his accession to power. He was fortunate in the first place in his colleagues—in William Mulock, a man combining intellectual eminence with long political experience; and in Clifford Sifton a right-arm of energy in the North-West. He was fortunate also in the moment of his success. It came just as the clouds of hard times gave way to the sunshine of reviving prosperity. It occurred just as the gold discoveries on the Yukon and the new mines in British Columbia opened the era of mineral production which has since altered the face and the future of Canada. The Yukon gold brought with it

Sir William 1902

Sir Clifford, 1915

the romance and danger of the Edmonton Trail and the White Pass, the attempted project of a Yukon railway, the expectation of El Dorado, the rise of Dawson City and the morning song of sourdough poetry. Even as it all subsided it left a dawning realization that beneath the acres of snow of Canada might still lie buried treasure. With this came also the imperial stimulus of the great Diamond Jubilee in 1897, with its London Canadian Arch that announced, *Free Homes for Millions*. There was a feeling that a new era had begun.

W. Ogilvie, "Early Days on the Yukon," 1913

Indeed it had. The earlier years of the century were to become halcyon days for the Liberal Party. Apart from any special excellence in their administration, they fell heir to the good fortune of the hour. After the close of the Boer War, the greater part of the world was at peace. There was indeed the war between Japan and Russia of 1904-5 but it was far away, did not disturb the intercourse of nations, while the fact that it was ended by a treaty made at Portsmouth, New Hampshire, seemed to give a foretaste of world solidarity. Not only was there peace but with it a background such as the generation born with the Great War can neither recall nor imagine, such as cannot conceivably come again within present lifetime. There was everywhere unimpeded trade and travel, and a flood of cosmopolitan migration. Two million people left Europe each year for the new world. Travellers moved without let or hindrance, with little even of formality, through what is now the stricken war area of Central Europe. Every city was as wide open as London. The gold standard of money supplied a universal medium of exchange, either direct or by simple and fixed conversion to local currencies. Finance and investment were international; the stock exchanges, as it were, a new brotherhood. The reign of the financial saints seemed close at hand. The business man inherited the earth and 'inspired millionaires' atoned for their sins by their benefactions. A book called *The Great Illusion*, of which millions of copies were sold in dozens of languages, explained the anachronism and fruitlessness of war and stated that "the majority of adult Germans have never seen a battle and never will." If the author was in error he had uncounted millions of us to share it with him.

G. S. Lee, "Inspired Millionaires" 1911

1908

Such an international environment reacted on all the new countries and most of all on Canada. "The new century," said Sir Wilfrid, "is Canada's." It was, till the Devil took it away. Bountiful harvests and good prices drew a flood of immigrants towards the West, utterly different from any movement seen before. The new Minister of the Interior, Mr. Clifford Sifton, inaugurated a vigorous advertising campaign for immigration. Lecturers spoke at the fall fairs of the United States and visited the British Isles. Leaflets and maps were sent all over Europe; agencies opened at the ports. Imperial Germany became alarmed. "The attempt to lure our fellow countrymen to this desolate, sub-arctic region," so complained Wilhelm's Street, Berlin, to Downing Street, London, "is to be denounced as criminal." But Main Street, Winnipeg, won out. Immigrants began to move in a flood. As many as 75,000 came to the Western Provinces in 1905, 90,000 in 1906 and in the last four years before the Great War an average of 120,000 a year. The year 1913 brought 400,870 immigrants to Canada, of whom 151,000 went to the West. So rapid a growth has seldom been seen. Winnipeg had 26,000 people in 1891, and 163,000 in 1916. Calgary was non-existent at Confederation. When the Canadian Pacific was built it was just a poor place, a few shacks. They moved it a mile or so, on ropes, rather than move the railway line. It had 4,000 people in 1901 and 56,000 in 1916. Lethbridge rose from nothing to 10,000; Saskatoon changed its 113 people to 21,000, and Edmonton's 4,000 increased to 54,000 in the same period.

J. Culliton, "Assisted Emigration and Land Settlement in Western Canada," 1928

G. Ham, "Reminiscences of a Raconteur," 1921

Not only did numbers increase but at the same time the complexion of the population of the North-West and even of the Dominion; the proportion of alien races in its population was seriously altered. At Confederation 61 per cent of the people of Canada (the Canada of that day) were British in origin; 31 per cent were French. Inasmuch as 5.8 per cent were of German origin, the remaining aliens were only a little over 2 per cent, a quite negligible quota. The census of 1871 knows nothing of Ukrainians, Russians, Poles, nor of eastern Europe in general. But the census of 1921 shows a population in its origin British 55.4 per cent, French 27.9 per cent, and hence nearly 17 per cent of alien races. Overwhelmingly this aspect appears in the

J. M. Gibbon, "Canadian Mosaic," 1938

Prairie Provinces. Part of this new element had come in even before the great invasion. Between 1887 and 1890, 10,000 Mormons had settled in what is now Southern Alberta. In 1899 a grant of 320,000 acres was set aside for a settlement of Doukhobors, or spirit-wrestlers, from Russia. About 4,000 of them settled in Alberta in that year, and in all as many as 7,500—excellent people except that their habit of periodically wrestling the spirit with very few clothes on was too metropolitan for prairie society. Early arrivals also were the 10,000 Icelanders whose presence was a compliment to the genial warmth of our North-West. Beyond this there were in the Prairie Provinces in 1916, 135,000 Austro-Hungarians, 63,000 Russians, 27,000 Poles, 36,000 Ukrainians—in all a British population of less than a million in a total of one million seven hundred thousand. In Alberta 40 per cent of the people were non-British. It must be remembered, too, that the bulk of these people were no longer refugees, loyalists or pilgrims. They were people on the make and on the move, exchanging European poverty for a new chance. Their new home they knew by advertisement only, and they faced no more danger in the transit than the doubtful coffee of an immigration shed. Yet we have to remember that their energy and their industry and their new patriotism towards their new home played a large part in the making of our Western Dominion.

F. Yeigh, "Through the Heart of Canada," 1911

It is only by recalling the spirit of the times that we can imagine a country exerting itself to attract so varied a population —Doukhobors running naked, Germans founding New Prussia in Saskatchewan, everybody talking everything, schools available for all languages, and people singing *Home Sweet Home* in all the tongues of Europe. There were more foreign-language newspapers in the Canadian West than anywhere else in the world. But these were still the 'melting pot' days, when a mixed population seemed as excellent as a mixed drink; days of a world in which world wars had been unknown a hundred years, and seemed gone for ever.

The only incoming element that worked the other way, and helped to keep unity of language in the Canadian West, was supplied by the Americans. In 1897 only 712 American citizens migrated to western Canada. In 1908, over 58,000 Americans migrated to Canada as a whole, the bulk of these going to the West. The number of people in the West of United States birth represented in 1916 almost twelve per cent, in Alberta over eighteen; to these, of course, must be added the rapid growth of young 'Americans' born in Canada. These immigrants were not like the paupers of the 'hungry forties' but substantial people, moving from old farms to new. Many came in caravans of prairie schooners—children, chattels and all. They brought, so the government said, at least a thousand dollars per person. Outside capital followed them as a fox follows a hen.

The larger part of the new settlement was rural. The homestead system put the people on the land. The system had been instituted in imitation of the United States and the huge rectangular survey on which it was based had already begun in 1869. The base used was the international boundary of 49° north, and a north-and-south line (principal meridian) close to Winnipeg (long. 97° 3'). Successive tiers of townships of 36 square miles (6 x 6) piled up like children's blocks, one on top of the other towards the North Pole. Each of the square miles was a section. A quarter of a section (160 acres) was a homestead lot. Two sections of each township were reserved for the benefit of schools, a part represented the railway grant, and the land reserved for the Hudson's Bay Company, one twentieth of each township. By 1912 as much as 183,918,171 acres had been surveyed, practically the whole available land of the provinces. Few people realized at the time that the system was suited only for one kind of farming, done in one way, in one kind of country. It shuts out all the old neighbourliness of the river group. Its application in a country of hills and dales like the Peace River seems utterly out of place. It means dependence on one or two kinds, principally on one kind, of grain crop, and on the export market and foreign trade. All this is its epitaph, written in the dust bowl of Kansas. In 1900 it was all bright with the colours of the morning. At least it served its day.

Of necessity the government of the North-West had to be reorganized. There followed the creation of the sister provinces

W. W. Swanson,
"Wheat,"
1930

Extension of Boundaries Act, 1912

Yukon Territory Act 1898

1920

Alberta and Saskatchewan in 1905 and the expansion of the boundaries of Manitoba. Since Rupert's Land was thus doomed, Ontario and Quebec took off the rest of it, the provinces thus reaching to the now familiar line of 60 degrees north and the Hudson Bay and Strait. Beyond that the Yukon had already been organized as a Territory with a Controller and an elected Council of three members, and the rest of the North, known and unknown, frozen or thawed, divided up as Mackenzie, Keewatin, and Franklin Districts under direct Dominion control. The North-West Mounted Police became everywhere the symbol of law and order.

Under such circumstances the general elections of 1904 and 1908 passed as in a dream. The government had become a legend;

INVASION OF THE NORTHWEST 1880-1914

a sort of mythology grew round them as if they created the good times, with the Minister of Agriculture as God of the Harvest and the Minister of the Fisheries as the Neptune of canned salmon. A hush fell upon the electorate as if the Ministry had been protected by a sort of highway sign, "Men at work; do not disturb." It will be recalled that when the party finally met disaster in 1911 they went down under the pathetic slogan, "Let Laurier finish his work."

But there was one phase of immigration into Canada in this halcyon period which occasioned difficulty and violent opposition. This was the oriental migration to British Columbia. The United States had long since realized the danger to American civilization of an influx of the Asiatic races to the Pacific coast. Asia could, and would, have flooded Pacific America, turning against Western Civilization its own invention of easy transport, and its own industrial demand for cheap labour. Welcomed at first as the coolies of the gold diggings, the Chinese soon became a menace to California. Bret Harte's mournful poem concerning *Ah Sin*, *The Heathen Chinee*, gives the views of *Truthful James* on "Chinese cheap labour" and represents a mosaic fragment of world history. The American exclusion law dates from 1882.

But British America was more slow in recognizing the Asiatic peril. In early days in Victoria, with labour scarce and dear and Chinamen cheap and handy, their coming met no opposition. Even when railway building began, the Chinese coolie labour was more than welcome. Indeed its import was encouraged. It accorded with the traditional doctrines of liberty, of the open-door, the traditional British privilege of refuge for exiles of all complexion and colour. People who had only seen Hindus as curiosities at Oxford or on the cricket field, and Chinese in the form of *Li Hung Chang* accepting an honorary degree, and who were in no danger of an invasion of the hop fields of Kent or the farms of Sussex by Chinese cheap labour, felt themselves singularly wide-minded as compared with the narrow selfishness of the Colonials. The British Columbian apparently did not realize that the Chinaman was his brother. Fuel was added to this flame by the unhappy episode of the import of Chinese coolie labour, under indentures, into the compounds of the South

L. Neame,
"The Asiatic
Danger
in the
Colonies,"
1907

1896

Reports,
Department
of Justice,
Ottawa,
1900-1905
African mines. British Columbian opinion, thoroughly aroused against the Asiatic peril, expressed itself in a series of Exclusion Acts. The Dominion Government set its face towards England and used its power of dissallowance. The quarrel went on for four or five years, until general opinion in Canada began to realize the danger, so obvious now, of unrestricted immigration. A statute of 1886 had undertaken to check Chinese immigration by an admission tax of $50 which was raised to $500 in the year 1904—a plan intended to combine a perfect liberty of entry with a perfect impossibility of entering. The Act only half succeeded. Capital could still sink $500 in a cheap Chinaman and take it out of him later. Moreover the United States complained that Canadian entry served as their back door. Canada got the $500 and the United States got the Chinaman. Later on an Act of 1923 forbade all immigration of the Chinese coolie class.

The case of Japan was different. Japan was now an armed nation. Britain had concluded a sort of general alliance, or at least *entente*, with Japan. It was felt that nothing must be done to hurt the pride of Japan. Chinese pride didn't matter. The suppression of the national movement—China for the Chinese —had seen to that. The nature and the justice of the Chinese movement was lost to most British and American people by its funny name of the "Boxers." The Chinese term corresponds in reality to such heroic terms as the "mailed fist." Nothing makes sadder reading to the idealist than the disregard of Asiatic rights by Europeans in the past, except the present disregard of European rights by the Asiatics.

For Japan was found a method of 'saving face' in the immigration difficulty by what was called a "gentleman's agreement." It was known, from the opening chorus of *The Mikado*, that there were then "gentlemen of Japan." One of them was found to *1908* make an agreement of good faith whereby Canada would not exclude Japanese labourers from immigration and that Japan would see that not too many immigrated. On the Canadian side a prominent part in the settlement was played by Mr. William Lyon Mackenzie King, then rising to eminence as Deputy Minister, and presently (1909) as Minister of Labour. It was one of the first of the many triumphs in finding the common

ADAM SHERRIFF SCOTT, A.R.C.A., MONTREAL, P.Q., 1941

*"The North-West Mounted Police became everywhere the symbol
of law and order"*—PAGE 208

ground of common sense which were to result later on in securing for Mr. King, as has been wittily said, "employment from time to time at Ottawa."

Hindu immigration to British Columbia was ingeniously side-tracked by the "continuous voyage" rule, as smart a piece of legislation as any that ever disfranchised negroes in the South. The Hindus were free to come, but only on a 'through' ship; and there were no through ships. Just before the war of 1914 somebody, or some government, supplied the money to fetch a direct ship with brown samples to Vancouver. The fat was in the fire but at that moment the war pot boiled over.

It was a new feature of the settlement of the North-West in the twentieth century, that it did not bring with it merely the population of the land and of stores and the workshops—the so-called "working people." It brought with them people to whom that title is commonly denied and whose activities are pre-sumably midway between work and leisure, the lawyers, the doctors, the clergy—all the round of the learned professions, and with them the whole apparatus of education and culture. Alberta and Saskatchewan began where older civilization ends—with Authors' Associations, Browning Societies and lectures on palæontology. The things in which older communities run to seed were the new seeds from which they drew life. The University of Saskatchewan rose, literally, on the empty prairie, on the high ground that overlooks the sweeping slopes of the Saskatchewan Valley. At the same time the University of Alberta emerged from Fort Edmonton as complete as Minerva from the head of Jove. It is a hidden secret, known only inside colleges, but unsuspected even by college trustees, that the most distinguished university in all the world can be made overnight by gathering to it the most distinguished scholars of all the world. The North-West guessed a part of this secret, and imported along with its harvest machinery, a working plant of scholarship that brought McGill and Toronto, Harvard, Oxford and the Sorbonne to the plains of the West. The vivifying example stimulated a new cultural activity in the older provinces of the West, themselves still young. Manitoba equipped itself anew. British Columbia shook off the leading-strings of McGill, and gave to its University a magnificent endowment of land beside the ocean that ought to guarantee its finances and its inspiration.

Nor should this expanding current of intellectual life be traced only in Western Canada. It was a part of a new life animating the whole country. The earliest era of war and wandering and danger gave way in Canada to the era of pioneer settlement, the fort to the farm. This was now giving place to the industrial age of all-round industry. The tone of the people altered with it. All observers of the period noted what began to be called the new Nationalism of Canada, and local patriotism and pride rang the changes on the idea that Canada was a nation. This was in part a political idea but in part also social, intellectual and literary.

R. Jebb, "Studies in Colonial Nationalism," 1905

It has not been possible in this survey to do more than glance at the development of art and letters in Canada. Nor was there, till the later nineteenth century, much more than what a glance might cover. Learning in the new world took its light from the old. A country with neither press nor public can do little else. Laval University and the classical colleges of French Canada accepted for education the old French models, undisturbed since Louis Quatorze. The British colleges reproduced the classics of Oxford, the mathematics of Cambridge and the surgery and philosophy of Edinburgh. Polite culture imitated Britain. A false quantity in a Latin quotation in the Parliament at Toronto would have called forth the same laugh as at Westminster—or an unconvincing imitation of it. Educated people of those days disclaimed all knowledge of such things as chemistry, as people openly disclaim sin. As with learning so with letters. There was but little that was not merely imitative, a lamp with old oil that burned dim in a wilderness. From the time of the humorist Lescarbot, of Port Royal, letters in Canada consisted mostly of things written about Canada such as Lescarbot's own history and that of Charlevoix. Till far on in the nineteenth century the whole output of literature in Canada, French or English, had not amounted to much. One may recall the scholarly *Histoire du Canada* of Francois-Xavier Garneau, published in 1848, the work of twenty-five years of research, and, in English, Robert Christie's *History of Canada 1791-1821* and later the ten volumes of Kingsford the mathematician, which have become of peculiar value

"Canada and Its Provinces," Vol. 12, 1914

1606

owing to their undiscriminating comprehensiveness. In the highest rank, vivid with the illumination of genius, and with the merit that crowns an unremitting toil defiant of a failing body, are the pages of Francis Parkman. But Parkman was an American and his theme continental. Goldwin Smith's polished work was that of Oxford in Canada. In fiction and poetry few voices from Canada reached home. John Galt of the 'Lone Shieling' and Tom Moore of the faintly tolling "evening chime," took a song home with them. Louis Fréchette reached the ear of France, but that was much later. A conspicuous exception is that of Judge Haliburton of Nova Scotia, reaching England as Sam Slick. He has been falsely accused as the father of the illegitimate child called American humour. But accurate history acquits him.

Stephen Leacock, "Humour, Its Theory and Technique," 1930

Nor is it possible to say that there was in the nineteenth century a *Canadian* literature, meaning literature written in Canada in a Canadian way which others may admire but did not originate. Most people would agree that there is still none. Canadian art there is, but not Canadian literature. The topic is delicate, with so easy an affront in it that it will stand a moment's elaborating. American literature (that of the United States) was similarly slow in coming. Sydney Smith, the famous cleric and wit of a hundred or more years ago, once asked, "Who reads an American book?" He had hardly said it when all England found itself reading Washington Irving's *Sketch Book* of 1819, absorbed in Hawthorne's gloomy fancies, weeping over Longfellow's *Evangeline*, and crawling breathless on all-fours through the forest with Fenimore Cooper, fearful of snapping a dry twig. Yet this was still not American literature; it was still part of the common stock, no better in its origin than Shakespeare or Milton.

It is exactly at that point that our literature in Canada still stands. There is not as yet a Canadian literature in the sense indicated. Nor is there similarly a Canadian humour, nor any particularly Canadian way of being funny. Nor is there, apart from varying accents, any Canadian language. We use English for writing, American for conversation and slang and profanity, and Scottish models for moral philosophy and solemnity. *Maria Chapdelaine*, may well be rated as one of the world's books. But it is only Canadian in the sense that it was written about Canada, seen better by a transient outsider than by ourselves. In the United States such writers as Mark Twain and O. Henry presently brought forth an American way of writing, greatly admired by great writers in England, who could not have written a line of it. Whether that will happen in Canada is doubtful. The times are against it. In all the Britains and in the United States, speech, thought and language now amalgamate, not diverge.

What is true of letters has not been true of art. All through the nineteenth century there were excellent painters in Canada, but little to distinguish their work from that of the overseas schools in which the most fortunate of them were trained. The topic changes but not the hand. The St. Lawrence looked like the Rhine and a waterfall was a waterfall. Then came a time when *ob. 1934* some one—was it Maurice Cullen first, or was it many people together?—discovered Canadian scenery and what to do with it—the breaking snow and the black water of opening spring, the intensity of dry cold, and with that a whole wealth of coloured sands and changing woods and the broken foam of rapids. The Latin inscription to Sir Christopher Wren in St. Paul's Cathedral invites anyone who seeks for his monument to look about him. The readers of this book, curious over Canadian art of the day, may do the same.

But if letters lay behind, science in the form of applied science has run ahead. The new century soon showed schools of engineering with which Great Britain had nothing to compare. Our country gave its open opportunity. Cambridge could teach hydraulic science; Canada could send the student over a waterfall. In this pre-war era hundreds of British students came to Canadian universities for applied science as humbly as Canadians used to go to Oxford for unapplied Greek and to Cambridge *A. S. Eve,* for inapplicable mathematics. More than that; it looked for a *"Lord* moment, when the century opened, as if one great Canadian *Rutherford,* College was to become the Mecca of all the world for pure *1871-1937"* physical science.

It was only natural that the quickening of intellectual life and the new sense of nationality should revive the question of the

"The University of Saskatchewan rose . . . on the empty prairie . . ." — PAGE 213

W. J. PHILLIPS, R.C.A., WINNIPEG, MAN., 1941

Empire. Universal peace, like free trade, was a lost dream. Separation looked too dangerous with a German Empire risen on the ashes of empire in France, with Russia 'at the gates of Herat,' harboured on the Pacific and reaching out everywhere for the open sea. Hence arose the impetus towards protection by union and strength in the Empire that brought the abortive Imperial Federation League (1883-1893). It held its meetings and it sang *God Save the Queen* on the veldt and on the prairie, in cities as old as Chester and as new as Portage la Prairie. Then it turned out that Federation meant federal taxes. Naval defence cost money. The colonies—they were still called that— claimed that they protected the Empire by opening new lands. With that the League went to pieces, broke up like Canadian ice, blew away like Australian sand, and dwindled like a South African river.

G. Parkin, "Imperial Federation," 1892

But the under-current still flowed. In place of formal federation came the pageants of demonstration of imperial power and the union of hearts, at the Golden Jubilee of 1887 and the Diamond Jubilee of ten years later. Out of these when the South African War had come and gone, grew the successive Conferences, Colonial till 1902 and Imperial after 1907. They occasioned an infinity of discussion and led, as far as any conclusion went, exactly nowhere. "If you want our aid," said Sir Wilfrid Laurier to Mr. Joseph Chamberlain, the Colonial Secretary, "call us to your councils." Mr. Chamberlain answered with equal grandiloquence to the same effect, "Come in, but pay as you enter." The Car of State stuck right there. Similarly the tariff problem was introduced at every Conference and got wedged, like a piano in a doorway. Canada gave a tariff preference that began in 1898. Mr. Chamberlain said it didn't prefer. Years later some one said what everybody thought, and called it humbug. The Conference of 1911 saw a complete scheme for an Imperial Federal Council presented by the Prime Minister of New Zealand. It was not really a child of his own. It had been fathered by a round-table group of Empire enthusiasts. This academic foundling he laid on the doorstep of the Conference. It turned out to be a dummy. Mr. Asquith, the Imperial Prime Minister joined with Sir Wilfrid Laurier in repudiating it. That was the end of imperial

R. Jebb, "The Imperial Conference," 1911

reorganization. People on the inside thought things ominous. A divided Empire seemed too weak to fight. But outside of the inside, nobody thought much about it. "We are happy as we are," said a leading French-Canadian jurist.

H. L. Keenleyside, "Canada and the United States," 1929

During all this period relations with the United States, as contrasted with earlier years, were singularly happy. The Alaska Boundary Question, which came to new life in the opening of the century, occasioned a brief flurry and led Sir Wilfrid Laurier to declare that Canada has been once more "sacrificed on the altar of British diplomacy." The reference was to the award made in regard to the boundary by a mixed tribunal, three Americans, two Canadians and one Englishman. In spite of the brilliant argument of Aimé Geoffrion, of Counsel for the Canadian case, the tribunal decided in favour of the United States the question whether the boundary separating the Alaskan Panhandle from British Columbia (the old boundary originally made in 1825 as between Russia and Great Britain) kept strictly back its ten leagues from the sea, even when the sea ran in as an inlet, or whether it cut across the inlets and gave Britain access in and out. Common sense shows at once that the meaning of the old Russian treaty was that Russia kept that part of the coast free from British access. When the false heat generated by argument was replaced by cold reason, Canadians at large knew that the award was just and another myth went the way of the North-West Angle of Nova Scotia. History has its little irony in making the impassable American Panhandle a part of our present protection.

The episode was forgotten. The Americans filled the West, and apart from muttered thunders caught by only a few apprehensive ears, the world seemed quiet to the Canada of 1911. Sir Wilfrid Laurier's government was obviously to last forever, along with the gold standard and international law and the freedom of the seas and western civilization. All this moved gently to the sound of the Vienna waltz called the Concert of Europe. The first break

L. E. Ellis, "Reciprocity 1911," 1939

came in Canada itself. In a rash moment Sir Wilfrid Laurier saw the will-o'-the-wisp of Reciprocity dancing beyond the frontier. This was to be effected by parallel legislation, like knocking out the boards of the boundary fence. It was to let western steers run through and keep heavy manufactured imports out. It was so good that some American enthusiasts said it would mean the annexation of Canada. That ruined it. The Conservative Party woke from apathy to hope and looked round for Sir John A.'s flag on a stick. Even the farmers got doubtful; the 'home market' of rising cities looked large compared with 1891. Manufacturers, though not immediately affected, thought that they knew what happens to a fence when you start knocking boards off. The winds of opposition rose to a gale. When the storm of election died down, it appeared that the Liberal Party had gone down to disaster.

Sir Wilfrid Laurier's career ended.

The new Conservative government of Sir Robert Borden had hardly entered office when the sunshine atmosphere began to darken. Immigration into Canada was still at its height—the year 1913 with 402,000 marking the all-time record. But already financial wisdom was shaking its head. The storm signals were up on Wall Street and without doubt a new fall into world depression was imminent. *Oct. 10, 1911*

Indeed worse apprehensions were abroad than those which agitated the stock exchanges. The new German peril had gradually risen from the horizon to the sky. Ever since the century began, Canadians had been trying not to see it. Germany was still supposed to be the land of tobacco smoke, fairy stories, pipe dreams, and philosophy. Vienna was a waltz, Hungary a dance, the Kaiser only a strutting figure, half comic, half mystifying, and a submarine an illegal contrivance, contrary to international law. That gradually changed. After 1897 huge naval votes built a threatening navy. The project of the Kiel Canal made a Baltic back door. Count Zeppelin's floating sausages began to look dangerous, except that here again international law forbade them to drop anything on anybody. What were whispers and rumours for the public were presently plain, if confidential, truths for the Borden Government. The Empire was in danger. Forthwith the Dominion House of Commons voted four battleships, and all England applauded. *Punch*, the mirror of opinion, presented Canada as the Viking's Daughter hauling four battleships on a string. Then it turned out that everybody had forgotten the

Canadian Senate. The Senate emerged like the forgotten old fairy out of the cupboard and put a spell on the ships. The jubilation was over. The Viking's Daughter couldn't swim. Yet even this passed as an episode, the world at large and Canada in particular still preoccupied with a thousand happier and better things.

Then came the war. The older generation recalls its strange, its seeming impossibility. For Canada it came out of a clear sky—the clear sky of vacation time, of the glory of Canadian midsummer, of summer cottages, of bush camps, and for the city population the soft evening sky, the canopy of stars over the merry-go-round resorts in the cool of the summer evening.

It is not the privilege of the present record to recount the story of the participation of Canada in the Great War. To those of us now in middle age and beyond, it still all seems yesterday. We recall the unbelievable outbreak of the war; the almost universal expectation that it would be over in a few months, stopped dead by the collapse of finance or by the power of finance to avoid collapse. We still recall the initial horror felt at the German methods of brutality and barbarity. There followed the long years of combat, deadlocked in the trenches in France and searching the world for battlefields. We recall the valour of Canadian soldiers, the military genius of our Canadian captains and our realization with pride that such names as those of Arthur Currie and Andrew McNaughton would rank second to none in the history of the war. Even the anguish of war, and its unending harvest of death helped to elevate Canadians to the consciousness of their full status as a nation. Then came the tumultuous joy of the Armistice, bringing peace to a people who asked nothing else, neither revenge nor gain. As the war closed in Europe the sun seemed to rise in Canada on a boundless and unclouded horizon.

"... the war closed ... bringing peace to a people who asked nothing else, neither revenge nor gain"—PAGE 222

ORIGINAL PAINTING BY HAL ROSS PERRIGARD, A.R.C.A., MONTREAL, P.Q., 1941

Hal Ross. Perrigard

CHAPTER IX

CANADA AS A NATION

After the Great War —Canada and the European Settlement —Reorganization of the Empire: the Statute of Westminster —Migration and Empire Settlement —The Ottawa Conference and Empire Tariffs —Collapse and Depression —Finance —Unemployment —Transportation —Dust and Social Credit in the West —The Brighter Side —Reciprocity with the United States: El Dorado: Panama —War.

Almost twenty-one years went by between the close of the Great War in 1918 and the opening of the war in 1939. In these years the peace and safety of the world might have been guaranteed by armed force in the hands of decent nations. In place of that it was guaranteed by pledges of criminals and by the sanction of a League of Nations with no more cohesion than a pyramid of billiard balls, no bond of more than a rope of sand. What should have been merely a clearing house of information, a broker's office for bargains, took on a mock sovereignty and spread an illusive security over a world all too willing to fall asleep. We can see it all in retrospect now, plain to the simplest. We were blind then and fast asleep. Nor anywhere more than in Canada. We have no right to blame our leaders; each and every one, we shared in the same sleep and the same blindness.

Winston Churchill, "The Aftermath," 1929

Winston Churchill, "Step by Step," 1939

The close of the Great War made Canada not only a nation in its own consciousness but even in the acknowledged sense of the term, as a signatory of the Treaty of Versailles and a member of the League of Nations. But as a matter of fact, Canada and Canadian public opinion turned gladly away from everything international. Canada rightly refused to accept a 'mandate' of

*The Chanak
Incident,
See
Stephen
King-Hall,
"Our Own
Times,"
1915-34*

anything. The Government of 1922 refused Mr. Lloyd George's invitation to participate in a new war of Turkey and Greece. We decided to let them run it out between themselves. The decision was natural to the hour. The Conservative war government of Sir Robert Borden, succeeded by Mr. Arthur Meighen, who had played a notable part in wartime as first lieutenant to Sir Robert, had gone down in the elections of 1921. Mr. Mackenzie King was in office at the head of reviving liberalism. The traditional imperial forward policy of a Conservative administration was changed for the equally traditional Liberal policy of minding one's own business. Without doubt, practically all people in Canada heartily endorsed Mr. King's refusal to interfere, and the subsequent British decision to let things alone. Yet, in the light of what we know now, we may wonder if it was not a first step in that failure to control Europe by military power while still controllable, which has proved so fatal.

For the moment the world went on. It had been understood in the War Conferences and in public discussions generally, that the Empire would be reorganized after the war. The general subject was discussed in the Conference of 1921 and a committee finally drafted a plan in 1926, accepted by the Conference of 1930, which, with becoming delay, became a British Statute in

*22 Geo. V,
c. 4*

five years and received complete Dominion ratification within the next seven. This is the famous Westminster Statute of 1931, which is generally now regarded as a sort of constitution of the British Empire. In reality it does little more than kick a dead mule and recognize a living truth. Such a dead mule, for example, is the Colonial Laws Validity Act which is expressly denounced and repudiated. But in 1931 hardly anybody, in Canada at least, had ever heard of this Act, and those who had, were foggy about what it meant. When adopted (1865) it extended colonial freedom by making any colonial law a valid one unless British legislation overruled it. But this once broad cloak of colonial liberty had shrunk to a little shirt beyond use. The Statute of 1931 took it off the line. The Statute is based on "the free association of the members of the Commonwealth of Nations . . . united by a common allegiance to the Crown." But it is as much a riddle of the Sphinx, a Delphic Oracle, as was the American Constitution of 1789 till the Civil War interpreted it with a sword. The Statute of Westminster, like its American predecessor, seems to create a permanent union with full right of secession. The Crown becomes as many crowns as there are Commonwealth members. Edward VIII ruled a day longer in Eire than he did in London, and in South Africa a day less. But the real meaning of the Act is that Canada and Australia and the other Dominions are admitted to have the full status that we all admit they have, though it defies definition in words. The understanding is suitably British. But an unfortunate oversight is that in disclaiming sovereignty over Canada the Statute failed to supply a means of our own for amending our constitution, such as Australia possesses. Failing that, as already said, we can only amend it by pretending that the British Parliament is still supreme, that is, by putting on again the shrunken little shirt of 1865.

A. B. Keith "Governments of the *British Empire*," *1935*

Equally inconclusive have been the attempts to reconstruct the economic life and the economic connection of the Empire. The close of the war was expected to open a new era of British migration overseas, to join in a common prosperity the unused resources of the Dominions with the surplus labour and accumulated capital of Britain. The Empire Settlement Act of 1922 was framed in this intention. The British Government offered to spend $15,000,000 a year from 1922 to 1927, to co-operate in any Dominion scheme of assisted migration. Australia and Australian States joined heartily in. The Commonwealth planned for 450,000 immigrants in ten years. The Act proved a failure. Each Western Australian farm family cost $7,500 to establish. Moreover, the event showed that the general attitude towards migration had altered. An immigrant was no longer a blessing, but a burden. Organized labour was now everywhere a power. Labour sees its own interest clearly, in the sharp light of necessity, but it sees with a special focus. It must not look too far ahead—a thing natural enough to people hard put to it to provide for the present. An immigrant seemed to mean a competitor to cut down wages. Hence Canada made no response to the Empire Settlement Act except to offer improved farms for families with something to start from, and to invite immigrants for jobs that no one else wanted—those of the house-servant and the hired man. Later, when unemployment set in, all immigrants without money seemed extra mouths to feed and all were shut out. Thus bad went to worse. With labour shut out capital stayed out. Presently migration began to drift the other way— from Canada and the other Dominions to the Mother Country, back to the little lighted streets and the corner pubs, where misery at least has company. Out of these vast errors of the past we must learn the wisdom of the future.

It was expected also that the new life of the Empire would include a new unity of trade, something approaching to the open door all round—the dream of the statesman and the nightmare of the colonial manufacturer. The moment of the Imperial Conference of 1930 seemed ripe for a forward imperial step. In Canada the Liberal Party had gone to defeat in the general election of 1930 and the Conservatives, now led by Mr. R. B. Bennett, were in power. But Mr. Bennett's overtures in London proved of little avail in a country still clinging, though with a loosening hold, to free trade, and unable to give preference to one customer without closing the door on the other. There was still also the lingering doubt whether Canadian preference preferred. The Dominions Secretary, Mr. J. H. Thomas, settled the discussion with the word 'humbug'; British statesmen had been too polite for thirty-two years to use it.

"The British Empire," Oxford Press, 1931

The renewed attempt at Ottawa in the further Conference of 1932 bore fruit, of what final ripeness we cannot yet tell. It was based on the sound idea of duties regulated to represent differential costs only; hence trade, if not free, would be at least equal. In practice the difficulty is to delimitate cost and hence the friction is still there. Many of the bilateral agreements of Ottawa have lapsed. But a part still stands. The removal of the duty on British books brought the consumer feebly back to life, whispering his thanks. But presently Ottawa and all that went with it was overwhelmed in the great cloud of the depression.

For the truth is that the whole economic life of Canada, as of other countries, was dislocated by the great industrial collapse of the years following 1930. This brought down the world's currencies to ruin and intensified the economic separatism already

JAMES CROCKART, A.R.I.B.A., MONTREAL, P.Q., 1941

*"Perhaps the brightest page in these short inter-war annals . . . . is the
record of the discovery and exploitation of the incalculable
mineral wealth . . . ."—*PAGE 237

commenced and now involving world trade in a common disaster. Great Britain abandoned the gold standard in 1931; currency, credit and banking collapsed in a heap in the United States in the opening of 1933. Canadian currency was already inconvertible. German currency, wilfully inflated, was multiplied by millions, by billions, by trillions, till it vanished in gas, leaving foreign bondholders holding an empty bag. All other European money followed suit till foreign exchange became a lottery and all foreign trade a gamble. In and out of the maze ran a new pernicious system of trade and exchange quotas that were strangling the remaining common life of Europe, when the war brought it to a quicker end.

J. P. Day,
"Introduction to
World Economic
History,"
1939

Canada felt the effect of all this to the full. This was partly because it still depends greatly on exports from primary industry, but also, in a new way, by its growth to a country of vast investment of capital. It was estimated that by 1937 there was some $2,684,000,000 of British capital invested in Canada and $3,932,000,000 of American. The British was predominantly in fixed obligations and in railway shares, the American in common stocks, municipal bonds and investment in subsidiary companies. All in all it represented a volume of interest payments, much of it contracted in terms of foreign currency. The whole of Canada now shared the fate of the old-time farmer of the middle seventies, sleepless over the six-months' interest on his mortgages ($17.50 on $500 at 7 per cent).

But the effect of the depression on capital and on those receiving dividends and interest, was only a part of its total industrial effect. It bore heavily on the whole class of industrial factory workers, on organized labour, and brought with it a widespread dislocation and unemployment unknown in the days of a simpler public economy. It has not been possible in this book to recount the changes which in Canada transformed the individual labour of the farm and forest to the organized labour of the factory and presently to the form of international federations covering all the field. The organized labour and trade unions in Canada, as late as 1911 included only 133,000 members, but in 1931 had reached a total of 310,000 members. As a consequence the whole industrial structure had acquired a sensitiveness unknown in the opening days of the Dominion. Hard times in those days were hard enough, for farmers holding out as best they could; but the new industry brought with it the new unemployment and the new public aid and relief, total or partial, extended to 870,000 persons in 1938. Just now the war is wiping the slate clean, but after the war we shall need a new slate.

Of necessity the decline of foreign trade and the cessation of migration reacted on the internal economy of Canada. In particular it helped to bring down into one vast wreckage the railway transportation system of the country. The trouble dated far back. With the opening century began the dream, and then the plan, of a second transcontinental railway. Part of it was to run in a great sweep from Quebec to Winnipeg and never hit a house. No traffic would get in its way. The other part, wisely enough, was meant to cross the prairies through a better country and by a better mountain pass than its great predecessor. Beside it grew up the adjacent enterprise of a Hudson Bay railway. The very activity of the hour launched a third transcontinental, the 'Northern' system of Messrs. Mackenzie and Mann, that put itself together in little pieces, a bit here and a bit there, passing the hat to municipalities.

The underlying impetus towards the great railway boom of 1903 to 1914 was the spirit of our people. Canadians 'fall' for public works as a farmer falls for peas under a thimble. We are all fascinated with our country. We'll build anything, remove it, dam it or damn it. Hence no one ever really counted the cost of the railway vision. To this was added the fact that the honeymoon of the West and the Canadian Pacific Railway had waned. The first locomotive came into Winnipeg all bells and flowers and with girls riding on the cow-catcher. No girls rode thus in 1913—not without paying. So the farmer began to call the railway an octopus and to look round for an octopus of his own. But more than all was the great revolution in traffic by which the motor car, the bus and the truck cut the track from under the railway. Till the roads are rebuilt there is no remedy. Meantime in Canada the great crash of 1930 completed the temporary downfall of all railway enterprise. Dividends stopped on the private line, and debt buried its subsidized competitor. This overbuilding of railways was to prove later on, when world war broke out, and called for transportation, a blessing in disguise. But for the time being not even the long experience of such a man as Sir Henry Thornton, nor the intellectual grasp and phenomenal industry of such a man as Sir Edward Beatty could stay disaster.

The accumulated hard times were bound to bring an upheaval of discontent. Hunger will not be still nor misery keep silent. It is not fair that able and willing people, trained and willing to enter on their work in life, should find themselves dispossessed in a closed world, dispossessed even of work itself. For the young at least this cannot be. Old age may die quiet in a corner. Youth will fight first. Hence the new onrush of hard times and unemployment brought to Canada a new social unrest, a dissatisfaction with the social quietism of existing political parties a demand for a new commonwealth, with the mirage vision of an imaginary Russia to lend it colour. *"Social Planning for Canada," Joint Authors, 1935*

Most of all did the new winds of doctrine sweep over the desolated Prairie Provinces. Hard times, poor prices and crops that withered to the dry ground, had done this. The dust blew from the dried-out valley of the Missouri to dry out the Canadian West. With the dust-wind came the still drier wind of defeatism, the farewell to hope. Till then farmers, in all ages since the Garden of Eden, lived on a cheerful confidence in Providence— one year bad, the next good—crops not as good as the farmer had expected, but then he hardly expected they would be. Thus he lived on a sort of Monte Carlo attitude of *rouge et noir.* Now *P. B. Sears, "Deserts on the March," 1935* came the growing fear, the alarm that the West was gone. Classroom theorists began to explain that the world's cultivation had been vain, that nature's deserts would come back, as if an angered deity of nature was to bury Saskatchewan under dust and make of it a new Palmyra in the desert. For a short time even the stoutest-hearted drew an anxious breath—watching each year—till presently mother nature showered the prairies with soft rain and buried them again in green. Nature passed a soothing hand over the human child's feverish forehead.

Most of all did the new doctrines sweep Alberta. To this province were imported certain economic profundities of British fog, impossible for most people to understand, which in sunny

Stephen
Leacock,
"My Discovery
of the West,"
1937

Alberta, by force of prayer, turned into Alberta Social Credit. The theory is an expansion of the idea of living by taking in one another's washing. It is suggested that if all the people collectively give twenty-five dollars each to all the people separately, then each of the separate people can call for work and goods from all the other people, whereby everybody has work and the work supplies everybody with bread. The theory is parallel to all the new doctrines of 'priming the pump,' pensioning all old men who promise to spend every cent—in other words all the theory of 'purchasing power.' Whatever may be in it, in Alberta it led to partial repudiation of public debt, and scaling down of mortgage interest, things done however, under other names, in Saskatchewan. This involved invasion of federal power by the province, and led to a sort of deadlock—waiting for the sunshine of prosperity to unloose its grip—and finding war instead. We cannot yet tell whether Social Credit was the end of something just ending, or is the beginning of something just beginning.

In this darkness of depression something like a twilight of dawn seemed to show in the long-sought conclusion of Reciprocity with the United States. It has been seen that when the imperial preferential system came at last it had somehow lost its outline. Still more unrecognizable was Reciprocity, the lost child of 1866 brought home at last in 1935. This again was partly due to the change of government. Political parties like all other lovers, still seek their first love. The Liberals, who came back to power in 1935, succeeded in obtaining bilateral legislation with the United States which at last brought Reciprocity, or the ghost of it, to Canada. But like the Ghost of Queen Dido's husband (in the first book of Virgil), how changed it was from its former self! Who could recognize in these intricate clauses and schedules, in this shifty give-and-take of movable duties, the broad, bold outline of the older Reciprocity. The new system was based upon the general Trade Agreement Act of Congress of 1934, authorizing the President to enter into reciprocal arrangements with any country and thereby reduce any existing duty, but not more than 50 per cent. It applied to any country. By 1940 Canada was only one of 21 countries with which it was

JAMES CROCKART, A.R.I.B.A., MONTREAL, P.Q., 1941

*". . . . the extraordinary advantages of water carriage. The cost of floating
things, once loaded, seems to vanish"*—PAGE 238

concerned. Moreover, the schedules seemed so complicated and so mechanical, as to lack any vital animating principle. It was the change from a gospel to a bill of goods. To the public at large it had lost interest, and to the individual also, except his own little subsection of an industrial clause.

Perhaps the brightest page in these short inter-war annals of years closing towards disaster is the record of the discovery and exploitation of the incalculable mineral wealth of the central wilderness of Canada between the Hudson Bay and the Lakes. This means far more than the wealth itself, great though it must be. It removes from our commonwealth its fatal geographical defect of an uninhabited and seemingly worthless central area which broke East and West forever apart. The touch of King

Midas is turning desolation into fairyland, a strange fairyland
indeed, where the poison-breath of smelters withers and obliter-
ates life and where uprooted trees and dynamited rocks show
how hydraulic plants can tear the heart out of primitive nature,
and yet a fairyland too, where the snug winter lights of happy
Noranda twinkle back at the sulky thermometer; and where in
summer the aeroplane hovers over still lakes as silver as its own
wings. The story of the discoveries is a romance. The Government of Ontario, building a railway, for fun, to James Bay (to
connect Moose Factory—with the contractors), ran into the
treasures of the land of Saguenay of which the Indians had told
Jacques Cartier. The Temiskaming and Northern Ontario Railway was found to be ballasted with silver rocks, and its roadbed
dusted with sand containing platinum. To this was added
the copper, already cut when the Canadian Pacific first cut
through the wilderness.

V. Stefansson, The old story of the northern climate comes true again. It
"Northward doesn't matter how cold it is out of doors; it's how cold it is
Course of inside. A blizzard doesn't matter to a man in a club. Vilhjalmur
Empire," Stefansson has told that the cold blizzards of Iowa made it seem
1922 utterly uninhabitable till houses were built. So with our new
North. Here, where once Red Indians froze white, are the lights
of happy Noranda—brick houses, apartments, electric lights,
hotels with bell-boys bringing ice—thirty below outside but
indoors, Rotary Club meetings, bridge, cocktails and a Ladies'
L. Laughlin, Club lecture on Browning and Freezing. Meantime from this
"History of frozen north there is produced each year $150,000,000 worth of
Bimetallism," gold—more than all the gold brought home by Cortez and
1897 Pizarro in twenty years.

Another feature of development over the same period, promis-
ing great things to come, was the unexpected effect on British
Columbia of the opening of the Panama Canal. The canal was
built as a military measure, camouflaged as commerce. Its con-
cealed object was to unite the American Navy; its unexpected
effect to create Pacific commerce. The canal was initiated in
1903 and opened in 1914. Its development remained for the
inter-war years. Now again appears the extraordinary advantages of water carriage. The cost of floating things once loaded

seems to vanish. It often costs less to float a ton across an ocean than to cart it uptown. Where time is not a factor water wins. In some cases the time factor is reversed. Wheat shipped from Vancouver to Liverpool via Panama would rather not get there too soon. It lingers on the way like Red Riding Hood among the flowers, gathering free storage and arriving on a better market. As a consequence all the wheat of British Columbia, most of the Alberta wheat and some from Saskatchewan goes out via Panama, constituting about one-quarter of the total Canadian export, for example, 39 million bushels out of 146 million for the season 1938-39. This trade via Panama and the trans-Pacific trade that had developed before 1939 are only the first signs of what the Pacific commerce of Canada must be in the future. The City of Vancouver had no people (none findable by our census) in 1880; in 1891, 29,000; and in 1931, Vancouver with its suburbs, 308,000.

But after all, and all in all, and when the worst is said, the depression and the difficulty and the hard times never broke ranks in Canada, never even began to. We knew nothing of the fierce hatreds that tore the vitals of Europe. We knew nothing of the inhuman concentration camps, the mass executions, the pogroms, the liquidations, the secret police—the things that have driven from Central Europe all prospect of human happiness under human freedom. Our people through all the minor divisions of race or province or social class, preserved certain ideals, stood firm on certain ground. Even the worst Conservative knew that even the worst Liberal had a touch of good in him and both knew that a Social Crediter with such a genial face as that of Mr. Aberhart couldn't be altogether bad.

So when the reality of war came, unexpected and scarcely believable, all Canada swung into a single front. It was not a question of whether Canada had to go to war if Britain went to war. That question had talked itself out years before, had run to seed, leaving nothing but academic chaff endlessly winnowed by vacant professors. The sinking of the *Athenia* and the massacre of the defenceless in Poland, settled for us the moral issue of the war at the outset. Nor were we prepared. No decent people were. Does a man walk the street prepared against murder ? But from the very righteousness of this anger, from the very fact that we had not prepared for war, had not gloated over blood or fashioned young souls to cruelty, the war in its coming has been able to bring out all that is best in our people—as adversity, as illness, as danger. We cannot doubt its issue.

The Peace River Valley. "We need immigrants—not thousands, millions . . . — PAGE 246

CHAPTER X

CANADA AS A FUTURE WORLD POWER

The Past as a Pledge for the Future—The New Horizon—World Security and Social Welfare—The Opportunity and the Responsibility of Canada.

NO ONE can read the record of the making of Canada without realizing that a great work has been done. Nor can any Canadian read it without realizing also how much our own efforts have been aided by the good fortune of our history. The growth of the United States to a single vast power reaching from ocean to ocean, speaking all one language and pursuing one democratic ideal, has produced a continent that knows nothing of the divisions of race, language and purpose which have brought down Central Europe in ruin. Nor has the proximity of the United States either overshadowed or endangered our institutions. On the contrary, there has grown out of it an abiding friendship and a mutual esteem beside which all the treaties of Europe are scraps of paper.

Nor has there been wanting to us for nearly two centuries the sheltering protection of the mother country. No overseas aggression could reach us, and those who came must come in peace. To that has been added the rugged gifts bestowed by nature, the great buttress of the polar seas and arctic islands, the safeguard afforded by two oceans over which ride the fleets of Britain and America.

Such is the past. But this protected infancy and sheltered youth are over now. The time has come when our country must make its full return for all that has been done for it in the past. For the present we best do this in making every effort to aid in beating back from Great Britain the war by which a brutal and degenerate nation tries to overwhelm it. When that is over we must look to the future, where a higher place and a higher responsibility than anything the past has seen awaits our country. From its very situation Canada must be reorganized as the central buttress of imperial power. Wedged, as it were, between Great Britain and the United States, our Dominion becomes the keystone of a new arch of mutual support and common security.

We have to take for granted the sad truth that after this war the European world can be ruled only by superior power—our enemies' or ours. Their rule would mean power with brutality, cruelty, injustice; ours a rule of decency and fair play with no further injustice than that of removing from a conquered nation every conceivable form of weapon of offence that could prompt a new treachery. This much we must do for our own preservation. There can be no question again of self-determined nations, all free, joining in a Free League of Nations to rule the world. It is well to be done once and for all and in time with the form of propaganda which still infests the British press and which pours over in leaflets to Canada. Here for instance is such a typical leaflet of the immediate moment, which urges a vigorous prosecution of the war to the complete destruction of German power, to be followed by setting up a new League of Nations, including Germans and such, but truly international in having its own armed forces, superior to those of any one nation in the League. This, of course, means winning the war and then handing over our lives and fortunes to a round-table vote, with a bunch of crooks among the voters. If idiocy can go as far as this, it is well to part company with it at the outset.

In point of force, then, it is plain that Canada must become, as it were, not exactly a fortified country in the old sense, but a country with a vast capacity, sufficiently developed to expand with ease, for producing armaments and munitions in places so safeguarded by natural obstacles that no war could impede the manufacture. Here is boundless water-power, as willing to run in subterranean channels as above ground; great battlements of rock that can be hollowed out into underground factories against which the largest bomber in the world is as harmless as a dragon-fly. With that is a store of minerals and metals that Pluto himself might envy. All hell can be raised in the bowels of northern Canada.

One speaks thus first in terms of war. To do so is a regrettable necessity of the hour. But we are here speaking of war only in the negative sense, of the means of protection and of potential war-power that would make an evil-minded nation hesitate to attack Great Britain. But all this is only to render possible our new destiny in peace.

It cannot be doubted that after the war there will be witnessed a great migration of population and capital to Canada from the British Isles. It is sometimes said—without thought—that Canada will become the centre and seat of Empire. That, to use a prayer-book phrase, is more than we either desire or deserve. History cannot be shifted and "1066 and all that" cannot be removed to Saskatchewan. Indeed we may well expect that in Great Britain, out of present tribulation, out of present heroism, there will rise on the ashes of burned cities, the wreckage of broken homes and the memories of lives given in sacrifice, a higher inspiration to great things than has been seen since the defeat of the Spanish Armada inspired the England of Shakespeare. No words that we may use of the coming greatness of our country should be so framed as to take away anything from the undying greatness of Great Britain. Both are needed. But undoubtedly a great migration of British people to Canada and still more a rapid natural increase among those who come, is a first necessity of our common welfare.

It would be a great mistake for us to divert attention from the present effort of the war by detailed peace-plans of the future. But the realization of certain broad ideals, to be achieved later on, can itself serve as a stimulus to the pursuit of victory.

The war effort seems all the more worthwhile if we can see the vision possible beyond it. We need immigrants—not thousands, millions—not gradually, but in a mass. Above all we have to realize that the best immigrants—in fact the best of all general imports—are children. We need them, imported and homegrown, in cradlefuls. That way lies security. In no time they grow up; see them there in the air above us, the children of yesterday!

It may well be asked, for there is a dense cloud of error that screens the subject, whether our country can take many more people. All kinds of silly little totals are put forward as the maximum, or the optimum, or the God-knows-what, of our population. The United States, it is said, is nearly full. We cannot take in immigrants, it is urged, except in proportion as our trade expands, or as our factories increase. In other words, since we cannot step out both feet first, we are told to step out with neither.

It is not possible in these brief pages to explore so large a subject. We need and we shall presently obtain a new survey of our economic life. We shall have to revise all our views of the relation of migration to natural assets, of the increase of population to social welfare. The views we have are just a shredded old patchwork, a 'coon-skin coat, dating down from days forgotten. Such studies, to be complete and convincing, would take much investigation and much labour of presentation. Yet even here a few suggestive considerations may be attempted. Within recent years the subject of the increase of population has received much scientific thought and statistical study. By science we mean thinking; by statistics, counting. We can easily understand that within the last fifty years the great advance of medical science, the increased control of epidemic disease, the progress of sanitation and the care of public health, must have greatly increased the average length of human life. We have to admit, indeed, that these things are partly offset by the fret, the worry and the congestion of modern life and by the change from the country to the city. No doubt an open-air cottager of the English countryside a hundred years ago, living with a maximum of breathing and a minimum of thinking, lived a long while. One recalls, as for so much of the social history of England, a picture in *Punch*. "And how old," asks a lady of an old cottager, sitting in the sunset on his door-step, "how old was your father when *he* died ?" "Bless you, ma'am," answers the cottager, "father ain't dead; he's upstairs putting grandfather to bed." But at best such cases were exceptions, survivals stranded in the backwaters of the vexed current of life. Even at that, in those days 'sixty' looked wrinkled and bent and toothless. With us men of that age would be out playing bridge.

We should therefore easily guess that life has lengthened. But few would realize by how much. Statistics show that once the first danger of being born dead, or half dead, is past, the average person in such countries as the United States and Canada now lives to be sixty years old. This contrasts with an expectation of life a hundred years ago that ran perhaps to forty years. Moreover, there is every reason to believe that the process of lengthening, as a consequence of improved medicine and hygiene, is still active and going forward all the time. In front of these average old men of sixty is a skirmishing line going forward to an average into the seventies, and scouts—old boy scouts—trying the ground out beyond a hundred. Scientists have it that the average man in another generation will be living to more than an age of seventy. Yet such lengthening must obviously stop somewhere.

Unfortunately this is only one side of the picture. This is the page of second childhood. Turn back to the first. With each successive decade, in a progressive civilized country, the proportion of babies born is smaller and smaller. Marriage is late, and gets later, or never comes. Married people have one baby, look at it, and never have another; or try two, perhaps three, and stop discouraged. Observe, this has nothing to do with human physiology. This is purely a social phenomenon. Statistics show that the birth rate in America in 1875 was 37 babies to every thousand people. In 1935 it had fallen to 17 and is still falling. The population, while still increasing, has every year more and more old people and fewer and fewer infants. This will mean, to the eye of the economist, queer changes in the structure of industrial life, more provision for the wants of old men and

women and less for that of children; the toy trade less important
than the wheeled chair industry; the tin trumpet beaten by the
ear trumpet, fewer children's books and ever so many books of
reminiscences; with infancy and senility joining forces to augment
the trade in macaroni and milk.

These economic conclusions are curiosities rather than apprehensions. But the statistician speaks in another tone. Under the
tendencies described, he tells us, the lengthening of life will end
and the falling birth rate presently meet it at an equilibrium
where the total of the population comes to a full stop, its maximum limit. The circumstances of the United States have best
fitted it for the theatre of these speculations. Great Britain
lives only in small part on and off the resources of its own land
and is more affected by migration. In many other countries the
outline of the whole picture is blurred with war or pestilence, or
indistinguishable for lack of evidence. Taking the continental
United States as a proper case in point, we find it in 1940 with
a population of 131,000,000. Statisticians tell us that the population will come to a halt at about 150,000,000 in about the year
1960; after that it will probably slowly decline.

Now it would seem at first sight that if we were to take these
estimates as a basis, the probable increase of the population of
Canada could not be very great. The continental areas of the
two countries are about equal and the proportion of unusable
territory is far greater in Canada. Hence Canada under the same
impulses and forces would fail like the United States to double
its present population, and reach its maximum—or optimum as
they call it—somewhere under twenty million. All this is a mix-
ture of ignorance and misunderstanding. The statistics in regard
to the United States are not based on, or concerned with, the
question of how many people the United States *could* support,
but of how many, under present social influences, it is likely to
support. Nations live, in the main and apart from localized
exceptions, on the ground under their feet, the food, the materials
of life that it supplies. Take the world as a whole and this is
self-evident. In one crowded spot (Belgium) a crowded square
mile of people can live on manufacturing things made from
material brought to them. Still more, an accountant in a City of

London financial house lives on the export of addition and subtraction; a novelist nearby in Fleet street, on the export of mystery.

But take a truly productive area, such as Java, and we find that a thousand people can live on a square mile just by growing things. At present the continental United States (1940) supports only 43 people per square mile, and Canada, even if you throw away all the territory outside the provinces, supported at its last census (1931) only 5.17. But the United States, in point of sheer production, could as easily support three hundred million as Europe can; and Canada, on what is under our feet, could easily support a hundred million before talking about 'optimums,' or 'magnums.' The whole issue is not one of feeding but of breeding. Humanity throws away food—melons float down the Potomac and coffee goes up in smoke in Brazil—throws away food and keeps the cradle empty. This is because there is plenty of room for children in the world at large but none in the world in particular—the little apartment island that dreads a maternity bill. The twist in our social system has a knot in the wrong place. This limitation of families threatens human destiny. Compare the world we know with the world that used to be. In the old colonial days that made America, children were a blessing and an asset, a widow with a flock of children a matrimonial prize. The smallest child could mind a hen or scare away a bird. The large family brought its care and sorrows but overpaid the debt in its reward; the mother of a grown-up family found her own life renewed in their comings and goings, as in a life that only slackened to begin again—a foretaste of immortality.

In what way we can alter our economy so as to favour and recall the vanishing 'family,' is too large a question for this page. It belongs with the whole discussion of altering our social environment so as to abolish hunger, poverty and want, and to set a universal basis of plain living and common opportunity, above which individual effort and individual merit may rise and fall. A decade ago all such discussion was apt to fly off at the tangent of Communism, Fascism or the totalitarian state. There will be no danger of that again. The world is learning that freedom must come first, that any attempt at social betterment that begins and ends with compulsion, must mean the iron bars of a prison, the slow death of a concentration camp. It almost begins to look as if even the bygone freedom to die in peace was something.

But there is no need to despair of what the social world may yet be made, nor of what part Canada may play in the making. When we have taken our share in beating down iniquity, we must take more than our share in setting up happiness. Our day is to-morrow.

FINIS

INDEX

HOUSE of SEAGRAM

THE AUTHOR

STEPHEN LEACOCK—Professor Emeritus of McGill University, was born in 1869 at Swanmoor, a suburb of Ryde in the Isle of Wight. His parents emigrated to Canada in 1876. He lived on an Ontario farm, in the township of Georgina on Lake Simcoe, for six years. He went to Upper Canada College from 1882 to 1887 and was Head Boy in 1887. He graduated from the University of Toronto in 1891 and taught at Upper Canada College till 1899. He entered the Graduate School of the University of Chicago in 1899 and was appointed a lecturer at McGill in January, 1901. He was made head of the department of Economics and Political Science in 1908 and held that position till his retirement in 1936. Professor Leacock has published over forty volumes of essays, biography, history, economics, political science, satire, humour and nonsense. In addition to two degrees received in course (B.A., Toronto; Ph.D., Chicago) he has received honorary degrees from Brown, Dartmouth, Queens, Toronto, Bishop's and McGill.

THE ARTISTS

THE following Canadian artists were selected by the House of Seagram and specially commissioned to furnish the original illustrations used in this book. They represent the outstanding leaders of contemporary art from Nova Scotia to British Columbia. In the choice of subjects, each was entrusted with the portrayal of those scenes and incidents for which his style and technique were most suited.

STANLEY ROYLE, R.B.A., R.C.A.

CHAS. W. JEFFERYS, R.C.A.

W. J. PHILLIPS, R.C.A.

A. SHERRIFF SCOTT, A.R.C.A.

F. H. VARLEY, A.R.C.A.

H. R. PERRIGARD, A.R.C.A.

JAMES CROCKART, A.R.I.B.A.

T. M. SCHINTZ

ERNST NEUMANN

THE PRINTER

A PART from its literary and historic value, this book provides a fine example of modern Canadian craftsmanship and especially in the fact that two distinctly different methods of printing have been used in its production. The body matter, including head and tail pieces, is letterpress printed in two colours, the secondary colour being also used for the marginal notes. Black-and-white illustrations are reproduced in single-colour lithography, the same process in six colours being used for the full colour plates. The crest of the Dominion of Canada on the cover is in quadricolour letterpress.

It may be interesting to the reader to mention that the sheets, after being letterpress printed, were passed to the lithographic department where the illustrations were added.

The type throughout the book is of the Caslon Oldstyle Family, the body matter being set in 12-point size with wide margins in the classic manner. The paper is a cream finish Paragon Book paper of Canadian manufacture which was made especially for the book.

The printing and production of this important book by the Gazette Printing Company Limited, was not inconsistent with the historic nature of its theme, the Gazette itself being founded by Montreal's first printer, Fleury Mesplet, in the year 1778.